THE LIFE OF THE LAW

THE
LIFE
OF THE
LAW

The People and Cases That Have Shaped
Our Society, from
King Alfred to Rodney King

ALFRED H. KNIGHT

Oxford University Press
Oxford   New York

Oxford University Press

Oxford   New York
Athens   Auckland   Bangkok   Bogotá   Bombay
Buenos Aires   Calcutta   Cape Town   Dar es Salaam   Delhi
Florence   Hong Kong   Istanbul   Karachi
Kuala Lumpur   Madras   Madrid   Melbourne
Mexico City   Nairobi   Paris   Singapore
Taipei   Tokyo   Toronto   Warsaw

and associated companies in

Berlin   Ibadan

First published in 1996 by Crown Publishers, Inc.,
201 East 50th Street, New York, New York 10022

First issued as an Oxford University Press paperback, 1998

Oxford is a registered trademark of Oxford University Press

Library of Congress Cataloging-in-Publication Data
Knight, Alfred H.
The life of the law : the people and cases that have shaped our society,
from King Alfred to Rodney King / Alfred H. Knight.
p.   cm.
Includes index.
ISBN 0-19-512239-9 (pbk.)
1. Law—United States—History. 2. Law—Methodology. I. Title.
KF385.A4K58   1998
349.73'09—dc21   97-49286

9 8 7 6 5 4 3 2 1

Printed in the United States of America

*This book is dedicated to
my dear wife and life companion,
Ruth*

CONTENTS

The seeds of England's criminal justice system are planted—inadvertently—when Alfred the Great enacts a law requiring citizens engaged in blood feuds to stop fighting for seven days and attempt to settle their differences.

Anglo-American law reaps magnificent and unexpected benefits when a stodgy medieval peace treaty between a king and his barons is made to operate under false pretenses, as a great charter of popular liberties.

That most necessary of evils and most evil of necessities, the professional lawyer, is brought into being by a busy monarch's on-the-run instruction to an underling.

The English judicial system begins to "follow" its own prior decisions in deciding cases, thereby making a Faustian bargain with itself, which trades creativity and reasonableness for predictability and consistency.

The bloody march toward legally protected individual liberties begins, with a most unlikely champion named Thomas More leading the parade.

The revolution that will lead to history's fairest criminal justice system is incited by the famously unfair criminal prosecution of Sir Walter Raleigh.

The most important doctrine of American constitutional law is invented by a sly English genius who receives no honor for it in the Old World and no lasting credit for it in the New.

INTRODUCTION

The life of the law has not been logic, it has been experience. . . .
The law embodies the story of a nation's development through
many centuries, and it cannot be dealt with as though it contained
only the axioms and corollaries of a book of mathematics.
In order to know what it is, we must know what it has been,
and what it tends to become.

OLIVER WENDELL HOLMES, *The Common Law,* 1881

A few years ago, trial lawyer Gerry Spence was asked to write an article for the *American Bar Association Journal* on trying complex litigation. The article began, "Well, it really is all just a matter of telling a story, isn't it?" "Affectatious," many of the *Journal*'s buttoned-down readers muttered, "like that damn cowboy hat he wears."

But Spence wasn't posturing, he was stating simple truth. Walk into any law library, and you will find yourself in the presence of countless individual stories about human beings in every conceivable circumstance of risk, dishonesty, bad luck, greed, carelessness, nobility, and passion. These stories were told, tested, denounced, and urged by lawyers, and the endings were written by judges. The constantly accumulating judge-endings are what we call law, and they are used to predict the probable outcomes of similar future conflicts. Contrary to popular belief, the law is not mechanistic, and the lawyers and judges who write it are neither mechanics nor—usually—charlatans. They are, in their own philistine way, a breed of artists painting on living canvases. The law is not an "it," it is a becoming, and like everything that is dynamic, it either grows or dies.

For more than thirty years I have pursued—and been pursued by—the practice of trial law in Nashville, Tennessee. I have represented personal injury victims whose disabilities increased and economic prospects decreased each time I interviewed them, personal injury defendants who had consumed two beers—never one or three, always two—just before the wreck, an occasional bank, construction company, national publication or TV station, and the politically active Nashville morning newspaper.

1

As an Assistant United States Attorney, I prosecuted bank robbers, milk dumpers, prisoner-beating deputy sheriffs and draft-dodging college graduates, and a gang of vicious thugs who killed a colleague to keep him from talking to the FBI.

As a defense lawyer, I have represented crooked preachers and honest gamblers, two kidnappers, an alleged murderer, and local politicians who had understandable difficulty distinguishing bribes from campaign contributions.

There was one thing all of them had in common when I met them—a story, to be gathered together, put into coherent form, and told as well as possible.

The first judge I ever appeared before had a set of scales on his bench, to represent the weighing and dispensing of justice. It was a false metaphor. Courts are more like theaters than laboratories, and the truth they produce is felt and apprehended, not carefully measured out. The raw materials they work with are recollections and impressions filtered through the memories, perceptions, and biases of witnesses, told with widely varying degrees of competence, and subjected to the distortions of cross-examinations. The facts found by judges and juries are mere versions of facts, which have no business masquerading as "truth." The most important of them tend to be unknowable intangibles—intentions, emotions, motives, and the like—which are within the province of courts not because they *can* be "found," but because they *must* be if legal disputes are to be resolved.

When cases are appealed, the facts found at trial are embodied in published opinions, which become legal precedents to be used in deciding future cases. By this process, the fate of one person can have a direct effect upon the fate of another, years and even centuries later. A decision holding a sixteenth-century English farmer liable for damage done by his rampaging bull may teach a legal lesson that results in liability for a twentieth-century pharmaceutical company which has sold a defective drug. A provision in a thirteenth-century peace treaty between the King of England and some rebellious barons, interpreted by seventeenth-century constitutionalists with motives of their own and run through a thousand subsequent judicial opinions, may have saved a North Carolina man from the electric chair in 1992.

For the intellectually fastidious, law seems disconcertingly haphazard in the making. Many years ago, when I was a young federal prosecutor, the U.S. attorney talked me into appearing with him on a local public television program. After some appropriately self-serving commentary on the current health of federal justice in middle Tennessee, the hostess turned to me and asked brightly: "And what will the priorities of the U.S. attorney's office be *next* year, Mr. Knight?"

"It depends on what the criminals do," I blurted out. The hostess could think of no follow-up to that one, except to exclude me from the remainder of the interview. I consoled myself with the knowledge (which was, I might add, unique to me among the participants in the broadcast) that my crude remark had the virtue of truth.

No one can begin to understand our legal system until he digests a seemingly obvious fact: The business of the courts is not planned; it occurs, and its principles are developed at the point of application. "What law will you make next year, Your Honor?" "It depends on what the people do."

The point is more elegantly stated in a parable I once read in a legal textbook. A university is expanding its campus and is designing walkways for the new grounds. The engineer suggests a geometrically efficient pattern, connecting the greatest number of destinations by the most direct routes. The architect proposes studying walkways on other campuses and copying the ones that seem most appropriate. "You want walkways that will *work?*" asks the university's lawyer. "Plant grass and wait a year. Then put the walkways down where the paths have been worn." Our law has been created by the tread of feet that did not necessarily know where they were going until they got there.

Most people, of course, encounter the law purely as an idea. For every person who sees the inside of a courtroom, there are hundreds who have hypothetical contacts with the law through the advice of lawyers, which consists of predictions as to what a court *would* rule in the circumstances presented, *if* called upon to do so. To the rest of mankind, the law is a vague universe of concept that empowers (they can't promote him ahead of me without giving a *reason*), limits (I better not hit him *first*), and informs (racism and sexism are wrong) their lives without any contact at all with lawyers, judges, or jailers.

Concept is what the stories in this book are mostly about. Not philosophy or wisdom, or even right and wrong, but the brand names the law gives to its ideas. If conflict is the root of the law, it is concept that causes it to grow and flourish. There is a magic power in the naming of a legal idea—the King's Peace, due process of law, liberty of conscience—that allows it to carry forward into the future as a transformed, better, more powerful idea. A Saxon king gives individual citizens guaranteed protection from physical harm and calls it his "peace." In later generations, his successors proclaim a "peace" in ever wider circles, until the King's Peace encompasses every English citizen—and a national criminal justice system has been born. The power in a named idea—a legal concept—can be greater than the specific judgments of a thousand courts.

When all that we have known and done is buried beneath the debris of time, what may be remembered most about us is our legal system. Nothing like it has ever been seen before on this planet, so far as we know. It is distinguished, more than anything else, by its breathtaking generosity to the individual.

The first job of law is to provide freedom from violence and the fear of violence that kills civilization at its roots. Until that job is done, nothing else about a legal system works. English law began as a secular answer to the terrified plea of the Book of Common Prayer: "Preserve us from the fury. . . ." The legal system that developed did not eliminate the "fury" of brutal men but made it more predictable by substituting public for private violence. When government acquired a monopoly on authorized violence, citizens were better able to anticipate when it would occur and avoid it. This was called obeying the law.

When the English felt safe enough, they began to devise ways to rein in the authorized violence called law with greater laws, which government itself was required to obey. These laws-restraining-laws became the great constitutions that are the Anglo-American legal systems' distinctive gifts to the world. For reasons having to do with geography, tradition, and accidental circumstance, the governments of England and America were able to get beyond pure force and threat of force in dealing with their citizens and acquired the luxury of defending their civilizations from internal violence by civilized means. They were able to grant broad free speech without inducing insurrection, freedom of belief without civil war, and—so far—decent trial rights without criminal anarchy.

Most of this has come about not by political negotiation or scholarly codification, but by innumerable painful clashes between authority and counterauthority, between haves and want-to-haves, between people with diametrically different views of humankind's destiny on earth; usually, but not always, in courtroom settings. After the fact, we tell the story of these clashes in words of logic and morality, but their guiding principle is always the grasp for power by disparate forces.

We should not be too self-righteous about the generally beneficent outcomes of these conflicts. As the stories told in this book demonstrate, we—the English and Americans—have been very lucky. Largely because of accidents of geography and history, the battles that have shaped our law have been waged in environments that allowed decency to survive, and even to prevail. Would England have used torture instead of jury trial if it had been geographically part of the savage European main? Probably so. Would America have developed its powerful bias for individual freedoms if attack from foreign cultures had been a realistic threat? Probably not.

It is the purpose of this book to tell, in episodic form, how some of the main contours of this unique legal system came to be. The twenty-one stories that are its focal points begin with Alfred the Great in the late ninth century and end with the Rodney King trials in 1993. Despite the time span, they are remarkably cohesive tales, tracing the unconscious unfolding of one of the true glories of our civilization.

Law is intended to apply to common life and should be comprehensible to ordinary folk, but increasingly it is not. Bookstores bulge with novels and treatises on the subject that oscillate between glitz and something resembling nuclear physics. Most law review articles discussing current legal doctrine are suited for minds that enjoy reading annotated chess games. Contemporary Supreme Court opinions on even the most basic issues, such as freedom of speech, have all of the grace and clarity of communist propaganda tracts. They are clogged with murky phrases such as "totality of the circumstances" and "heightened scrutiny," and propose complex "three-pronged" tests of constitutionality. Gone are the lucid poetry of Holmes, the stirring rhetoric of Brandeis, and the thunderclap prose of Marshall. The meaning of the law is becoming inaccessible, not only to the public but to the bar itself.

There are consequences to this, of course. We are more likely to lose the meaning of our freedoms through ignorance and carelessness than through intentional governmental evil. Despite the fulminations about contemporary constitutional liberalism, we are already, in many ways, measurably less free today than a century ago. The jury is less powerful, and more subject to control from the bench. The constitutional protections against unreasonable governmental searches and seizures have steadily shrunk over the last quarter century. There are current judicial and congressional attacks on the writ of habeas corpus that threaten to restore us to the dreadful era of the Leo Frank debacle. Our federal criminal justice system has been saddled with a congressionally inspired horror called the sentencing guidelines, which require judges to eschew individualist judgment and to impose punishment on human beings in accordance with a bureaucratic point system that Stalin would be proud of.

Obviously, this book is no antidote for any of the above. On the other hand, it couldn't hurt. Knowledge is power, and the law is badly short of people power just now. Besides, legal history as it happened is more entertaining by far than anything "L.A. Law" ever thought of. It is worth the telling—much *more* than worth the telling—in and of itself.

AUTHOR'S NOTE

These essays are works of opinion and interpretation, not primary research. In the endnotes, I have provided references for a few of the more important quotations that readers may wish to review in context, but I have made no attempt to be exhaustive in this regard.

I have added emphasis to some quotations where it seemed appropriate, but—in the interest of sparing readers annoyance—I have not followed the academic practice of inserting "[emphasis added]" all over the place. My goal has been to enhance clarity, not to slant the meaning of anyone's words. No attorney would ever do *that*.

1

NATIONALIZING ENGLISH JUSTICE

(The King's Peace)

Good order is the foundation of all things.
EDMUND BURKE

For more than a year the people had been boiling mad at government. The Clinton administration had taken office promising to ratchet back big government but then proposed a giant health care plan that threatened to smother the country under a bureaucratic blanket. In November 1994, Democratic majorities were ousted from both houses of Congress by opponents who echoed Ronald Reagan's potent promise "to get government off the people's back." Former Tennessee governor Lamar Alexander launched a bid for the Republican presidential nomination with the suggestion that the people "cut [Congress'] pay and send them home." Reduce spending, the people said, and the taxes that feed it. Eliminate welfare, impose term limits, cut through the accumulation of red tape. We don't know what we're for, they said, but we know what we're against—government, in all of its invidious manifestations.

Then, at 9:02 A.M. on April 19, 1995, some murderous thugs blew off a third of the federal court house in Oklahoma City with a fertilizer bomb. First came pure shock. Then anger. Then fear. Who were these people, how many were there, what were their motives, where would they strike again? If the heartland of America could so easily be made a war zone, was anybody safe? Then the people saw their president and attorney general on television, promising swift justice to the "evil" ones. Fifty FBI agents were on their way to Oklahoma City, with more to follow. They expertly picked through the wreckage and followed every lead, and within forty-eight hours an arrest had been made. The case would be solved, the people thought, the culprits identified, their motives exposed, and due punishment imposed.

The people were still angry, but their anger was diluted by relief. They had suddenly remembered what a government of law most fundamentally means. Not taxes or benefits or civil rights and freedoms, but simple physical security from violence and the corrosive fear that violence breeds.

English justice had its beginnings almost in a state of nature. The Saxons who overran the island in the sixth century A.D. replaced the Roman culture they found there with tribal ways of life. They were not one people, but a motley collection of independent clans that had crossed the Channel throughout the preceding century. When the dust of the last battle had settled and the fires of pillage had burned out, the political makeup of the island had been transformed into a maze of tribes and subtribes led by ruffians politely called kings. Legal systems in any sense recognizable to us did not exist.

For the next five hundred years, much of law enforcement was self-help. The law of *Infangthief* required everyday folk to act as policemen, judges, and executioners. When crimes occurred in their neighborhoods, the hue and cry was sounded, hoes and sickles were dropped, and packs of farmers gathered to chase the culprits down. If the pursuers caught their quarry and were satisfied of his guilt, they were authorized to hang, decapitate, or otherwise dispose of him virtually on the spot.

If a criminal suspect could not be caught in hot pursuit, and suspicion of his guilt was strong, he might be summoned before a local court. If he did not appear—and he was likely not to—he might be outlawed. Outlawry was a declaration of war by society against an individual and had terrible consequences. An outlaw was permanently vulnerable to his neighbors, like a perpetually fleeing felon constantly subject to capture and death. It was the duty of every man to hunt him down, to kill him on sight, to burn his fields, and to demolish his homestead. The formula for imposing outlawry, "Let him bear the wolf's head," signified the culprit's status as not only a "friendless man" but a "wolf."

Outlawry was no exotic rarity; ten men were outlawed for every one who was hanged. For centuries after the Saxon invasion, the bogs and forests of England were full of desperate fugitives who were a greater threat to life and limb than they had ever been prior to their encounters with the law.

Those who did appear in court, if first offenders, might buy their freedom by paying money compensation to the victim or his kin. If a trial occurred, there would be no testimony or fact-finding. The defendant would swear a complex oath of innocence, supported by oath-helpers who swore to his truthfulness and honor. If these oaths were "broken" by faulty recitation, the defendant would be put to trial by ordeal. He might, for example, be required to appear in church to have his hand burned by hot iron, his guilt or innocence to be determined by whether the burn festered or healed within three days.

The king had little to do with all of this. For the most part, he concerned himself with legal disputes only to the extent his interests, or those to whom he specifically owed protection, were affected. Kings might from time to time proclaim rules for conducting trials across the land, but the business of rendering everyday justice was as local from vill to vill as the suppers served in village taverns.

Centuries later, all English justice would be the king's or queen's and would be, the English would plausibly assert, the best the world had ever seen. The confused, layered patchwork of lynch law, local courts, barons' courts, church courts, and regionally unique courts that had sprung up over the years would yield to a seamless national justice system to which all were equally subject— at least in theory.

This centralization happened as part of a gradual concentration of political power in England. It was accelerated by the coming of the Normans, who brought exceptional administrative skills with them when they conquered the island in 1066. It was made easier by the smallness of England and its island isolation, which allowed for an efficient consolidation of power.

Not least important, this nationalization of justice was facilitated and rationalized by a legal concept called the King's Peace. Without this useful juristic tool, the development of English law enforcement might have been quite different, and much more turbulent.

There was a rustle of parchment sheets in the dark-timbered room. The tall man bending over them erupted into a barking cough and turned to confer with the cleric who was assisting him. Alfred, king of the West Saxons, was engaged in his continuing effort to implant civilization in his primitive land.[1] One day in the distant future, he would be memorialized by a statue in Winchester as "the founder of the English nation." Perhaps no one person ever "founds" a nation—even Romulus had a brother—but the many-faceted Alfred came close.

As he stood in that scroll-cluttered room in the year 887, he was by far the most important figure in his people's long history. The youngest son of a tubercular royal family, he had been forced to assume the throne when his elder brothers died unseasonably, and led his people to safety in mortally perilous times. Alone of all the English kings, he had found the means to halt, and then subdue, the ferocious Danish pirates who had spent most of the century pillaging England. He had made Christians and farmers of the Danes, convincing them to settle after baptism in a prescribed area of England known as the Danelaw, northeast of London and apart from precious Wessex.

He was an even greater statesman than warlord. Having experienced the catastrophic effects of seaward vulnerability, he had created his people's first navy. Understanding that civilization is impossible without learning, he had worked to bring literacy to the land. Believing that a nation must know itself in order to realize itself, he had authorized a national history called the Anglo-Saxon Chronicle. He was the last English king to write books personally until Henry VIII undertook to do so 650 years later, and his were much better than Henry's.

His present effort was less noticed by his contemporaries but was equally important. He was undertaking to proclaim the laws of Wessex so that the few who could read would know what they were and future generations would know what they had been.

These laws were nothing like the floods of paper churned out by modern legislators. Alfred had a reverence for tradition that would baffle an American congressman. He was, in fact, not so much a legislator as a collector. His own description of his under-taking was both modest and accurate: "I, then, Alfred, gathered [the old laws of the Saxons] together and commanded many of those to be written which our forefathers held, those which to me seemed good. I dared not venture to set down in writing much of my own, for it was unknown to me what of it would please those who should come after us."

Saxon noblemen of Alfred's time could recite their lineage, an-cestor by ancestor, back to Noah himself, and Alfred's laws reflected that sense of immediate connection with the remote past.[2] Although some were original with him, he culled many of them from the reigns of "Ine, my kinsman" (688–725) and "Ethelbryht" (540–616), "who first among the English race received baptism"; they, in turn, had derived many of them from the ancient forest tribes that migrated to England from Germany in the fifth and sixth centuries. It was as though the Massachusetts legislature had adopted the Body of Liberties of 1641 as the law of 1990s' Massa-chusetts.

Alfred's laws were unlike ours in another fundamental way. Far from separating themselves from religion as ours do, they de-rived their very authority from Christianity. They began with the Ten Commandments ("The Lord spake these words to Moses") and proceeded to list the harsh criminal laws of Exodus: "He that smiteth his father or mother, let him perish by death"; "For thrust-ing out another's eye, let him give his own for it"; and so on.

As Alfred conceived it, these brutal measures had been tem-pered by Christianity into the more lenient laws of the Saxons. "[H]appened it," he wrote, "that many nations received the faith of Christ. . . . They then ordained out of that mercy which Christ had taught that secular lords might without sin take for almost every misdeed for the first offense the money-*bot*." In other words, Christ's merciful intervention meant that crime could be atoned for by paying the victim and giving a cut to the king, as the Saxons had done for generations. There was an exception: "Cases of treason against a lord [such as Alfred] to which they dared not assign any mercy, because God Almighty judged none to them who despised Him . . . and He commanded that a lord should be loved as one's self." Death to traitors, in other words, and the possibility of monetary settlement to all other first-time criminals.

The result was that the laws collected by Alfred were not, for the most part, what we would think of as criminal laws at all. They were an elaborate code of payoffs that priced every conceivable type of physical injury with extraordinary precision: "If within the hair there be a wound an inch long, let one shilling be given as *bot*. If before the hair . . . two shillings." Striking off an ear cost the assailant thirty shillings unless deafness resulted, in which case the ante was upped to forty shillings. Many of these provisions read like classified ads for body parts: "For each of the four front teeth, six shillings; for each of the teeth which stand next to them, four shillings; then for each tooth which stands next to them, three shillings."

The compensatory laws of the Saxons would in time be overtaken by the stern justice of the conquering Normans, which lopped off the limbs of felons or strangled them from gibbets without giving them a chance to buy Christ's mercy. Despite his qualms, it was, ironically, one of Alfred's "own" laws that most "pleased" the future. Without intending to do so, he dropped a seed upon the soil of English justice that eventually grew into a national criminal law enforcement system.

The ancient curse of Saxon society was the incessant cycle of private violence known as the "blood feud." Attack, vengeance, counterattack, and countervengeance were waged continuously between noble clans, with little interference by the king. Overlords such as Alfred were like modern Mafia chieftains compelled to tolerate turf wars among lesser dons, or Old West marshals whose practical authority was confined to ensuring that murders were conducted face-to-face. There was no clear distinction between violent crime and private war, and the few prohibitions that applied to such crime were, in essence, rules of warfare. The king did not judge and punish private violence so much as he refereed it. He prescribed the rules citizens were required to follow as they went about the business of killing, maiming, and laying waste the property of one another.

It was against this backdrop that Alfred proclaimed his "home-sitting" law. In his violent world, safety and quiet were prized possessions, and the law protected them fiercely. Every man from the king on down was entitled to his own *mund*, or peace, which was centered in his home. The ancient laws made unauthorized intrusions into the home a serious crime, called *hamfare*. They also punished house violence more severely than street violence: If you knocked out a man's front tooth, you must pay him six shillings, but if you broke his peace by doing it in his home, the fine was multiplied.

Alfred used the concept of "peace" to effect some mitigation of private violence by requiring a warrior seeking blood vengeance to pause for an interval of time at his enemy's doorstep. "I proclaim," he said, "that a man who knows his foe to be home-sitting fight not before he demand justice from him." He must give his enemy seven days to come out of his house to negotiate a truce before resuming the fight. Alfred treated violations of this peace with great severity as an offense against himself.

Giving the king's protection to specific persons, such as royal attendants, was an old Germanic practice that long predated Alfred. But his "home-sitting" law was different in that it applied that protection to a circumstance—a private siege—that might occur at any time, in any place, to anyone. Such applications gave the English peace a uniquely flexible quality that eventually led to the creation of a national criminal justice system.[3]

This flexibility shored up a weakness in the English kingship. Continental kingdoms exercised more undiluted power and generally imposed universal legal systems upon their peoples from their founding. English kings had to compete for power with local magnates who commanded strong loyalties of their own. The King's Peace was a versatile instrument for gradually extending governmental authority without undue resistance or bloodshed.

For generations after Alfred's death, private warfare remained the natural state of things, and the King's Peace was a special, narrowly circumscribed boon. Royally punishable crime occurred when that tenuous peace was broken. Having one's lawless act declared a breach of the King's Peace had its good and bad points. It made it, according to Maitland, "an act of personal disobedience, and a much graver matter, than an ordinary breach of the peace."[4] On the other hand, the king's justice was less brutal than that of, say, the barons of King Stephen's reign (1135–54), who were known to drown prisoners in mud.

By the early eleventh century, the peace had settled upon the king's highways, and royal prosecutors increased the scope of their power by fictitiously charging that crimes committed elsewhere had been committed on a highway and were subject to the king's jurisdiction. When William conquered England in 1066, he drew a sharp line across the face of English justice by announcing that his peace extended to "all the men [he had] brought with him." Under Henry II (1154–89), the quality of justice dispensed by the king greatly improved. Henry formalized the accusation process by inventing the grand jury, and his judges were generally more enlightened and humane than the men who presided in the local courts. The king's justice became the preferred brand, and its expansion was generally welcomed.

Eventually, a nationwide proclamation of peace applicable to all citizens was made at the beginning of each reign, effective until the king's death. For a few decades, a window of anarchy existed between the death of one king and the coronation of the next, during which crimes could be committed without royal punishment. In the thirteenth century that too was closed, and the King's Peace became universal in time and space. English law had fulfilled the definitional requirement of a fully mature criminal justice system: It had acquired the exclusive right to kill, maim, and lay waste the property of its citizens.

All future English criminal indictments would be required to state that the defendant had acted "against the peace of the King (or Queen)." It was the breaking of the peace that made the citizen's act a punishable crime: Geoffrey's breaking of John's head broke the King's Peace, which—after due adjudication—authorized the king's minions to break Geoffrey's head, not incidentally depriving John and his family of the ancient entitlement of doing likewise if they got to Geoffrey first.[5]

By and large, it was a reasonable bargain for all concerned.

Hundreds of years in the future and thousands of miles to the west, a man named Rodney King was beaten savagely by officers of the state. The elaborate criminal justice system went into action to determine whether a violation of the peace had taken place. When twelve citizens reported back that the peace had been observed, the spirit of the blood feud reappeared. Impromptu armies gathered, raging in the streets, entering buildings, burning, looting, killing, harming, in anger and in greed. Many causes were assigned, but one struck terrifyingly true: An ancient covenant had been broken, and the people sensed it in their blood and bones. Break it again, and it would happen again. Break it often enough, and the state's care of the peace would be forfeited.

2

THE RULE OF LAW

What is history but a fable agreed upon?

NAPOLEON

In thirteenth-century England, noblemen maintained drowning pools for disposing of people convicted in their private courts. (Bayard's castle in London had a special franchise to drown miscreants in the Thames.) Particularly egregious criminals were hanged, "cut down while yet living," disemboweled, castrated, and quartered.

The cruelty of the punishments fit the destructiveness of the crimes. Gangs of marauders roamed the English countryside, controlling towns for years at a time, robbing, murdering, raping, invading churches and attacking people at Mass, stealing women and children, and in general making a hell of common life.

Tragically for law-abiding people, justice was as weak as it was bloody. In a typical year, the Northumberland Roll listed seventy-two murders, with eighty-one identified culprits. Three were hanged, one imprisoned, one fined, and the rest, upon failure to appear in court, were outlawed and left to roam the countryside.[1]

As a potential birthing ground for the rule of law, thirteenth-century England seemed about as fertile as Lord Bayard's spayed bitch. Nonetheless (we are told), there appeared in the midst of this black night an aurora borealis of justice. The king and noblemen of England met on Runnymede Plain and produced an unprecedented charter of liberties for the protection of the English people. This great charter is the source of many of the provisions of the American Bill of Rights, which were adopted more than five hundred years later in a far more civilized environment. Its creation in the circumstances in which it was created was an act of genius that cannot rationally be accounted for. It is close to miraculous.

Isn't it?

King John's dark features were contorted into a look of even greater petulance than usual. He was about to encounter his greatest humiliation. He sat brooding in his tent as he had for most of the last five days, waiting for the scrivener to finish drafting the instrument. It was an instrument of surrender for a ruler who had failed on almost every front. His quarrels with the pope had resulted in the laying of an interdict upon England, which among other nuisances had prevented Christian burial of the dead. His ill-advised military adventures had depleted the limited wealth of his countrymen, who despised him for it as they had never despised his far more wasteful brother Richard. He was later to cap his reign (it was said) by losing the crown jewels in a creek bed while fleeing his enemies. On this day, June 19, 1215, he would be forced to acknowledge that the nobility and freemen of England were entitled to a great catalog of rights and privileges that John, they claimed, had sought to deny them.

The document confirming these rights recited that John had "granted" them "for the good of his subjects and the health of the King's soul." John the Lawgiver? The English Justinian? The Anglo-Norman Moses? Not quite.

As everyone who has seen a Robin Hood movie knows, John's oppressiveness as a ruler was mitigated only by his ineptness. He "granted" the rights set forth in the charter at the point of a sword, for the health of his carcass, and as he sealed the legal instrument that would live in the hearts of his countrymen forever, he was heard to mutter: "Will they ask for my kingdom too?"

A contemporary account of the scene at Runnymede makes the reason for John's "generosity" painfully clear:

They in their great joy appointed the fifteenth of June for the king to meet them, at a field lying between Staines and Windsor. Accordingly, at the time and place pre-agreed on, the King and Nobles came to the appointed conference, and when each party had stationed themselves apart from the other, they began a long discussion about terms of peace and the aforesaid liberties. . . . At length, after various points on both sides had been discussed, King John, seeing that he was inferior in strength to the barons, without raising any difficulty, granted the underwritten laws and liberties.[2]

John's capitulation was the climax of many years of struggle. For almost a decade, he had waged intermittent war in France, desperately seeking to retain the provinces of Anjou and Aquitaine as part of his English kingdom. Weary of the sacrifices they had made on behalf of Richard, many barons refused to provide military support for these adventures; and when John demanded exorbitant scutage (money payments in lieu of service), they refused that as well. Conditions became ripe for civil war. Armies were formed, and swords were sharpened. England was a powder keg waiting for a spark.

The spark was supplied by Stephen Langton, archbishop of Canterbury. In 1213, John had made peace with Rome by the astonishing gambit of becoming the pope's vassal. He tendered his kingship to the pope, who returned it two days later upon receiving an oath of personal loyalty from John. As part of the deal, John promised the pope that he would provide good government for his English subjects. Archbishop Langton vowed to take him at his word.

On August 25, 1213, while the king was busy with an insurrection in the north, Langton convened a meeting of the barons in the south. They came to St. Paul's Church in London, in creaking saddles and battle dress, to hear what this activist bishop had to say. He brought with him a copy of the coronation charter of John's great-grandfather, Henry I. Not many of the barons could have read it, but Langton held it aloft and reminded them of what it was—a royal promise to uphold the ancient laws of England. He said that John should be compelled to renew that promise. The barons—so the story goes—responded by swearing to "fight for those liberties, if it were needful, even unto death."[3] So had begun the struggle for legal primacy that ended almost two years later with John's grudging acceptance of Magna Charta.

After he emerged from the shadow of the barons' swords on June 19, 1215, John made his feelings about the charter even clearer. He applied to his papal liege lord to nullify Magna Charta and set him free from the obligations he had undertaken to his people. The pope responded with alacrity. Almost before the wax had hardened on the historic agreement, Pope Innocent III issued a bull that might have strangled English constitutionalism in its crib:

> [B]y such violence was John forced to accept an agreement that was shameful, illegal, and unjust, impairing his royal rights and dignity. Therefore, we utterly reject and condemn this settlement, ordering under threat of excommunication that the king should not dare to observe it nor the barons require it to be observed, and we declare the Charter, with all undertakings arising from it, to be null and void forever (August 24, 1215).[4]

John later went to war with the barons who sought to enforce the charter and very nearly prevailed. His efforts to nullify the historic compact might have succeeded, and its provisions might never have taken root, if he had not died in 1216—reportedly from eating unripe peaches.

The barons believed that the charter of Runnymede merely guaranteed ancient rights that they had inherited from the acts and proclamations of earlier kings. They believed that John was a lawbreaker who was being forced to observe long-established principles he should have observed voluntarily. In the far distant future, the barons' descendants would take a different view of the proceedings. They would call the instrument the "Great Charter," and would mark the birth of English constitutional law from the moment John set his seal upon it. Magna Charta would become the great legal myth of our culture—the goddess of English law looming out of the mists of time.

It has been said that all of English constitutional law is but a commentary upon the charter. The origins of the right of habeas corpus, of due process of law, of no taxation without representation, of freedom from private monopolies, of the privilege against self-incrimination, and especially of trial by jury have all been traced to this ancient document. For more than seven hundred years it was the unanswerable authority in constitutional debate, often invoked by both sides.

It was a potent force in American law from the beginning of the republic. In 1793, the first Supreme Court chief justice, John Jay, instructed a Philadelphia grand jury that "Magna Charta's strict regard for the rights of the [common man]" would be the hallmark of American justice. The American legal culture was by this time already saturated with Magna Charta. Although England was identified as America's oppressor, its law was the law of America. Founding Father John Rutledge of South Carolina said that "Coke's *Institutes* [for centuries, the 'bible' of English jurisprudence, which treated Magna Charta with nearly mystical veneration] seem almost to be the foundation of our law," and as a law student, Founding Father John Adams was sternly told, "You must conquer the *Institutes.*"[5] Eighteenth-century English devotees of Magna Charta such as Edmund Burke, William Pitt, and John Wilkes inspired the American Revolutionaries emotionally and provided much of the intellectual substance of their Bill of Rights. As the English historian Trevelyan gracefully put it, "America revolted in [Magna Charta's] name and seeks fellowship with us in its memory."[6]

Although much abated, the charter's vitality continues to the present day. Since the end of World War II, it has been cited in no fewer than 373 federal court decisions and 734 state court decisions. Its influence on modern decisions is sometimes amazingly direct.

Faced with deciding whether a punitive damages verdict was "disproportionately" large, a 1993 federal court based its ruling entirely on Chapter 20 of Magna Charta. Chapter 20 limited the king's power to impose monetary penalties by providing that "a free man shall be immersed saving always his position; and a merchant in the same way saving his trade; and a villein shall be immersed in the same way, saving his tillage." The court read this archaic language to mean that "the penalty inflicted should not, in any event, destroy the offender's means of making a living in his particular trade or calling"; concluded that the 778-year-old principle had not been violated by the punitive damages verdict in the case before it; and affirmed the trial court judgment.

On the other hand, veneration for the Great Charter sometimes succumbs to the court's sense of relevance—and sense of humor. In another recent case, a federal judge rejected a prisoner's argument that his rights under Magna Charta had been violated by his transfer to a more secure prison. The court reasoned that "the plaintiff was not a 'free man'[7] at the time of his reclassification and transfer, and no one could possibly have imagined that King John, in placing his seal upon the great Charter at Runnymede, was consenting to limitations on his power to upgrade classifications for convicted murderers." Moreover, the court continued, "if the plaintiff had been convicted of murder in the King's court in 13th century England . . . his security classification could not possibly have been a live issue for very long, [for] any punishment short of death by hanging would have given the defendant more than his due."

Considering its awesome reputation, reading the charter for the first time is a disappointing experience. For the most part, it bears no resemblance to the splendid declaration of rights and liberties we imagine. It deals mostly with obscure medieval issues such as wardship, relief, and scutage, and with mundane problems such as bridge-building, obstructions to navigation, and standard measures for wine, ale, and corn. It is sometimes startlingly specific, as in Chapter 50, which reads like a medieval eviction notice:

> We will entirely remove from their bailiwicks the relations of Gerard of Athee . . . namely, Enelard of Gigone, Peter, Guy and Andrew of Chamceaux, Guy of Cyguyne, Geoffrey, Martigny with his brother, Phillip, Mark with his nephew Geoffrey, and the whole brood of the same.

More than anything else, Magna Charta was a tenant's relief act, with the barons in the role of tenants and John the greedy landlord. Many of its provisions were, essentially, rent-control measures. For example, Chapter 2 froze the "relief" payable to the king at "one hundred pounds for an earl's barony; and for heirs of a knight, one hundred shillings at most for a whole knight's fee." A prudent hedge against inflation, but nothing to bring tears to the eyes of a constitutional theorist.

The main basis for the charter's fame is the grand language of Chapter 39:

> No free man shall be taken or disseised or exiled or in any way destroyed, nor will we go upon him, nor send upon him, except by the lawful judgment of his peers, or by the law of the land.

But even this stirring declaration is not what it seems.

For centuries, the phrase "judgment of his peers" was interpreted to mean trial by jury. Many American state constitutions use the phrase in their provisions guaranteeing jury trial. In 1896, the U.S. Supreme Court went so far as to rule that a Utah jury of eight persons was unconstitutional because "when Magna Charta declared that 'no freeman should be deprived of his life but by the judgment of his peers . . .' it referred to a trial by *twelve* jurors."

This ruling graphically illustrates the human capacity for viewing remote history through contemporary lenses. The author of the opinion, the brilliant John Marshall Harlan, read the phrase "judgment of his peers" and saw, not a council of barons, but a jury of twelve ordinary citizens. Without being conscious of doing so, he saw a nineteenth-century vision of justice in the words of men who never glimpsed that vision.

The fact is that when Magna Charta was drafted, the criminal trial jury did not even exist. Trial by battle had been introduced by the Normans 150 years previously and was still in vogue. Criminal trials were not a matter of evidence but of ritual. Most cases were tried by the ancient method of ordeal, presided over by priests. Suspects were bound hand and foot and thrown into water, or were scalded with hot metal or boiling water. If they sank, or if their wounds healed within three days, they were declared innocent. If they floated or their wounds festered, they were declared guilty. The church decreed in November 1215 that the clergy could no longer participate in ordeals, and that method of trial disappeared in England. The men who sealed the Magna Charta in June of that year had no way of anticipating this, however, and in any case could not have intended to replace the ordeals with the as yet nonexistent criminal jury trial.

What, then, did the phrase "judgment of his peers" mean? Most fundamentally, it meant that the king would not go to war against a baron unless the other barons consented. Secondarily, it meant that if a freeman (a fairly restricted class) was tried, he could not be judged by one of lower rank. In this sense the provision was designed to prevent the king's justices, who were not nobility, from conducting judicial proceedings against the barons. Hardly a progressive idea.

Most of the other claimed constitutional offspring of the charter are equally illegitimate.

The Petition of Right of 1628[8] falsely stated that Magna Charta established the writ of habeas corpus, which prohibits arbitrary imprisonment. In fact, John, Stephen, and the barons never heard of habeas corpus, or anything like it. What the Petition of Right may have been referring to was the "Writ of Life and Limb," granted by Chapter 36 of the charter. "Life and Limb" sounds as though it might have something to do with habeas corpus ("having the body"), but it does not. The Writ of Life and Limb was a process that allowed accused persons to avoid trial by battle under certain circumstances—not a very useful right in 1628.[9] Whatever the source of the confusion, it is undeniable that the one privilege uniformly exercised by every English monarch from 1215 to 1628 was the arbitrary imprisonment of enemies of the Crown, contrary to the principle of habeas corpus.

In the 1590s, the Puritan Robert Beale invented the outrageous fiction that Magna Charta prohibited compelling a person to testify against himself. Of course, testimony in the modern sense did not even occur in the trials of 1215, and the participation of defendants in the trials that did occur—the ordeals—was always compulsory. The first clear application of the privilege against self-incrimination occurred in 1568—about thirty years before Beale wrote—during the trial of Thomas Leigh for unlawful participation in a Catholic Mass. In crediting the privilege to Magna Charta, Beale was exactly 353 years wrong.

Lord Edward Coke's seventeenth-century claims that the charter prohibited monopolies (it came closer to guaranteeing them) and taxation without representation (it did require the barons to be consulted about increases in feudal rents, but neither taxation nor representation existed in 1215) are equally anachronistic.

The imagined right to jury trial and the other aspects of the Magna Charta myth are spectacular examples of an old lawyer's trick. Lawyers need precedents. It is difficult to stand up and ask that things be done that have never been done before. A right that has no age on it carries little weight. As new constitutional principles began to emerge, particularly in the early years of the seventeenth century, English lawyers learned to "discover" those rights in the obscure and stately language of the charter. The result was one of the most brilliant and productive uses of the power of myth in the history of our civilization.

The road from reality to myth was long and tortuous. Throughout the thirteenth century, the charter was at the center of English political life, a practical focal point for power struggles among the ruling classes. But when Parliament became fully formed in the fourteenth and fifteenth centuries, it displaced the charter in the nation's political consciousness. With the establishment of Parliament, the struggle for governmental power between nobility and king had found a new battlefield, and a new mechanism for resolving political grievances was in place. By the time of the Tudor monarchies (1485–1603), Magna Charta had all but disappeared from view. Shakespeare's play *King John,* otherwise rich in historical detail, does not even mention the events of Runnymede or the great charter they produced.

Then, by a leap of genius now difficult to reconstruct, lawyer contemporaries of Shakespeare—Beale, Coke, and their parliamentary colleagues—saw meaning in Magna Charta that had not previously been conceived of. Rules of warfare were seen as guarantees of trial fairness and prerogatives of barons as the rights of common men.[10] The historical remoteness of the charter did not weaken these interpretations; it gave force to them, like the biblical pronouncements of ancient Israel.

The events that caused Magna Charta to "walk again" in seventeenth-century England were a distant replay of the events of 1215. Once again, an inept, belligerent king unwisely provoked governmental rivals whose authority was second only to his own. In 1603, King James rode down from Scotland to take the English throne, asserting his divine right ("Kings are not only God's lieutenants ... but even by God himself they are called gods") and determined to keep the newly power-conscious members of Parliament in their places—and in prison, if need be ("I am surprised that my ancestors should ever have allowed such an institution to come into existence"). By the time his even more obnoxious son, Charles I, had been deposed and beheaded forty-five years later, the Parliamentarians who opposed these assertions of arbitrary royal power, headed by Lord Coke, had transformed the ancient charter into a legal Goliath that no one who lived prior to 1600 would have recognized.

This was not merely a matter of reinterpreting a four-hundred-year-old document, as an American scholar might reinterpret provisions of the Bill of Rights. Coke was "calling spirits from the vasty deep" in a way no modern lawyer would undertake to do. He said that Magna Charta was the embodiment of "the immemorial common law" that came from an unremembered time, before the Norman Conquest, before the forest Saxons, back perhaps to the laws of King Arthur himself. The rights he asserted against the king had always been implicit in this law, he said; if not in its letter, then certainly in its spirit. His writings and speeches on the subject were not scholarly reports; they were sermons in support of a secular religion.

The disparity between the myth and fact of Magna Charta does not, of course, diminish it as a force in legal history. What is believed about it has taken on an independent life that does not depend upon historical verification. The Great Charter[11] has had two existences: It was the extorted treaty of 1215, which settled the contemporary grievances of powerful men; it became the justifying reference point for men of later ages, who made its archaic phrases fit the needs of their times. Magna Charta as a great instrument of liberty was the creation not only of its own age, but of later ages that strove for the idea that government is something greater than the naked exercise of power.

Yet the power of the myth was there from the beginning. From its inception, the fundamental meaning of Magna Charta was that *the King is subject to the law*—whatever that law might be. By bowing to the demands of the barons, however unwillingly, John made those words flesh. From Runnymede on, the people of England *knew* that the king was under law because they had, in a sense, seen it with their own eyes.[12] That concrete vision was the source of all of the constitutional rights that followed, and in that sense, Magna Charta gave birth to them all.

3

THE BAR IS BORN

It is shameful to be a lawyer.
ADOLPH HITLER

American trial lawyer F. Lee Bailey once gave a newspaper interview in which he said "the public regards lawyers with great distrust. They think lawyers are smarter than the average guy, but use their intellects deviously. Well, they're wrong; usually [lawyers] are not smarter." Bailey was engaging in one of America's most popular indoor sports—the systematic denigration of the legal profession.

It is by no means a new pastime, even among lawyers. Thomas More, chancellor of England under Henry VIII and author of the sixteenth-century classic *Utopia,* explained that he had provided no lawyers for the citizens of his ideal society, "for [Utopians] consider them as a sort of people whose practice it is to disguise matters." When Abraham Lincoln came upon a cemetery headstone with the inscription "Here lies a lawyer and an honest man," he remarked, "I didn't know that things were so bad that they were putting two to a grave." Nineteenth-century English prime minister Benjamin Disraeli was quoted as saying in all sincerity, "To be a great lawyer, I must give up my chance of being a great man."

Nonlawyers have been even more hostile in denouncing the profession. "I think we may class lawyers in the natural history of monsters," wrote English poet John Keats. English novelist Anthony Trollope was only slightly more polite: "Is it not the case that the body of lawyers is supposed to be the most roguish body in existence?" American poet Carl Sandburg put it poetically: "Why is there always a secret singing when a lawyer cashes in; Why does a hearse horse snicker hauling a lawyer away?"

On the other hand, it is difficult to contest the objective accuracy of Alexis de Tocqueville's assessment that "in America . . . lawyers form the highest political class of society. . . . If I were asked where I placed the American aristocracy, I should reply without hesitation that . . . it occupies the judicial bench and the bar." The creation of the American nation was announced in what was essentially a lawyer's brief called the Declaration of Independence. Its government was conceived in a legal document called the United States Constitution. Many of the nation's greatest heroes, from John Marshall to Daniel Webster to Oliver Wendell Holmes to Clarence Darrow, have been members of the bar. Even today, when lawyer jokes are rampant, there remains a sort of hostile respect for the bench and bar, based largely on a feeling of unavoidable dependence.

The hostility is real, and so is the dependence. No nation ever really wants professional lawyers, and in the beginning most nations try to do without them.[1] Like cancer surgeons, dentists, and undertakers, however, lawyers are as inevitable as the calamities they deal with.

Edward I was another of those magnificent Plantagenet kings: warrior, lawmaker, and administrator *extraordinaire*. His one fault may have been that he was *too* perfect, like a woman who is so beautiful and brilliant that no one can stand her. The admiring descriptions of him in the histories are interesting at first, but they tend to make the eyes glaze over after an effusive paragraph or two. Winston Churchill, no slouch in the hero department himself, described Edward as "of elegant build and lofty stature," "eloquent," "a mixture of the administrative capacity of Henry II and the personal prowess and magnanimity of Coeur de Lion," "animated by a passionate regard for justice and the law," and "masterful, but not tyrannical."[2]

His greatest achievements fell short of perfection, but only just. He never quite subdued the Scots in his incessant wars with them, but he beat them half to death and took their sacred Stone of Scone back to Westminster Abbey in London, where it still resides beneath his sculptured feet. He did not exactly create Parliament, but he gave it a coherent form and was the first king to use it as an effective royal ally. He was also the first true English legislator. Although his statutes supposedly declared preexisting laws instead of inventing new ones, they had a potent impact on the lives of his contemporary and future countrymen, in a few cases surviving well into the twentieth century.

In the midst of these grand accomplishments, he is said to have given a quiet, casual order in 1291 that may have been the most important single thing he did as king:

> Concerning attorneys and apprentices the Lord King enjoined Mattingham and his fellows to provide and ordain at their discretion a certain number, from every County of the better, worthier, and more promising. . . . And that those so-chosen should follow the Court and take part in its business; and no others.

In issuing this order, Edward was merely applying his administrative instincts to another segment of government. To him it only made common sense to limit practice in his courts to the ablest advocates and to exclude the bunglers. His predecessors in kingship had tended to rely upon the "amateurish assistance of great feudalists staggering under the weight of their own dignity" to conduct public affairs.[3] Edward believed in using the best and the brightest, blokes who knew what they were *doing,* by God.

When he created this specialized cadre of court pleaders, however, he did something revolutionary. He inadvertently launched the legal profession as we know it today by providing the essential ingredient of monopoly power. The class of men admitted to "practice" as a result of his order to Mattingham achieved a special status that would in time replace ecclesiastical office in the English social hierarchy and rank only slightly below the exalted station of Parliament men. More importantly, once these professionals got ahold of it, the law of England would never be the same again.

* * *

Lawyers were late arrivals in the English justice system, for obvious reasons. The early English trials were personal verbal tests performed by the parties themselves, in which professional advocates had no place. People who sued and those they sued were required to stand before the court and repeat complex pleading formulas that defined the issues and asserted the rightness of their cause.[4] If they made significant misstatements, they lost. Sending a surrogate to perform in these verbal ordeals would have been the ethical equivalent of cheating on a college examination.

As pleading became more a matter of logic and less a matter of iron-headed repetition, litigants were allowed to bring friends with them to do their pleading for them—but for those advocates, it was a hazardous undertaking. Since the pleading was the litigant's statement, he could repudiate his representative's version of it if it proved to be erroneous. In 1208, William of Cockham brought a land dispute before the king's court and persuaded his more worldly friend, John de Planez, to plead on his behalf. John had never previously represented another person in court and was extremely nervous. He cleared his throat and began to describe the complex chain of title that supported William's claim. In the first few minutes of his recitation, still nervous, he referred to a land conveyance forty years previously as having been made "in the reign of Henry, grandfather of our Sovereign Lord, King John." When he paused in confusion, his client alertly intervened to repudiate the blunder, correctly identifying Henry as John's *father*. John de Planez was duly chastised by the justice and amerced (fined) for "breaking" William's plea! So much for helping out a friend.

As in all human endeavors that last long enough, skill came to be prized in the pleading process, and only effective stand-ins were invited back again. William probably did not ask John to plead for him in his next trial, but he may have asked Geoffrey, who had done well for William's Uncle Richard in another case, and perhaps he induced Geoffrey's appearance as counsel by agreeing to pay his "expenses."

By the time of Edward's decree, there was already a group of men such as Geoffrey holding themselves out as semiprofessional pleaders. The decree weeded out the weak ones, bolstered the effective ones, and made the entire process legitimate. Within a year, the first case reports, called Year Books, were being published, and they reflected that a few lions of the bar—Lowther, Spigurnel, Howard, King, Huntingdon, and Heyham—had already cornered the market on the great litigation of the realm. Undoubtedly their offspring have enjoyed a similar lucrative stranglehold on justice down to the present day.

But more was created by Edward's decree than another monied class. The real creation was the future shape of the law itself. Until 1291, the justice system had basically been the property of government. The law supposedly consisted of the customs of the people, but those customs were interpreted by the king's men, who were the only professionals on the scene. Justice was the king's justice and law was the king's law, however benign and impartial the interpretations might purport to be. Without a professional bar, without a class of advocates asserting the interests of individual subjects, the law might have remained essentially the servant of those in power.

From the date they were granted their monopoly status, lawyers became the engines of legal definition and change. Over the centuries, the legal system became a capitalistic, consumer-driven institution, with lawyers constantly pushing for redefinition and improvement on behalf of their litigant customers. England and America could not have progressed legally as they did without professional lawyers, any more than they could have progressed commercially as they did without entrepreneurs. Almost every inch of progress our law has made originated in a lawyer's brief. The people have good reasons not to like the professional bar, but it was the lawyers who preserved ownership of the law for them.

Don't take a right that's given to you, said Mr. Dooley, there's always something wrong with it. Americans have not had to put up much with the indignity of conferred rights. Their lawyers have wrested from government most of the fundamental rights and freedoms they have needed.

The most basic precept of our most basic freedom—that true statements cannot be punished by the state—was established by lawyer Andrew Hamilton over the contemptuous resistance of a judge. Protection from unreasonable searches and seizures was first proposed by lawyer James Otis in a stirring speech to a bank of un-responsive judges. The twentieth century's most important constitutional idea—that separation of the races is incompatible with legal equality—was introduced by lawyer Thurgood Marshall to a Supreme Court that came late and reluctantly to the idea. The revolution in press law that began in 1964 with *New York Times* v. *Sullivan* might never have occurred but for the brilliant impetus provided by *New York Times* lawyer Herbert Weschler. None of the above were governmental gifts, and if the people had waited for government to confer them, they might still be waiting, in patience and in ignorance.

Every day, in every court, competing lawyers push and pull, assert and contradict. In the process they disclose law to judges who seldom know it as they are supposed to, and reveal facts to juries who are always hungry for them. If knowledge is power, the relentless, self-interested, digging-up and framing of law and fact by professionals have made our judicial system more powerful, by geometric multiples, than any conceivable judge-driven system. No other aspect of our government has integrated private energy and motive one-tenth as well.

Edward was as unidealistic in all of this as were the hard-eyed opportunists he empowered. His goal was efficiency, not people-driven law. He helped create the most successful popularly based legal system the world has ever seen, without in the least meaning to do so. That seems to be the norm in the progress of our legal system. It has more or less muddled through to greatness.

A Scottish lawyer (Peter Watson) who represented some of the plaintiffs in the 1991 Lockerbie plane crash cases recently gave a speech to a group of American lawyers. His theme was the American legal system as a force for social betterment. The litigation process in this country, he said, with its potential for large judgments and the incentive of contingent fees, empowers ordinary people by empowering their lawyers. "When corporate America screws up," he said, "the American bar sends it a message loud and clear. American lawyers make industry accountable. If a car design is proven dangerous in a lawsuit, and a large enough judgment is returned, the design is modified. The American lawyer is a white knight for ordinary people; a power equalizer for the otherwise powerless."

The Lockerbie tragedy was, he said, a convincing case in point. "As the catalogue of incompetence, deceit, dishonesty and risk taking" emerged during the investigation of the crash, "the insurance industry rigorously examined security practices at airports and as operated by airlines." The "huge pay-out" they faced in the pending cases "was bad enough for one crash, but they would ensure it would not happen again. The way to ensure that was to make sure security standards were in place which would prevent unaccompanied bags getting on board planes they insured." Such remedial measures would probably never have been taken, he said, but for the investigative efforts of plaintiffs' lawyers pursuing large fees and the threat of similar efforts by other lawyers in future cases. The lawyers' intensive, profit-motivated diligence had benefited every person who rides on airplanes.

"That's very nice," said a young female lawyer during the questioning. "But if it's true, why are we, of all the lawyers in the world, so disliked?"

"No, no," the speaker replied. "It's not just *you*. You must understand, we are despised *everywhere*. No one likes a lawyer until he *needs* one.

"But think where this Country would be without them. Just think."

4

BINDING PRECEDENT

Because I have been wrong once, I don't intend to be wrong forever.

VAUGENQUES

About once in every generation, a constitutional whale surfaces in the American judicial sea. A massive issue is presented to the Supreme Court, which traverses deep fault lines in the American psyche. The species has included *Dred Scott* v. *Sandford* (1857), which held that slaves had no rights under the U.S. Constitution; the *Legal Tender Cases* (1870), which legalized paper money; *Lochner* v. *New York* (1905), which limited Congress's authority to regulate business on social policy grounds; and *Brown* v. *Board of Education* (1954), which ended legalized segregation.

Such cases force the justices to decide the limits of their own power under circumstances of extreme social and political pressure. They test the strength of the rule of law in America and even its continued viability. Because they approach the outer perimeters of settled legal concept and traditional values, they provoke storms of intellectual and emotional resistance; and, however they are decided, they fundamentally affect the nation's culture.

Such a leviathan appeared before the Court in 1973, in a case called *Roe* v. *Wade*. As the world knows, *Roe* decided that the Constitution affords women a qualified right to abortions that cannot be abridged by criminal antiabortion statutes.

A sleeping, ill-tempered giant was awakened by the decision. Prior to *Roe,* America's deeply divided views about abortion had been mostly latent. Now, pro-lifers joined forces to oppose what they considered a genuinely evil exercise of judicial power. They were supported by respectable legal scholars, who claimed that the justices' discovery of a constitutional abortion right in *Roe* was intellectually obtuse, if not outright fraudulent.

Over the ensuing years, the "right to life" of embryos and the "right to bodily integrity" of women became political battle cries, just as the "Southern way of life" and "racial justice" had been in the years following *Brown* v. *Board of Education.* Unlike *Brown,* however, no consensus about *Roe* was ever reached. If anything, the controversy grew sharper over time. Nominees for the Supreme Court were scrutinized by the opposing forces for signs of pro-life or pro-choice leanings. As a series of supposedly conservative justices was appointed by the Reagan and Bush administrations throughout the 1980s, the hopes of the pro-lifers for a reversal of *Roe* progressively increased, and the fears of the pro-choicers deepened. These hopes and fears came home to roost when the appeal in *Planned Parenthood* v. *Casey* was argued in April 1992.

At issue was the constitutionality of a Pennsylvania statute that imposed a variety of restrictions on abortion, including a requirement that women contemplating abortion give their husbands advance notice and that they submit to counseling regarding the risks of, and alternatives to, abortion. The contending factions were not so much interested in the details of the statute as they were in the opportunity the case presented for the Court to overrule *Roe* v. *Wade.*

The betting was heavily against the survival of *Roe.* Four of the justices—Chief Justice William Rehnquist, Antonin Scalia, Byron White, and Clarence Thomas—would certainly vote to overrule it. Only Harry Blackmun, the author of the *Roe* opinion, and John Paul Stevens could be counted on to uphold the embattled precedent. The other three—Sandra Day O'Connor, Anthony Kennedy, and David Souter—were moderate-to-conservative Republican appointees who were thought to have personal misgivings about abortion. Surely one of them would be moved to join the other four in administering a death blow to *Roe.*

Most Americans saw the case as a contest between the "right to life" and the "right to choose." Legal scholars and serious lawyers saw another issue, perhaps even more profound. They saw *Casey* as a rare acid test of the principle of *stare decisis* (to stand on decisions), on which the very integrity of the judicial process depends. What meaning would the rule of law have if the Court could discard so important a precedent after nineteen years simply because of a turnover in Court personnel? On the other hand, what kind of a system of justice would require its judges to apply law they believed to be bad simply because it had existed for two decades? The very meaning of the rule of law appeared to be at issue.

The Court announced its decision on June 29, 1992. The three "swing" Justices—O'Connor, Kennedy, and Souter—had written the majority opinion jointly, something that had not occurred since 1976, when the Court reinstated the death penalty. When the case was called for presentation, each of the three justices read a portion of the opinion. They were plainly seeking the shelter of solidarity.

They needed it. Most observers agreed that the majority opinion was a diligently reasoned mess. It purported to reaffirm the "central holding" of *Roe* while rejecting much of its substance. The legality of an abortion would no longer depend, as *Roe* had mandated, upon which trimester of pregnancy it occurred in, and restrictions on abortion would no longer be subject to "strict" judicial scrutiny, as *Roe* had held. Legislation would be valid if it did not place an "undue burden" upon the right to an abortion—an exceedingly mushy standard for such an important issue, most observers thought.

Both factions expressed bitter disappointment. One abortion rights activist was quoted as saying that *Casey* represented the "first time in history" the Supreme Court had "weakened protection for a right it once deemed fundamental." The decision was "devastating for women," she said, and "moved them one step closer to the back alleys."[1] Abortion opponents were "equally unhappy." The president of the National Right to Life Committee said that the ruling was "a loss for unborn children and a victory for pro-abortion forces."[2]

The debate over the jurisprudential soundness of the decision was equally shrill. One commentator thought that the Court's purported adherence to the "central holding" of *Roe* was a "resounding reaffirmation" of precedent, "an amazing act of courage and intellectual honesty [and] a blow for the rule of law."[3] Another thought that the decision should "worry all Americans—whether supporters or opponents of abortion rights"—because it "proclaimed a formidable and frightening barrier for correcting erroneous precedents."[4] A third thought that it was "a head-scratching opinion that accomplishes nothing."[5]

It seems remarkable that the honest efforts of competent judges could produce such conflict and confusion, and wind up pleasing almost no one. And yet it has happened before and will happen again. *Planned Parenthood* v. *Casey* was merely a particularly troubling chapter in an old familiar story.

In the Year of Our Lord 1454, a group of young apprentices sat in the rear of a darkening courtroom, half listening to the advocates. The argument was swinging back again, in a great repetitive arc, having ceased making any forward progress. It had gone on past its time, producing enough verbiage to fill four quartos, thirty-two pages, of transcript. All but one of the apprentices had stopped taking notes.

The attorney addressing the judges laboriously pressed a thrice-made argument once again. It was based on a line of reasoning followed by a judge in a similar case several years before. The logic of that case, the attorney insisted, should be applied to the present one.

After a period of frowning, lip-pursing, and throat-clearing— all unnoticed by the tedious advocate—the patience of Chief Justice Prisot came to an end. He abruptly cut off the lawyer's argument. "If we have to pay attention to the opinions of one or two judges," he snapped, "which are contradictory to many other judgments by honorable judges in the opposite sense, it would be a strange situation." This was particularly true, he said, because the more numerous judgments were older ones, by judges "nearer to the making of the statute than we are, [who] had more knowledge of it." Moreover, he continued—glancing toward the back of the courtroom— "if we were to rule as you suggest, it would assuredly be a bad example to the young apprentices . . . for they would never have any confidence in their books if now we were to adjudge the contrary of what has been so often adjudged in the books."

Centuries later, Prisot's words would be remembered as the first clear hint of a legal doctrine called *stare decisis,* which would come to dominate English law. But no particular importance was attached to them by those who heard them. Indeed, the advocate to whom they were directed was probably puzzled by them. Bad example to the apprentices? Well, what of that, so long as it be the *law?* And yet, he might have conceded to himself, "the law" *could* at times be a most elusive thing.

A French lawyer has at least one advantage over his English counterpart: He knows where his law comes from and when it came into being. On March 15, 1803, the French government promulgated the Code Napoléon, 450 pages of superbly wrought text setting forth the whole of French law. In 1811, an English translator enviously praised the code's "unrivaled" "closeness of language . . . correctness of wording and extent of application" and commended it to "all admirers of jurisprudence."

No such elegant coherence is to be found on the other side of the Channel. Ask an English lawyer to identify the source of his country's general law, and you will get a baffled stare, a history lecture, or perhaps an evocation of Coke's "unremembered past."

The English (and American) common law is—as its practitioners love to say—"judge-made" and therefore without discoverable origin. In a practical sense, it can *have* no origin, since the first judge to decide an "English" case, whoever he may have been, was necessarily relying on *some* preexisting notion of what the decision should be. In this sense, Coke's "immemorial common law" is something more than jurisprudential moonshine.

Historians have ascribed the invention of the "common law" to Henry II and his traveling judges, who administered the first nationwide justice system in England in the mid- to late twelfth century. This law was, simply, the "custom" of the courts: not codified rules, but an accumulation of practices that were developed and modified as they were applied to individual disputes.

By the time Chief Justice Prisot spoke his piece in 1454, this customary law was complicated, having been modified and manipulated—and occasionally misrepresented and mangled—by generations of clever practitioners. Its meaning had been influenced by decisions in individual cases, of course, but—and this was the essential fact—the law was not the decisions *themselves*. The common law remained "legal custom" as "known" to the deciding court, and the law as construed by that court need not be—might even be contrary to—previous case decisions. The idea that a court might be "bound" by a prior decision, or that such a decision might be the law itself, was entertained by no one in 1454.

Prisot's statement made such an idea at least thinkable. It suggested that consistency for consistency's sake should be a principle of judicial decision-making; that the fact that a previous court had applied a given principle was, in and of itself, a reason for applying it again; that maintaining the "confidence" of the "apprentices" might be a sufficient reason for a court to rein in independent thinking and adhere to the reasoning of a predecessor court.

Prisot's concern for the mental quietude of law students—and, obviously, practicing lawyers as well—marked the beginning of a process that would, in the end, make judges the creators of law and the prisoners of their own creation. When the doctrine of binding precedents reached full force in future generations, it became the intellectual glue—the general hallmark and sometimes curse—of the Anglo-American legal system.

The foundations of *stare decisis* were laid two centuries before Judge Prisot spoke by Henri de Bracton (1215–68), a judge of the court of common pleas. Bracton had an idea that would prove as important to English law as the theory of gravity is to physics—the recording and analysis of cases. The idea was much easier to conceive than to implement. In Bracton's time, the records of court cases were as inaccessible as the crown jewels and, even after one got general access to them, they remained practically inaccessible because of their form. They consisted of hundred weights of closely guarded, unindexed, unorganized pipe rolls on which were recorded, end-to-end, the records of pleadings and decisions in literally thousands of cases.[6]

If genius consists of "an infinite capacity for taking pains," Bracton was the legal genius of the ages. He somehow obtained possession of the pipe rolls and recorded the reasoning and results of two thousand decided cases in his celebrated notebook. No other English lawyer made any similar use of precedent for generations afterward, and even Bracton's notebook was not published during his lifetime. After several years of Bracton's mining in the pipe rolls, the authorities abruptly demanded that he return them to the bolted cellars from which they came, and his noble work was ended, never to be taken up again.

Why did Bracton undertake this arduous, thankless labor? To demonstrate that the law, as applied in his time, was inferior to that applied in the previous generation. How omnipresent is the myth of a better past! Here was Bracton, writing at the dawn of English law, longing for the good old days when cases were decided *right*. According to him, the contemporary judges were "ignorant" and "foolish," not fit to sit on benches once occupied by his heroes, Justices Bereford and Pateshull. By definition, Bracton recognized that the older, superior decisions were not law but only illustrations of what the law should be.

Bracton's efforts inspired an interest in precedents and probably the development of England's first regularly circulated case reports—the famous Year Books (1291–1535). These were really legal newspapers produced by lawyers who attended trials and recorded the verbal give-and-take between the advocates and judges. The early year books are full of the joy of combat and dwell at length on the personalities of the participants, honoring the heroes, criticizing the inept, and applauding clever efforts to make weak arguments prevail. They include many rambling conversations and witty asides that modern lawyers would consider irrelevant to a case report.

The earliest year books were not, in fact, like modern case reports at all, but more like modern news coverage of sporting events. Like all journalism, the truth they conveyed depended upon the interests and competence of the reporters who conveyed it, and there were multiple reports of single trials. It was, therefore, often difficult to tell with any clarity what a reported case was about, or what it decided. These early year books were a step up from reliance on oral memory, but only a step.

By Prisot's time, this was beginning to change. The year books had become more precise and businesslike. They omitted the jokes and repartee, and stuck to business. More importantly, they had become more uniform, to the extent that there appears to have been only one reporter at a time.

The clarity and consistency of these reports made Prisot's call for consistent decision-making predictable. The year book cases were now definite entities, and everyone's version of them was the same. Now one read them, not just to get a sense of the general direction of the law in given areas, but to study specific lines of legal analysis. Since the decisions had a clear, agreed-upon content, they could be cited in court, and judges and opposing lawyers had to take them into account. Consistency in decision-making became a touchstone of legal argument. As lawyers acquired the means to confront judges with precise information regarding past treatment of similar disputes, consistency took on the moral force of even-handedness, and hence of justice itself. Prisot's statement did not propose an innovation; it merely called attention to what was already taking place.

In the year that statement was recorded—probably with a quill on parchment—the first book ever printed with movable type, the Gutenberg Bible, rolled off a German press. Twenty-two years later (1476), William Caxton introduced printing into England. In time, this technology made it possible to record case law and commentary in universally accessible form. As the exact words of prior decisions became widely and easily available to lawyers and judges, those decisions naturally began to be seen as "the law itself."

By the time of England's second great case commentator, Edward Coke (1552–1634), the dissemination of printed case law had revolutionized the idea of precedent. The decisions Coke recorded could be studied, refined, and applied in various permutations over the years because they were fixed and widely distributed in the enduring medium of print. They were an accessible body of knowledge, a storehouse of legal ammunition, that eventually lined the library walls of every substantial law school, lawyer, and judge in the land.

In a cultural sense, the rise of case law and *stare decisis* was part of the vast sea change called the scientific revolution. By 1454, pragmatic analysis was replacing a priori reasoning, not only in law but on many other fronts. In law's sister discipline of medicine, religious charms such as church door keys were giving way to scientific cures such as quinine (as an antiseptic), tobacco (as a narcotic), and comfrey (as a cure for bronchitis). No longer the refuge of mystics and barbers, medicine and surgery were becoming licensed professions that required the application of learned knowledge to analytically defined problems.

Lawyers unconsciously sought a similar scientific status. Medicine and the hard sciences dealt with objective realities, such as the human body and the properties of matter, which lent themselves to knowledge-oriented, analytic treatment. Printed case law provided an objective reality for lawyers that could be subjected to similar "scientific" analysis. It was not entirely coincidental that Coke was examining old English precedents at the same time Galileo was examining the heavens through the first telescope; or that Coke's description of the case law as "an artificial perfection of reason, gotten by study, observation and experience" echoed the language of the laboratory.

There was, of course, a logical trap in all of this, for unlike the objects of true scientific investigation, decisional law was the creation of those who "observed" it. A planet was a planet was a planet, but a precedent was the law only if, and to the extent, the judge examining it said it was. This gave rise to a troublesome question unlike any encountered by doctors or scientists. If past decisions were law, when, if at all, did they *cease* to be law? When a court disagreed with them? Then precedents were meaningless, and law was nothing but the present exercise of power. When the disagreement was violent? That, more or less, became the rule.

Requiring consistency in judicial decision-making is by far the most important idea ever introduced into our law. Compared to it, due process is a superficial notion and the presumption of innocence a passing fancy. Today, the art of lawyering largely consists of dealing, one way or another, with the results and reasoning of previous case decisions. *Stare decisis* has become a definitional reality. Not only is fidelity to precedent a required method of deciding cases; it has come to represent the very meaning of our law.

For a long time, the legal system was comfortable with rigidly binding precedents. They went hand in hand with the so-called discovery theory of law, which was in vogue in England and America until the end of the nineteenth century. The discovery theory held that the rules that make up the common law preexisted any court decision, and that the task of judges in deciding cases is simply to discover those rules. When a judge refused to apply a rule that had been announced in a prior case, he was not changing the law; he was discovering and applying it correctly. The theory was that "the old rule never existed," that "the judge who announced [it] in the former decision must have had bad eyesight, for he had [made] a mistake in 'finding' the 'Law.' "[7]

This notion of a fixed, preexisting law tended to support a strict application of *stare decisis*. If legal rules were permanent fixtures, judges could not be innovators. Once the applicable rule was discovered, it must be applied, regardless of the judges' personal notions of fairness and justice.

This led to a kind of "dignified cruelty" in decision-making, in which judges acknowledged that they were inflicting injustices while claiming an inability to do anything about it because of a higher duty to the law.[8] A dramatic example of this occurred in a slander case that came before the English Court of Common Pleas in the 1880s.[9] The plaintiff had been falsely accused of lewd sexual behavior and sought to recover damages from the slanderer. In a 1593 case, the same court had refused to hear a similar claim on the ground that charges of sexual immorality were within the sole jurisdiction of the church courts. By the 1800s, church courts had long since ceased to exist, and the logic of the 1593 ruling had evaporated.

The presiding judge nonetheless applied the three-hundred-year-old precedent and dismissed the slandered woman's claim, declaring his impotence in the matter with masochistic eloquence: "I may lament the unsatisfactory state of our [judge-made] law," he said, "according to which the imputation of words, however gross, however public, upon the chastity of a modest matron or a pure virgin is not actionable . . . but I am here only to declare the law." Having once been discovered, the rule in question could not be reconsidered; it could only be "declared" in its everlasting, original form.

Sensible commentators never accepted this metaphysical view of judicial decision-making. Writing in the early nineteenth century, John Austin derided the "childish fiction employed by our judges, that judiciary or common law is not made by them, but is a miraculous something made by nobody, existing, I suppose, from eternity and merely declared from time to time by the judges."[10] By the end of the century, the discovery theory and the strict application of *stare decisis* it supported were both in retreat. They have been displaced in the twentieth century by a pragmatic approach to applying precedents, which acknowledges that judges do create law and requires, at least theoretically, a rational blend of fairness and consistency in the creation process.

This approach has worked well in the everyday decision-making of state and lower federal courts. Most of the commercial, tort, and regulatory rules applied by these courts are morally and politically neutral. As long as they are rational and consistently applied, they serve their purpose. Adherence to precedents in this context is largely a matter of convenience. As Judge Benjamin Cardozo noted, "[T]he labor of judges would be increased almost to the breaking point if every past decision could be reopened in every case, and one could not lay one's own course of bricks on a secure foundation of the course laid by others who have gone before him."[11]

The process of overruling common-law precedents is rational, almost technical. The court asks itself such questions as, How well is the existing rule working? Will the proposed change effect a real improvement? Have social or economic conditions altered since the previous rule was adopted, so that its overruling will not appear to be mere whim? Have a large number of people taken actions in reliance upon the prior rule, so that changing it will unfairly injure them?

Judges have used this methodology to effect a gradual transformation of the common law throughout the twentieth century. The technological explosion America has experienced has, for example, led courts to impose strict liability upon manufacturers and sellers of dangerous products that would not have been recognized a century ago. For similar reasons, the old rule barring purchasers of defective products from suing the manufacturer has been abolished, and the rule preventing all recovery by a plaintiff whose negligence contributed to his injury has been generally replaced by a rule of comparative negligence, which apportions recovery according to the respective fault of the parties. These and similar overrulings have been generally well received. They have shown rational respect for precedent while moving the law forward at a reasonable pace.

Conditions have been starkly different on the constitutional front, where Supreme Court battles are fought. There the issues tend to be both moralistic and controversial. Whereas common-law rules are considered largely technical and within the special province of the court, constitutional rules have no such insulation. Every citizen is his own expert on the great rights and freedoms applied in Supreme Court decisions. Large sections of the population feel a personal stake, pro and con, in constitutional precedent and respond vociferously to the Supreme Court's handling of it.

Moreover, the subject matter of constitutional adjudication lends itself to overrulings. The broad, vague commands of the Bill of Rights—that freedom of speech and press shall not "be abridged," that there be no "establishment of religion"—permit a great variety of plausible interpretations. At the same time, the values they express are too profound to be applied without the aid of individual conscience and belief. A judge may trade a rule of "contributory negligence" for one of "comparative negligence" with cool objectivity, but to uphold the validity of the death penalty he must consult his soul.

Thus, as the personnel of the Supreme Court changed throughout the century, views were imported into the Court that produced terrific pressures for overruling precedents.

The late 1930s and 1940s were a virulent era of Supreme Court overrulings. The mostly conservative "nine old men" who had dominated the Court for two decades had been replaced by a cadre of enthusiastic activists appointed by FDR. These new justices viewed many of their predecessors' constitutional rulings as simply wrong and moved to correct them in a straightforward manner. Eschewing the traditional bag of judges' tricks—"distinguishing" prior cases on their facts, overruling the substance of precedents while preserving their form—they swept an array of established rulings out of existence. Because much of this activity occurred while the Court's personnel was in the process of being replaced, one of its striking features was the lightning-quick reversals of just-established precedents.

One of the shortest-lived precedents in Supreme Court history was *Jones* v. *Opelika,* decided on June 6, 1942, and overruled on May 3, 1943. The issue was whether a privilege tax on the door-to-door sale of religious literature violated the freedom of religion clause of the First Amendment. Absolutely not, said the *Jones* Court, in a 5-4 decision. Although the vote was close, the Court's language was emphatic. "It is difficult to see a *shadow of prohibition* of the exercise of religion" in such taxation, the justices proclaimed. Eleven months later, that barely detectable shadow had become a crushing presence. In *Murdock* v. *Pennsylvania,* the Court smothered the infant *Jones* under an avalanche of dire verbiage that cast doubt on the Court's own mental competence in ever giving birth to it. "This method of disseminating religious beliefs [i.e., door-to-door] can be *crushed and closed out by the sheer weight of the toll or tribute* which is exacted town by town, village by village," said the newly enlightened Court.

The brief time interval between decision and overruling naturally arouses suspicion that some form of religious conversion may have taken place. The true explanation is less exciting. On October 5, 1942, James Byrnes, a member of the 5-4 *Jones* majority, resigned from the Court, and on February 11, 1943, Justice Wiley Rutledge took his place just in time to become part of the 5-4 *Murdock* majority. The Supreme Court's rapid footwork is sometimes remarkable but seldom miraculous.

Similar decisional nimbleness was shown in other pairs of Supreme Court cases. On June 3, 1940, the Court held (8-1), in *Minersville School District* v. *Gobitis,* that Jehovah's Witness schoolchildren could be compelled to salute the American flag even though doing so violated their religious beliefs. "To hold [that such compulsion is unconstitutional] would in effect make us the [unelected] school board for the Country," said the majority opinion. Almost exactly three years later, in *West Virginia Board of Education* v. *Barnette* (June 14, 1943), the Court reversed itself by an identical 8-1 vote. "One's right to . . . freedom of worship . . . may not be submitted to vote; they depend on the outcome of no elections," said the Court, in precise contradiction of its former words.

In *Grovey* v. *Townsend* (April 1, 1935), the Court held that excluding Negroes from voting in the Texas Democratic party primary did not violate the Constitution because the Texas Democratic party was a private organization and the Constitution applies only to governmental action. "The primary is the party primary; the expenses of it are not born by the State, but by members of the party seeking nomination; the ballots are furnished, not by the State, but by agencies of the party; the votes are counted and the returns made by instrumentalities created by the parties." Nine years later, in *Smith* v. *Allwright* (April 3, 1944), the Court held that excluding Negroes from voting in the Texas Democratic party primary *did* violate the Constitution because the Texas Democratic party was a *government agency*. "The party takes its character as a state agency from the duties imposed upon it by state statutes; the duties do not become matters of private law because they are performed by a political party," said the remarkably flexible Court. It was this opinion that moved Justice Owen Roberts to make the famous remark that "adjudications of this tribunal [are being brought] into the same class as a restricted railroad ticket, good for this day and train only."

Roberts was hardly one to talk, having been the "hero" of the most spectacular personal flip-flop in Supreme Court history. In June 1936, he had voted with the 5-4 majority in *Morehead* v. *Tipelo* to invalidate New York's minimum wage law on due process grounds. In March 1937, he had executed the notorious "switch in time," voting with the 5-4 majority in *West Coast Hotel* v. *Parish* to reverse the *Morehead* decision and uphold Washington's minimum wage law against an identical due process attack. If any justice understood how to punch "one-day railroad tickets," Roberts did.

The public reaction to the Court's direct approach to overruling, particularly from conservatives, was predictably vociferous. "Because of the packing of the Court with leftists, New Dealers, bigots and political hacks, there is no law today," read a typically truculent editorial. "Precedent is only a word in the dictionary."[12] In 1944, the Texas Bar Association passed a resolution bitterly complaining that the Supreme Court had "over-ruled decisions, precedents and landmarks of long standing."[13] And many of short standing too, it might have added.

Realizing that their image had become wobbly from the overrulings of the 1930s and 1940s, the justices modified their tactics during the 1950s and 1960s. They didn't stop overruling, they simply denied that they were doing it. The Court plowed more new constitutional ground from 1954 to 1969 than it had plowed in the preceding fifty years, but you would never know it from reading the opinions. You would think the Court was merely scratching the topsoil.

When the justices outlawed legalized segregation in *Brown* v. *Board of Education* (1954), they offhandedly noted that the reasoning of *Plessy* v. *Ferguson* (1896), which had upheld segregation, was "rejected" *to the extent* it was inconsistent with the *Brown* decision. That was like Grant saying the South could no longer wage war to the extent doing so was inconsistent with unconditional surrender. In *Colgrove* v. *Green* (1953), the Court held that how legislatures apportioned themselves was a "political question" a court should not decide. In *Baker* v. *Carr* (1962), it held that reapportiontment was a proper judicial question—blandly denying that *Colgrove* had held the opposite.[14] Justice Frankfurter, who had *written* the *Colgrove* opinion, protested incredulously in a dissenting opinion—to no avail, of course.[15] When the Court applied the First Amendment to a libel case for the first time in *New York Times* v. *Sullivan* (1964), it was acting contrary to several previous decisions that had refused to do so. These inconvenient precedents were swept deftly under the judicial carpet, receiving only passing mention in Justice Brennan's historically sweeping opinion. The Court had learned that changing constitutional doctrine was like adultery: much less painful if you don't admit it.

The opinion in *Planned Parenthood* vs. *Casey* raised such judicial obfuscation to the level of an art form. The majority justices stated, no doubt sincerely, that their aim was to preserve the integrity of *stare decisis* and the rule of law. In fact, their puzzling opinion grievously undermined both. For a law to have meaning, it must be capable of being understood by those who are expected to abide by it. The *Casey* opinion is filled with sentences like this one: "In any event, because *Roe*'s scope is confined by the fact of its concern with post-conception potential life, a concern otherwise likely to be implicated only by some forms of contraception protected independently under *Griswold* and later cases, any error in *Roe* is unlikely to have serious ramifications in future cases." Constitutional rights defined this opaquely in a practical sense do not exist. Uncommunicated law is no law at all.

John Marshall's announcement of the crucial Doctrine of Judicial Review covered seven pages. The Supreme Court's adoption of the historic rule prohibiting the use of unconstitutionally seized evidence, six pages. Its first prohibition of prior restraints against the press, ten pages. These great opinions were written in relatively ordinary English. Love them or hate them, educated people could at least understand them. Not so the *Casey* opinion, which consists of thirty-eight pages of convoluted analysis only a narrow specialist could love—or comprehend.

The *Casey* opinion exudes a smell of overripeness. It conveys a sense that the practice of *stare decisis,* with all of its analytic possibilities, has been on the judicial vine too long and is beginning to decay. In this respect, *Casey* is typical of much of the Court's recent work product. For more than a generation, Supreme Court opinions have been turning in upon themselves, building on arcane phrasing and narrow analysis from case to case, giving instructions on our basic rights that even lawyers do not fully grasp and certainly cannot communicate. This is perhaps natural in a legal system that is based upon the constant elaboration of its own prior reasoning, but it is deadly to the rule of law.

Half a millennium after the law began to strive for consistent decision-making—and largely because of the intellectual contortions produced by that very effort—the "apprentices" find themselves more confused than they have ever been.

5

MAN AGAINST THE STATE

(Images of Justice)

Power concedes nothing without a demand.
FREDERICK DOUGLASS

In the 1960s, Robert Bolt's play and movie *A Man for All Seasons* brought the story of Thomas More's treason trial into popular focus. More was a lord chancellor of England who was beheaded in 1535 because he would not acknowledge Henry VIII's self-proclaimed status as head of the English church. Bolt's More was a strong but gentle defender of liberty of conscience for all people. Consumed though he was by his own faith, he retained an objectivity about it that kept him from imposing it on others. He was a surpassingly tolerant man who hoped that others would share his beliefs but conceded them the same right to theirs that he wanted for his own.

More's prospective son-in-law, William Roper, was a heretic according to More's beliefs, which temporarily disqualified him from marrying More's daughter. But the old boy couldn't help admiring the young man's integrity:

MARGARET: Is that [More's refusal to permit the marriage] final, Father?

MORE: As long as he's a heretic, Meg, that's absolute. (warmly) Nice boy ... terribly strong principles, though.

When More confronted the king's interrogators prior to his treason trial, Lord Cranmer challenged More's tolerance directly:

CRANMER: So, those of us whose names are there [on the oath affirming the king's supremacy] are damned, Sir Thomas?

More passed the test with flying colors:

MORE: I don't know, Your Grace. I have no window to look into another man's conscience. I condemn no one.

CRANMER: Then the matter is capable of question.

MORE: Certainly.

This More is truly a man for all seasons, and particularly a man for ours. His tolerance for the beliefs of others has a striking modern quality that seems to separate him from his own time and bring him into ours.

As is so often the case, however, More's life "reads much better than it played." The More of *A Man for All Seasons* is a classic example of an historical figure mythologized to fit modern biases. The footlights of the theater and the klieg lights of Hollywood have given him an artificial glow; he looked quite different in the light of a sixteenth-century sun.

They were an assemblage of power and respectability convened to do a colossally dirty job. England had often done prominent citizens to death, but Thomas More was something special. He was considered his country's greatest man: its most distinguished lawyer, its foremost man of letters, its most righteous public servant, and, until recently, the confidant and friend in whom the king had placed his greatest trust. Samuel Johnson would later call him "the person of greatest virtue these islands ever produced." It all meant nothing now. When More appeared before the court, hobbling on a cane, his proud face drawn from months in prison, his eighteen judges knew that they were looking at a dead man. His physical condition was not fatal, but his legal one most definitely was.

Accounts of his treason trial have the prisoner complaining that the indictment was so long, he "could scarce remember the third part of it" as it was read to him. This is strange because the statement of charges was, in fact, distressingly succinct. The only truly lethal accusation it contained was a charge of high treason based on a statement More allegedly made while in prison. According to the indictment, More had told the king's solicitor general, Richard Riche, that the recently enacted statute making the king the supreme head of the English church was ineffective.

Lord Chancellor Thomas Audley gave a cruel cat-and-mouse aspect to the proceedings by offering More the hope of "the pardon and favor of the King" if he would but "change his opinion." More answered "cheerfully," it is said, that he returned "thanks to your Honors, but I beseech Almighty God that I may continue in the mind I am in, through His grace, unto death."

More's principal accuser, Solicitor General Riche, was also one of his prosecutors. After some preliminary fencing over the lesser charges, in which the skilled and learned More was an easy victor, the trial got down to serious business. Calling himself as a witness, Riche testified that he had engaged More in a sort of Socratic dialogue while he was taking his books away from him in his Tower of London cell. In the midst of the discussion, he stated, he had said to More: "The King is constituted supreme head of the Church on earth. Why should you not, Master More, accept him as such, as you would me, if I were made King?" According to Riche, More made the fatal response: "The case is not the same, because a Parliament can make a King and depose him, but a subject cannot be bound in a case of [church] supremacy."

More flared back at Riche, calling him a notorious liar and "gamester." Then he used his ultimate weapon, his reputation as a true Christian believer: "If I were a man, my Lords, that had no regard to my oath, I had no occasion to be here at this time. . . . If this oath, Mr. Riche, which you have taken be true, then I pray I may never see God's face, which, were it otherwise, is an imprecation I would not be guilty of to gain the whole world."

It was no use, of course. In sixteenth-century England, the defendant could not "give evidence" on his own behalf, and the uselessness of a defendant's courtroom denial has never been more clearly demonstrated than in More's case. After witnessing one of the most compelling defensive efforts of the age, the jury deliberated exactly fifteen minutes before returning a guilty verdict. One week later, More's head was struck from his body by a headsman's ax and was hung from London Bridge until it became a skull.

The message conveyed to history by More's trial and death was not at all the one Henry VIII intended. With this brutal set piece of political theater, Henry created the first great martyr to the ideal of individual liberty that came to characterize English and American law.

Henry would have been stunned if he could have foreseen More's future reputation as an apostle of religious tolerance—as would More himself. The beliefs of Thomas Jefferson and James Madison, as embodied in the religious freedom clauses of our First Amendment, would have made More apoplectic. He had approximately the same attitude toward freedom of religious belief that Carrie Nation had toward drunkenness. As a devout Catholic, he believed passionately that it was the duty of government to identify and stamp out unorthodox religious doctrine by whatever means it took. As lord chancellor in the years immediately preceding his trial and death, he was the most committed heretic hunter in the English government. "The burning of heretics," he wrote with unintended black humor, "is lawful, necessary and well done." He imprisoned heretics in his home and was accused of beating and otherwise physically abusing them. He wrote grotesquely false accounts of the deaths of heretics, intended to make them look bad and the Catholic religion look good. A recent biography by Richard Marius summarizes More's views on religious toleration with the bark off:

> Heretics were the enemies of God . . . More believed that they should be exterminated, and while he was in office he did everything in his power to bring that extermination to pass. That he did not succeed in becoming England's Torquemada was a consequence of the King's quarrel with the Pope and not a result of any quality of mercy that stirred through More's own heart.[1]

Far from "condemn[ing] no one," he considered condemnation of religious error a sacred obligation.

This dichotomy between reputation and reality becomes understandable when More's trial is looked at in its own time. He was prosecuted under the recently enacted statute of treasons, which made it a capital offense to say that the king was a "heretic, schismatic, tyrant, infidel or usurper of the Crown." Parliament was terrified of this statute—any king who was called a tyrant often enough to need it obviously could not be trusted with its enforcement—but was convinced to pass it by the addition of the word "maliciously" to the definition of the offense. This was supposed to ensure that words alone would not be punished unless they implied an intent to commit treasonous acts.

The legal heart of More's defense was that a belief expressed in harmless private conversation could not be "malicious" in that sense. Even if he had engaged in the Socratic dialogue testified to by Riche, he argued, "it was spoken but in familiar secret talk, nothing affirming, and only in putting of cases, without other displeasant circumstances [and therefore] it cannot justly be taken to be spoken maliciously." In other words, it cannot be a crime—let alone treason—for a citizen to express an abstract belief on any subject without an intent to translate that belief into unlawful action. An expression of pure conscience is immune from punishment by the state.

More gave this idea wings in a great, simple speech: "I am the King's true, lawful subject and daily bondsman and pray for his Highness and all his and all the realm. I do nobody harm; I say none harm; I think none harm, but wish everybody good. And if this be not enough to keep a man alive, in good faith, I long not to live."

To a modern reader, this reads like a general plea for liberty of conscience, but the issue was more technical. More's argument addressed the state's power to punish treason, not the church's power to authorize the punishment of heretics through governmental processes. This distinction means little to us, but it meant everything to him. To him, it was the difference between earth and heaven.

More's great speech would have been inappropriate in a heresy prosecution—the beliefs of a heretic were, after all, the worst "harm" imaginable. But he was certain that he was guiltless of heresy as well. Not because erroneous religious beliefs should not be punished, but because his beliefs were right and the king's were wrong! In the final analysis, More's basic complaint against his accusers was not that they were intolerant, but that they were blind to the truth. In his last speech, given after the jury had sealed his doom by returning a guilty verdict, he admitted that he did not accept the king's supremacy over the church. He then reminded his judges that "of the learned and virtuous men now alive . . . they are ten to one of my mind in this matter" and many more among the dead. "And therefore, my Lords, I do not think myself bound to conform my conscience to the counsel of one kingdom against the general consent of all Christendom." Such a man might die for his own liberty of conscience, but not for yours or mine.

More and the martyrs who came after him brought about religious tolerance not by exhibiting it, but by forcing the state to eventually yield it through courageous, self-centered resistance to authority. The quality that allowed More to die courageously, and take his place in history, was not generosity of spirit but an unyielding sense of self. Bolt portrayed this trait as well, in one of the most revealing passages in his play. "I will not give in [on the question of the king's supremacy]," More tells his friend Lord Norfolk, "because I oppose it—*I* do—not my spleen nor any other part of my appetites, but *I* do—I!"

From the date of his death, historians treated More with admiration, even though they were put off by his Catholic zealotry. But it was not until the nineteenth century, when religious differences ceased to matter so much, that he truly came into his own as a constitutional hero. His image underwent a secularization process that transformed him into the English Socrates of Bolt's play.[2] He was seen through a pleasant historical haze as a man who stood up to tyranny—of some kind—and died for his beliefs—whatever they may have been. In the popular mind he had done it not only for himself, but for all of us.

Wendell Phillips wrote that "every step of progress the world has made has been from scaffold to scaffold and from stake to stake." More occupies a place of honor in that bloody procession because of what he gave the world with his last words and actions, misinterpreted though they may have been. It will be objected that he is traveling in disguise, but, as we will see, he is not the only marcher who is doing so.

More's execution was the true beginning of religious civil warfare in England. For centuries, Europe had stunk from the burning flesh of heretics, but the English air had been relatively free of such unpleasantness. The English people had accepted orthodox Catholicism without much questioning and had given the church few excuses to punish them. In 1220, a priest who had converted to Judaism was burned by a local sheriff, but no other Englishman died for his religion until a relapsed heretic named William Sawtre was burned at the stake in March 1401.

The smoke from Sawtre's execution was the beginning of a slowly growing cloud of persecution that would eventually darken all of England's skies. From his death to the death of More 135 years later, fifty heretics perished in the flames of Smithfield, the official place of execution for English heretics. After More, they numbered in the hundreds.

The fifty who preceded More were mostly Lollards, disciples of John Wycliffe, burned by the Catholic church for preaching denial of the pope's authority, reliance on individual reading of the Scriptures as the source of faith, and denial of transubstantiation (the belief that Christ's blood and body are actually consumed during communion). These executions were largely motivated by sincere beliefs. To men who accepted church doctrine as literal truth—which presumably included most of those who fired up the faggots—heretic-burning was logical. If murderers who took mortal lives were justly executed, what punishment could be enough for heretics, whose preaching endangered immortal souls?

This logic became strained when Henry made himself head of the English church in 1534. Such towering political narcissism had not been seen since the Emperor Caligula declared himself a god and his horse a Roman senator. Loyalty to God became equated with loyalty to Henry, and Henry's commands acquired the force of Holy Writ. Errors in faith became treason, dissenting political views became heresy, and either, if detected, could result in excruciating death.

Inflicting death to save souls had seemed a cruel necessity, but killing off political opponents in the name of religious purity was a game sincere believers would not tolerate forever. When religious verities began to change with kingships, and with changes in the attitudes of kings, popular resistance surfaced. What had been seen as the appropriate enforcement of piety was now seen as the laying of governmental hands upon the consciences of the people—and, in the end, the people would not stand for it.

After More's execution, the king's enforcers declared what

amounted to a holy war on anti-Anglican believers. To the date of Henry's death eleven years later, his government burned as many heretics (51)—mostly good Catholics—as had been put to the torch during the entire reigns of Henry IV, Henry V, Henry VI, Edward IV, Richard III, and Henry VII combined.

When Henry VIII's daughter Mary, the wife of King Philip of Spain and a committed Roman Catholic, took the throne in 1553, the doctrinal pendulum swung viciously back to pure Catholicism. The flames of Smithfield were stoked even higher—this time against Anglicans—and popular resentment rose with them. The unprecedented scale on which the queen slaughtered heretics fully justifies the infamous title "Bloody Mary," which history bestowed on her. During the five years of her reign, she burned an estimated 273 Protestant heretics. In 1557, the Italian ambassador noted in his diary that "two days ago, to the displeasure as usual of the population here, two Londoners were burned alive, one of them having been a public lecturer in Scripture, a person sixty years of age, who was held in great esteem. In a few days," he predicted, "the like will be done to four or five more; and thus from time to time to many others who are in prison for [heresy] and will not recant, although such sudden severity is odious to many people."

Indeed it was. Mary's inquisition poisoned the public well for English Catholics, making them a feared and hated "enemy within." A tidal wave of anti-Catholic fury carried into the reign of Anglican Elizabeth (1558–1603). Catholics were easy for Protestant Englishmen to hate, being guilty (by association) of the worst religious bloodbath in the nation's history, during Mary's reign. They were disloyal by definition, having spiritual allegiance to a foreign pope, which conflicted with their secular duty to queen and country (a conflict made stark in 1570, when a papal bull deposed Elizabeth as queen and commanded her subjects not to obey her laws, on pain of excommunication). While Catholics were enough of a threat to invite retribution, they were politically weak and safe to bully.

Anti-Catholicism propelled, and was propelled by, the publication of perhaps the most influential book in Anglo-American legal history. *Foxe's Book of Martyrs* (1563) was for more than a century the most widely read work in the English-speaking world, the Bible only excepted. It reported, in detailed question-and-answer form, the trials of the hero-victims of England's Catholic inquisition. As Foxe's verbose title put it, it described "the Acts and monuments of these latter perilous days, touching matters of the Church, wherein are comprehended and described the great persecutions and horrible troubles that have been wrought and practiced by the Romishe Prelates, specially in the realm of England and Scotland from the year of our Lord a Thousand unto the time now present." It did all that, and more.

Foxe's martyrs fit well-known images of English heroism. They were like the paladins of King Arthur, facing death and dying for their faith. More to the point, they were like Robin Hood and his men, standing against the power of the state, seeking—no, demanding—their inherent rights as Englishmen. These images revived the half-forgotten dream of Magna Charta and gave it a more populist form. They encouraged the belief that royal power was subject to higher principles of right and justice that were—or ought to be—assertable by the lowliest persecuted citizen.

In future times, Karl Marx, Charles Darwin, and Sigmund Freud would produce writings that would turn the consciousness of nations inside out, but theirs would be elitist works, whose effects would filter down from top to bottom. *The Book of Martyrs* did not reach the common mind by osmosis from on high, but by telling simple tales of courage that every yeoman could relate to.

The Book of Martyrs had specific resonance for its first readers because the hated Catholics were its villains. But its themes were universal and eventually lost their doctrinal cast. Oppression was oppression, belief was belief, courage was courage. In the far reaches of the future, it would cease to matter who had been oppressing whom. The lessons were the same in any case. Persecuted immigrants to America—Puritans and Quakers—as well as their Anglican oppressors, would keep copies of the remarkable book on their bedstands for nightly reading. Its central message was universally inspiring: the sovereignty of the individual against the power of government and institutionalized religion.

This message predictably incited demands for freedom of religion, speech, and press. What was less predictable were the side effects of such incitements. It soon became clear that, if conscience was to be free, the people could not be compelled by official questioning to reveal "the secrets of their hearts." Thus, the privilege against self-incrimination, now embodied in our Constitution's Fifth Amendment. If written expressions of conscience were private matters, governments must be prevented from rooting at will in the homes of citizens in hopes of finding writings that offended them. Thus, the prohibition against unreasonable searches and seizures, now embodied in our Fourth Amendment. The American Bill of Rights might have been written as it is if Foxe's galvanizing book had never existed, but that is a supposition no American patriot would ever wish to bet on.

Foxe's portrayal of the Protestant martyrs was even more distorted than latter-day portrayals of a tolerant More. *The Book of Martyrs* was, in fact, "a monumental piece of anti-Catholic propaganda, filled with errors, bowdlerizations, and expurgations."[3] But however false Foxe's accounts may have been, they created real popular perceptions that stimulated demands for individual rights and liberties. Foxe's martyrs were a progressive force in history, whatever they may have been in flesh and blood.

The familiar figure stood in a rural Tennessee courtroom, hands thrust into his pants pockets, voice rising in genuine passion. "If today you can take a thing like evolution and make it a crime to teach it in the public school," he said, "tomorrow you can make it a crime to teach it in the hustings or in the church. . . . After a while, Your Honor, it is the setting of man against man and creed against creed, until with flying banners and beating drums, we are marching backwards to the glorious age of the sixteenth century when bigots lighted faggots to burn the men who dared to bring any intelligence and enlightenment and culture to the human mind."

The orator was actor Spencer Tracy, performing the role of Clarence Darrow in the 1950s movie *Inherit the Wind*. The movie told the story of a brave young schoolteacher named John Scopes, who was prosecuted in 1925 for violating a Tennessee statute making it a crime "to teach the theory that denies the story of Divine creation of man as taught in the Bible, and to teach instead that man has (sic) descended from a lower order of animals." Scopes had defied that law by teaching Darwin's theory of evolution to his class and—according to the movie—had been thrown into jail and prosecuted for doing so. The prosecution took place in a tiny Tennessee town (Hillsboro in the movie, Dayton in real life) that the movie depicted as a hotbed of fundamentalist bigotry and hatred.

The movie portrayed Scopes as a fearless hero, but his real-life prosecution was nothing to inspire fear. Far from being a calculated persecution, it was not even the state's idea. Scopes had volunteered to be prosecuted in order to test the validity of the so-called "Monkey Law." His friend George Rappelya obtained a misdemeanor warrant against him, and the district attorney had no practical choice but to proceed. Scopes was never jailed.

He was defended by Clarence Darrow, who was pitted against William Jennings Bryan, whom the state hired as a special prosecutor. Eloquent as both lawyers were, their performances seemed more directed toward the hordes of spectators and reporters that packed the spacious courtroom than the judge and jury.[4] When the histrionics were over, Darrow agreed to a directed verdict of guilty so that the case could be appealed. The judge assessed a fine of one hundred dollars, which the Tennessee Supreme Court later reversed on a technicality.

After the verdict was returned, the lawyers, the judge, and a member of the local bar took turns making graceful little speeches to each other and the spectators, referring to the greatness of the event just completed and expressing thanks to all concerned. Except that they were not all winners, the scene was vaguely reminiscent of a series of Academy Award acceptances.

Those who thought it was all a waste of time, however, were expressing an outdated viewpoint. The Scopes trial was one of legal history's first calculated media events, and as such it was a huge success. It attracted journalists from all over the United States and from Canada, England, and France. The proceedings were heard by the entire country on an unprecedented nationwide radio broadcast. In a post-trial statement, Bryan noted the trial's unique worldwide notoriety: "We are told that more words have been sent across the ocean by cable to Europe and America about this trial than has ever been sent in regard to anything else in the United States."

Despite their technical defeat, Scopes and Darrow had done what they had set out to do. The trial had generated a surge of press coverage ridiculing and demeaning the Monkey Law and the "boobs" who attempted to enforce it. Scores of radio broadcasts and press reports had communicated to the world Darrow's scathing anti-fundamentalist oratory, and his humiliating cross-examination of Bryan, who testified as an expert on the authenticity of the Bible. This tide of anti-creationist publicity swamped nationwide efforts to enact statutes similar to the one under which Scopes was prosecuted.

Superficial, even silly, as some of its aspects seemed, the battle was a serious one. The Tennessee Monkey Law was the first fumbling grasp of what might have become a religious stranglehold on freedom of thought throughout much of the United States. The Northern journalists who covered the trial—most prominently, the acerbic H. L. Mencken—ridiculed the supporters of the Monkey Law as ignorant hicks and redneck clowns who were terrified of scientific thought in any form. But the more perceptive of them knew that the creationist movement was no laughing matter. History had amply demonstrated that religious dogma, however valid for individuals, makes a deadly brew when mixed with governmental power. Moreover, once religion is introduced into government in any proportion, there is no way of controlling the mix. If a particular dogma can define a school's curriculum, it can potentially define every aspect of a society's law and culture—or try to do so, in savage competition with other dogmas.

If the creationists were not exactly threatening to march the nation back to the sixteenth century, they were threatening to turn it in a disquieting backward direction. The Scopes trial and the publicity it generated stopped that effort cold.

But important as it was to the progress of intellectual freedom, the Scopes trial bore little real resemblance to the important constitutional prosecutions of the past. It differed from a prosecution such as Thomas More's, not only in its lack of severity, but in its essential nature. More's trial had not been a show produced by the defendant to prove a point. It had been a battle for survival in which ideas were used as weapons, not a battle of ideas only with nothing else at stake. When More lost his case, he lost his life. When Scopes lost his, he went back to teaching school.

Great constitutional trials had always thrown long, distorted shadows, but they had not been shadows themselves. Always at their centers had stood endangered people whose physical fate was the reason the trials were conducted. In the Scopes trial, substance and shadow became one. The trial was *about* the ideas, not the man.

Many a martyr had gone bravely, even willingly to his fate, but few, if any, had created their own prosecutions, for their own purposes. The Scopes trial demonstrated that a court could be a platform for addressing the conscience of the people, not incidentally, as an effect of governmental process, but primarily, as a chosen forum for debate. With the help of the modern media, the trial had converted what might have been a generation of struggle into an instantly decisive event.

This lesson was put to brilliant use thirty-five years later, during the struggle for legal equality by America's blacks. The beachhead in this struggle was won by traditional use of judicial process: suits by injured parties, appeals to the U.S. Supreme Court, and opinions declaring fundamental changes in the law. But the interiors of the country were won for desegregation by taking a leaf from the book of the Great Monkey Trial.

The leaders of the civil rights movement exposed the evils of segregation by inciting enforcement of its laws—and seeing to it that the results appeared on prime-time television. Like Scopes and his allies before them, they planned the times and places of their public victimizations. They demonstrated in towns with the meanest sheriffs—Bull Connor in Birmingham, Jim Clark in Selma—and they marched at times convenient to television camera crews.

The object of such legal jujitsu was not to win in the traditional legal sense but to publicize injustice, win or lose. Like the constitutional martyrs of history, many a courageous civil rights protestor was punished by the system, beaten, jailed, convicted, and imprisoned by the laws they sought to wipe away. But they knew something their opponents had not yet learned. The battle was not in the jails or in the courts, or in the streets, with the dogs, the firehoses, and the billy clubs. It was in the living rooms of America, where the televisions glowed. There was a chant that went up from the streets of Birmingham in those days that gave the game away: "The whole world is watching, the whole world is watching."

It was a victory cry.

6

THE RIGHT TO CONFRONT ACCUSERS

It is abominable to convict a man behind his back.
JUSTICE JOHN HOLT

In the latter thirteenth century, Pope Boniface VIII worsened the already hideous Inquisition by granting anonymity to accusers of heretics. Without the ability to confront their accusers, suspects were helpless prey to an arbitrary power of life and death. "Every defense was trampled, every avenue of escape closed, leaving the accused at the complete mercy of his judge, the inquisitor."[1]

Until the mid-seventeenth century, most English criminal defendants were not advised of the charges against them or the identity of their accusers until the day of trial. Any semblance of a successful defense required great luck and an ability to perform spontaneously under pressure. We sometimes condemn modern trials for their resemblance to fights, but that is, in fact, their saving grace. Due process in our system simply means a fair fight: the opportunity to contend for truth with a known and present adversary. It took one last outrageous trial, a manifest travesty of justice, to teach the English that necessary definition, but learn it they finally did.

* * *

Except that it used the same words—jury, grand jury, judge, prosecutor, evidence, indictment, and so on—there is little about the justice dispensed during the English Renaissance that a modern citizen would recognize, or want anything to do with. The commotion and stench of ordinary criminal trials made them something resembling cattle auctions. Defendants appeared in ragged groups before the judge, without counsel, to hear the charges against them read rapidly and carelessly. Repetitions and clarifications were discouraged. Those who had the presence of mind to plead not guilty were put to trial in amazingly rapid succession, with the same overworked jury often hearing as many as six or eight cases back-to-back. The judges participated vigorously in the give-and-take debates that served as trials, almost always to the defendant's disadvantage, and were not above threatening juries that seemed reluctant to convict. They tended to grow ominously impatient if a routine case lasted more than half an hour.

The English legal historian Sir James Stephen, who never wasted any sympathy on defendants, was moved to write of these trials that "the principles of evidence were then so ill-understood and the whole method of criminal procedure was so imperfect and superficial, that an amount of injustice frightful to think of must have been inflicted at the assizes and sessions on obscure persons, of whom no one ever heard or will hear."[2]

Meanwhile, England was conducting more elaborate prosecutions of a horde of *unobscure* persons, whom *everyone* had heard of—Sir Thomas More, Mary Queen of Scots, the Earl of Essex, Sir Walter Raleigh, Sir Francis Bacon, King Charles I himself—in the great state trials at Westminster. Stephen's comment seems to imply that, in comparison with the poor anonymous devils who were being drilled "at the assizes and sessions," these upper-class defendants may have been getting some sort of break from the authorities.

Aesthetically, they were. Westminster was certainly cleaner and probably smelled better than most of the courtrooms on the hustings. It was physically safer and freer from disease. Its highborn defendants were not hustled through their trials; they received the undivided attention of judges—sometimes of as many as ten or twenty judges. Points of law were learnedly bandied about, clever repartee abounded, and fine rhetoric filled the air—like beautiful organ music at a funeral. The judges were definitely politer than those at the lower levels, often telling the convicted paragon how "sorry" they were to see him "come to such a pass," before ordering his head removed, or his limbs sawed off and his guts burned before his eyes.

But being a high-ranking defendant had its disadvantages, too. Whereas judges at the assizes acted on an indiscriminate impulse to cleanse the world of lower forms of human life and were usually indifferent to the fate of any given specimen of it, the Westminster judges had a particular interest in the destruction of the prisoners who appeared before them. The king, after all, did not go to the trouble of assembling his heaviest judicial artillery so that he could sit back and watch it misfire. In fact, a state trial defendant's chances were inversely proportional to the amount of attention he received. He could pretty well calculate the odds against himself by counting his judges and multiplying by, say, ten.

All of this reached a sort of shuddering climax with the 1603 treason trial of Sir Walter Raleigh for conspiring with Lord Cobham to place Arabella Stuart on the English throne. In addition to being charged with a crime, which was a sufficient disadvantage for most defendants of the time, Raleigh had two other strikes against him. He was generally despised, and his prosecutor was Edward Coke.

Coke was on his way to becoming chief justice of England, leader of Parliament, and his country's most renowned legal scholar, and he was in a hurry to get there. Raleigh was potentially an obstacle on the path to greatness. Determined to make him a stepping-stone instead, Coke took it upon himself to walk all over Raleigh, contrary to every due process principle he would later espouse.

There was also something personal involved. Coke was an angry, humorless man. As was later said of Thomas Babington Macaulay, he "overflowed with learning and stood in the slop." He had worked his way to power by diligent scholarship, a relentless will, and a rhetorical style that tended more to burying the opposition than persuading the audience.

Coke was a perfect foil for Raleigh. Raleigh was a gentleman rather than a scholar, tall, elegant, witty, and worldly. He was learned and exceptionally intelligent, but in an urbane sort of way. He did not bellow Latin sayings as Coke did, but spoke so softly in his Devonshire burr that fellow members of Parliament often complained that they could not hear him during debates.

His effect on Coke during the trial was something to behold. Coke would launch into a windy speech, studded with ancient maxims and old case citations; Raleigh would interrupt with cool courtesy, making some on-the-point remark; and Coke would explode with invective. The result was, by general consensus, the most verbally brutal prosecution of the age. The cause of Coke's "rancorous ferocity" is hard to determine from the printed record. One gets the sense, however, that Raleigh was inwardly laughing at Coke, and Coke knew it. Some of the exchanges have a definite matador-bull quality:

COKE: You are the absolutest traitor that ever was.

RALEIGH: Your phrases will not prove it, Mr. Attorney. . . . If my Lord Cobham be a traitor, what is that to me?

COKE: All that he did was by thy instigation, thou viper.

RALEIGH: It becometh not a man of quality and virtue to call me so. But I take comfort in it, it is all you can do. . . .

COKE: I protest before God, I never knew a clearer treason.

RALEIGH: You speak indiscreetly, barbarously and uncivilly.

COKE: I want words sufficient to express thy viperous treasons!

RALEIGH: I think you want words, indeed, for you have spoken one thing half a dozen times.

The nadir was reached with Coke's thundering assault upon Raleigh for allegedly taking pleasure at Lord Essex's execution for treason some years previously. Coke had prosecuted Essex with almost the same ferocity he was showing toward Raleigh, but now he piously said that Essex "had died a child of God," whereas Raleigh had responded to Essex's death like a blood-lusting beast of prey. "*Lupus et turpis instinct moventibus ursae,*" he bellowed. "Wolves and bears press close upon the dying."

But this was only shameful window dressing. Raleigh could have stood being yelled at by a berserk antiquarian until Christmas, if they had let him go home when it was over. The problem was, they didn't. They convicted him of treason, kept him waiting for fifteen years, and finally chopped his head off—*without producing a single word of human evidence against him*. Like the yelpings of a toothless dog, Coke's verbal assaults on Raleigh concealed a lack of substance in his case. The echoes from his rantings soon died away, but the memory of an unjustly inflicted death lived on for generations.

What passed for evidence in Raleigh's trial was a twice-retracted written statement by his alleged coconspirator, Lord Cobham, accusing Raleigh in the most general terms of approving a plot to make Arabella queen. (Arabella—not much of a threat, apparently—was an unaccused, mildly interested spectator at Raleigh's trial.) In addition to being rank hearsay, Cobham's contradictory statements were factually incoherent. Coke and Raleigh went through an unfunny comedy routine alternately producing documents setting forth conflicting versions of the Truth According to Cobham. By the time Raleigh read Cobham's second renunciation of his once-confirmed accusation, the jury was probably sick of the whole thing, certain that *something* had gone on and ready to convict anyone in its path.

The stench that arises from Raleigh's conviction is not that of perjury. Whether Cobham was lying or telling the truth is beside the point. What turns the stomach is the way the conviction was reached: A court of supposedly learned judges let Cobham's pitiful accusation into evidence, and let the jury use it to take away a life, without giving the accused a chance to confront and question his accuser in person. There was nothing of process, let alone due process, about it. If a piece of paper was sufficient for conviction, why not just read out the indictment and chop off Raleigh's head? If there was not going to be a real trial, why have any trial at all?

Raleigh was, for all practical purposes, as helpless as a victim of the Inquisition. He was accused, condemned, and effectively executed by an adversary he was never permitted to engage. Again and again he sought, with calmness and patience and whatever legal knowledge he had been able to accumulate, to persuade his judges to give him the most basic component of an adversarial trial—to let him at least die on his feet, slugging it out with his opponent:

RALEIGH: The proof of the common law is by witnesses and jury; let Cobham be here, let him speak it. Call my accuser before my face and I have done.

RALEIGH: I beseech you, My Lords, let Cobham be sent for, charge him in his soul, in his allegiance to the King; if he affirm it, I am guilty.

RALEIGH: My accuser ... is alive and in the house. ... Good My Lords, let my accuser come face to face and be deposed.

But Coke and the judges, who certainly knew that Raleigh's legal position was sound, turned deaf ears to these entreaties:[3]

COKE: You have read the letter of law, but understand it not.

CHIEF JUSTICE: This thing cannot be granted, for then, a number of treasons should flourish. The accuser may be drawn by practice, whilst he is in person.

JUDGE WARBURTON: I marvel, Sir Walter, that you being of such experience and wit should stand on this point; for so many horse stealers may escape, if they may not be condemned without witnesses.

Raleigh's trial was the most important of its generation because it was one side of a watershed in English justice. It was like the climactic fever of a person who has been sick for a long time, just before it breaks. It showed the English the worst of their justice system, and they didn't much like the view. When the people understood the system as it was, they wanted something better.

The earliest manifestation of this unease was in the post-trial treatment of Raleigh himself. He went to trial a despised suspect and came out a convicted hero. He was spared death for fifteen years, even temporarily freed to lead an expedition to the New World, because public opinion would not tolerate the carrying out of his execution. The ferocious unfairness of his trial became a public byword, and the feelings inspired ultimately paved the way to better justice. As the distinguished biographer Catherine Drinker Bowen put it:

> To say that from Raleigh's trial dated a change in the laws would be to say too much. Yet from that day there entered, it is said, the possibility of change—a groping after procedure which might give to the unfriended single prisoner fair chance against the solid power of the state.

Somewhat amazingly, the revolution in trial process spawned by Raleigh's conviction was led by none other than the "rancorous" Edward Coke himself. If any one person can be said to have laid the foundation for the modern concept of due process of law, this ill-tempered, overly ambitious, complex, profoundly self-centered man did so in his later careers. As a judge, he invented the doctrine of judicial review, which gave courts the power to invalidate unconstitutional (i.e., unreasonable) laws. (See chapter 11.) As a leader of Parliament, he sponsored the famed Petition of Right, one of the earliest models for the American Bill of Rights. As England's most influential legal scholar, he was the main architect of the myth that Magna Charta conferred basic rights and liberties on ordinary subjects, which overrode the power of the king. (See chapter 2.) In retrospect, it is hard to imagine that this was the man who so brutalized justice in Raleigh's case.

What caused Coke's "astonishing metamorphosis" from principal assailant to principal defender of the fair trial rights of Englishmen?[4] Apparently nothing more than a change of occupation, coupled with a driving personal ambition. As a prosecutor, it had been his job to get convictions for the Crown, and he got them with a flat-out effort, using every means the system would allow. As chief justice and member of Parliament, he became a representative of the common-law system, which was the natural adversary of the absolutism of the king, and he did those jobs with equal energy. A modern trial lawyer would recognize the type. Like all committed legal advocates, Coke was a rightful heir to the armed champions of old, who were paid to fight in trial by battle on behalf of others. He was skilled, he was courageous—and he was for hire.

Like most great legal changes, the movement toward better justice begun by Raleigh's trial took a long time to reach its goal. It took the amputation of Pyrnne's ears, the whipping and cruel punishment of John Lilburn, the horrifying oppressions of Justices Scroggs and Jeffreys, and hundreds of other judicial crimes before the law was moved to treat defendants with basic decency.[5]

Due process of law as we know it did not truly begin to take hold in the English trial system until after the Revolution of 1688. When it did, it was built upon the simple idea that a trial should be a live contest over disputed facts between a defendant and his accusers. None of the more famous elements of due process—the right to counsel, to subpoena witnesses, to refuse to testify, to jury trial itself—is more basic to a fair trial than the right to confront one's accusers. Without that right, the very concept of fairness falls apart. The best defense counsel cannot cross-examine a piece of paper; the most conscientious jury cannot judge the credibility of an absent witness. Without contending witnesses there can be no trial at all, and the trial rights given the defendant are mere rituals. The enduring lesson of the Raleigh prosecution was that direct confrontation between accused and accuser must lie at the heart of every criminal case.

Students of the modern law of evidence encounter a monstrosity of interlocking logic called the hearsay rule. This rule (a misnomer, since it consists of many rules and exceptions of subtle application) is the product of the law's fixed determination not to repeat the injustice of Raleigh's trial. Its premise is that all trials, both civil and criminal, should be contests between live witnesses, who can be punished for perjury, tested by cross-examination, and observed for credibility.[6] Exceptions are granted only when the risk of factual inaccuracy is small, and the opportunity for increased trial efficiency substantial. The result—so far—has been a complex but reasonably workable shield against oppression. In an age that values convenience and abhors personal conflict, modern American justice has done a remarkably good job of preserving the spirit of the live witness trial.

If a modern Lord Cobham were to write letters from his jail cell accusing a modern Raleigh of a crime, an elaborate truth-detecting process would be set in motion. If the accusations were taken seriously, Cobham would be questioned before a grand jury, and if his testimony were deemed creditable and sufficient, an indictment would be returned. At the command of the hearsay rule, Cobham would then appear in person as a witness at Raleigh's trial. He would take the stand, swear an oath, and testify in the presence of the subject of his accusations. Raleigh's counsel would examine him, searchingly and vociferously, exposing past sins, motives to lie, and the contradictions in his various letters. The jurors would have a chance to see any shame in his face, hear any tentativeness in his voice, detect any falseness in his bearing. Whatever the verdict, justice would be done so far as mortals have learned how to do it.

The hearsay rule, with its nagging insistence on live witness testimony, is the foot soldier of due process. While other trial rights have had the dubious honor of public recognition, the hearsay rule has fought a quietly effective war for everyday justice. Attend any criminal trial, and you are likely to hear recurring arguments over whether a witness can testify about "what the other guy told him" or whether the "other guy" must himself appear in court to testify. These battles are unheard by the jury, and boring to spectators, but they are the mainstay of the integrity of the criminal trial system. The right to confront one's accusers is the one indispensable trial right we have.

Preserving it has not been intellectually easy. If evidence is a science, the hearsay rule is quantum physics, and probably two out of every three hours spent studying evidence are devoted to it. As law students labor through declarations against interest, spontaneous utterances, and vicarious admissions, some of them may be heard to curse this semantical Leviathan. They should bless it—Raleigh most certainly would have.

7

JUDICIAL REVIEW

There must in every society be some power from which there is no appeal.

SAMUEL JOHNSON

In 1610, a run-of-the-mill false imprisonment case came before Edward Coke, chief judge of the Court of Common Pleas of England. A London physician named Thomas Bonham had been denied a license to practice medicine, having been deemed deficient in medical knowledge. He had practiced anyway. When the licensing authority, the Royal College of Physicians, found out about it, it had Dr. Bonham arrested, fined, and thrown in jail. Bonham sued the board of the college for damages, claiming that his fine and imprisonment were unlawful. Exactly why he thought so is not clear.

An ordinary judge would have seen very little in the case. After all, a statute of Parliament gave the college exactly the authority it had exercised: to license or refuse to license putative physicians, and to fine and imprison them if they practiced without permission. But my Lord Coke was, as we have seen, far from ordinary.

If being an effective judge means making the undisciplined exercise of power palatable by garnishing it with rhetoric and massive learning, Coke was a Hall of Famer. He in essence grabbed English law by the scruff of the neck and made it fit his personal conceptions of it. He got away with this because case law was still relatively inaccessible in his time, and he was one of the few lawyers in England who was willing to invest a major portion of his earthly existence researching the old, unindexed year books and pipe rolls in which the ancient cases were recorded. He dug the law out, translated it into his own terms, and made the finished product available to other lawyers and judges in easy-to-read form. For the most part, they were glad to accept it.

By this process, Coke "became regarded more and more as the second father of the law, behind whose work it was not necessary to go." His vast intellectual energy, combined with an awesome capacity for convenient inaccuracy, produced a good deal of original law during his tenure on the bench.

So it was in *Bonham*'s case. Instead of applying the clear terms of the statute, dismissing the case, and hurrying off to an early dinner, Coke saw an opportunity to increase the scope of his authority. In reading the statute, he noted that fines imposed by the college on violators such as Bonham were to be divided between the college and the king. This meant that the college could award itself a fine by deciding that a doctor was practicing illegally and profit by its own decision. Such self-dealing violated the common-law maxim that "no man [may] be a judge in his own case."

Bad statute. Fundamentally *unreasonable*. But no harm had been done, since Bonham had clearly violated the act and deserved the fine. If there was any question about that, Coke could review the board's decision and make an independent, unbiased decision of his own. *At most,* Bonham might be entitled to a refund of the fine.

Not so, said Coke, warming to his task. What Parliament had done was contrary to Law itself. Thus, no part of the statute could be considered valid or enforceable. This conclusion was dictated by well-established precedents. "In *many* cases," he wrote, "the Common Law will controul an Act of Parliament, and sometimes adjudge it to be utterly void." *When*, my Lord? "[W]hen an Act of Parliament is against common right and reason, or repugnant, or impossible to be performed the Common Law will controul it and adjudge such Act to be void." Being most of the above things, according to Coke, the Physicians Licensing Act was no law at all, and the fortunate—and soon to be famous—Dr. Bonham was entitled to full damages.

It was vintage Coke. If *"many* cases" stated that courts had the power to nullify statutes, they were hermetically sealed in some dark cellar, never to be revealed. Certainly Coke cited none of them. He did cite three extremely old cases that said nothing at all about unreasonable statutes being unenforceable. In discussing this and other Coke opinions, his perennial critic Sir James Stephen grumbled, "a more disorderly mind than Coke's and one less gifted with the power of analyzing common words it would be impossible to find."[1]

The bench and bar of England greeted the decision in *Bonham*'s case with a collective yawn. That fellow Coke was always telling *someone*—the king, other courts, other judges—that his power exceeded theirs; why not Parliament too? Coke himself seems to have thought his stunning assertion too obvious to merit discussion. His reports devote little space to *Bonham*'s case, and his comments about it are pedestrian. He thought the case "worthy to be reported and published" because it was "the first judgment . . . concerning fine and imprisonment which has been given since the making of the said Charter and Acts of Parliament. . . ." Ho, hum.

Actually, the case was worth reporting because it introduced the most important constitutional principle ever announced. The ultimate question in any legal system is, What is the ultimate source of law? In England, it had always more or less been the monarch, as God's representative on earth. But Coke and his colleagues had lately been creating a secular religion derived from Magna Charta and the rest of the unwritten English constitution, which would change the locus of the ultimate legal power in England. The text of this new religion was the "right reason" of the all-encompassing common law.

Two years before the *Bonham* decision, on November 13, 1608, Coke had attempted to explain this new religion to the king. Five years earlier, James I had arrived from Scotland to replace Queen Elizabeth on the throne, asserting that *he* was the embodiment of law. Coke had a semi-comical meeting with the upstart monarch, in which he explained that in England, the king was "under God *and* the law." James had not taken it well. He had gone into a tirade, shouting that it was "a treasonous speech"; then "his Majestae . . . looking and speaking fiercely with bended fist offered to strike him, which the Lord Coke perceiving, fell flatt on all fower." (The king's reference to "treason" probably had a certain resonance with the prosecutor of Sir Walter Raleigh, who was still in the Tower of London awaiting the removal of his head.)

With his dictum in *Bonham*'s case, Coke quietly dropped the other shoe in this domestic quarrel. If the Law (with a capital L) is the ultimate authority, the question becomes: Who determines what the Law *is*? Who are the priests of this secular religion? Coke's answer was: I am. I and my colleagues on the bench.

This assertion was never taken very seriously in England. To the extent it was noticed at all, it tended to be ridiculed. After Coke's fall from judicial power in 1616, Parliament became more and more the bastion of English liberties, and the people became less and less interested in having its powers curtailed by unelected judges sitting as philosopher-kings. Lord Campbell summed up the English attitude toward Coke's allocation of legal power 240 years later. "A foolish doctrine," he wrote, "alleged to have been laid down extra-judicially in Dr. Bonham's case ... a conundrum that should be laughed at." When a feeble effort was made to resurrect the "doctrine of judicial review" in the mid-nineteenth century, Justice Wiles curtly rejected it, saying, "The proceedings here are judicial, not autocratic, which they would be if we could make laws instead of administering them." He was shooting a long-dead horse.

Meanwhile, the horse was alive and in full gallop in America. Colonial Americans did not revere Parliament, they despised it, and did not object to judicial limits on legislative powers. Long before the Bill of Rights was drafted, American Lawyers were arguing that all government authority was limited by the "right reason" of the common law. James Otis's argument against general search warrants in the *Paxton* case (1761) was a reprise of Coke's words in *Bonham*'s case:

> No act of Parliament can establish such a writ. . . . An act against the Constitution is void. An act against natural equity is void. The courts must pass such acts into disuse.

Four years later, Massachusetts made America's debt to Coke explicit. Arguing against the hated British Stamp Act, Otis again thundered that "an act against natural equity is void." The Massachusetts General Assembly responded by declaring the Stamp

Act "against Magna Charta and the natural rights of Englishmen, and therefore, according to Lord Coke, null and void."

In 1803, a run-of-the-mill mandamus case came before the U.S. Supreme Court, presided over by Justice John Marshall.[2] At the end of his term in office, Federalist president John Adams had made forty-two appointments to the post of justice of the peace for two counties in the District of Columbia. The commissions had been drawn up and approved but had not been delivered by the time Republican president Thomas Jefferson was inaugurated. Jefferson confirmed twenty-five of the commissions and withheld the rest. Four of the excluded nominees, including William Marbury, applied under the Judiciary Act of 1789 for a writ of mandamus from the U.S. Supreme Court to compel Secretary of State James Madison to issue their commissions.

By the time the case came before Marshall's court, it meant almost nothing from a practical standpoint. The terms for justice of the peace were half expired, the appointed justices were handling the available work, and Jefferson was not likely to recognize an order requiring the appointment of the Marbury Four expeditiously enough to make any difference.

The piddling dimensions of the case did not concern Marshall. It was the size of the concepts he could squeeze out of it that counted. First, he decided—by some fairly tortuous logic—that the statute authorizing the Supreme Court to issue writs of mandamus violated the Constitution. Then he did what he had set out to do. He ruled that the Supreme Court had the power to declare statutes that violated the Constitution null, void, and of no effect. The unconstitutional Judiciary Act did not give the Court authority to issue writs of mandamus, and Marbury's suit must therefore fail.

If Coke had cited bad authority for the doctrine of judicial review, Marshall cited none at all—not even Coke. He seemed to need none. The power he asserted for his court had been widely disputed, but the organ tones of his opinion made the disputable seem inevitable:

> It is emphatically the province and duty of the Judicial Department to say what the law is. . . . So if a law be in opposition to the Consti-

tution; if both the law and the Constitution apply to a particular case, so the court must either decide that case conformably to the law, disregarding the Constitution; or conformably to the Constitution, disregarding the law; the court must determine which of these conflicting rules governs the case. This is the very essence of the judicial duty.

If, then, the courts are to regard the Constitution, and the Constitution is superior to any ordinary act of the Legislature, the Constitution, not such ordinary Act, must control the case to which they both apply.

The silence that greeted Marshall's pronouncement was almost as complete as that which had greeted Coke's, and some of the subsequent comment about it has been similarly unflattering. A recent book by an outstanding legal scholar calls *Marbury* v. *Madison* "an opinion of slight merit, distorted reasoning, and galloping activism."

In any case, Marshall had seized the day just before the sun went down. It would be fifty-five years before the Supreme Court had another chance to declare an act of Congress unconstitutional (*Scott* v. *Sandford,* in which the Court held that Congress could not constitutionally prohibit slavery in new territories). If the Court had let the inconsequential *Marbury* case go by while waiting for a better one, it might have been too late for it to assert the vital power.

For the remainder of the nineteenth century, judicial review was of relatively minor consequence. The Supreme Court had not yet begun applying the Bill of Rights to state legislation *via* the due process clause of the Fourteenth Amendment, and the opportunities to question federal legislation on due process grounds were rare. Beginning in the 1920s, however, the Supreme Court used the power of judicial review to catapult itself into the center of American political life. From that day to this, scarcely an important issue of governmental power has arisen of which the Court has not been the final arbitrator.

In 1927, the state of Minnesota had at its disposal an extraordinarily useful device for dealing with the excesses of the press. Its Public Nuisance law authorized courts to permanently enjoin the publication of "malicious, scandalous and defamatory" newspapers. The theory was that such publications pollute the intellectual environment, just as a stinking rendering plant pollutes the physical environment, and should be equally subject to abatement by a court. It was a popular idea that might have diminished the role of a free press in this country, if it had survived and spread.

The Minnesota law was used to terminate the existence of a garbage can of a newspaper called the *Saturday Press*. Later dubbed the "Minnesota Rag," the *Press* made false, vicious, and concerted attacks upon selected politicians on a weekly basis. It was shut down by a court order pursuant to the Public Nuisance law after nine weeks of publication, to the dismay of almost no one. Its publisher, Jay M. Near, appealed to the U.S. Supreme Court, arguing that the nuisance law provided for "prior restraints on publication" in violation of the First Amendment. In its first great freedom of the press case, the Court held the law invalid, thereby ensuring a bright and powerful future for the American press.

In 1963, police in Phoenix, Arizona, conducted a routine interrogation in a rape case. After being questioned for two hours, the suspect, Ernesto Miranda, admitted his guilt. The interrogation was not coercive and, according to the officers, Miranda was told that anything he said "could be used against him." All of the laws and regulations applicable to police interrogation were observed. Miranda was convicted and sentenced.

He appealed, arguing that the use of his confession violated his Fifth Amendment privilege not to be compelled to incriminate himself and his Sixth Amendment right to counsel. The legal standards pursuant to which he was questioned were constitutionally inadequate, he argued, because they did not require the police to advise him that he had a right to consult a lawyer before answering questions. Acceptance of this argument would invalidate police procedures throughout the country, and, according to many experts, would all but end the ability of investigating officers to obtain confessions. To the outrage of most of the nation, the U.S. Supreme Court accepted Miranda's argument, reversed his conviction, and changed the essential quality of police interrogation in America.

During the 1988 presidential campaign, George Bush draped himself in the American flag. His opponent, Governor Michael Dukakis, had vetoed a Massachusetts law requiring the Pledge of Allegiance to be recited in public schools, and Bush pictorially reminded voters of that fact by appearing on television visiting a series of flag factories. After he was elected, Bush continued to exploit the "flag issue" by vigorously supporting passage of the Flag Protection Act of 1989, which made it a federal crime to burn or to otherwise physically afflict a "Flag of the United States."

A group of protestors was soon arrested in Seattle, Washington, for burning a flag—in protest of the Flag Protection Act of 1989. Trivial as it seemed to some, the case symbolized a spiritual chasm that sorely divided the American people. It seemed to one-half of the people that the republic might collapse if the flag could not be legally protected, and to the other half that the republic might collapse if the meaning of the flag were lost in efforts to protect its physical integrity. In an atmosphere of bitter public acrimony, the U.S. Supreme Court struck down the Flag Protection Act of 1989, holding that it violated the First Amendment's freedom of speech provision.

In each of these cases the vote on the Court was 5-4. The three justices whose votes made the difference in these decisions wielded power as pervasive as that of any English king, Roman emperor, or Egyptian pharaoh. By the exercise of final and purely personal judgment, they changed the very character of the society they served. The "conundrum" to be "laughed at" had proven to be anything but a joke. It had turned out to be the greatest bloodless acquisition of political power in the history of the world.

An America without judicial review is hard to conceive of. At the end of the twentieth century, the fabric of our society is completely interwoven with its effects. Desegregation. An unrestrained press. Strong due process protection for accused persons. Legal abortion. What important aspect of our society *hasn't* been profoundly touched by Lord Coke's doctrine?

John Marshall's biographer Albert Beveridge wrote brilliantly about *Marbury* v. *Madison,* but then he wrote: "This principle [of judicial review] is wholly and exclusively American. It is America's original contribution to the science of law." That is like saying Macy's invented Christmas. We have made the most of judicial review, but we certainly didn't think it up. That distinction belongs to a sly English genius who understood, better than anyone, how to counterfeit history and translate it into power.

8

THE DEATH OF A SCAMEGOAT

An apology for the devil—it must be remembered that we have only heard one side of the case. God has written all the books.

SAMUEL BUTLER

Once, when things were going badly for Senator Joseph McCarthy during a televised congressional hearing, he broke in and complained that the chairman was conducting a "Star Chamber proceeding." He meant that the proceedings were oppressive, in violation of standards of due process, and foreign to the American way. With his usual genius for such things, the adroit demagogue had selected the perfect mudball. *Everyone* knows that the Star Chamber was bad.[1]

The chamber's evil reputation is institutional, like the Inquisition's or the Gestapo's. No one can name a single judge who sat on that infamous tribunal, but that makes no difference. It is the tribunal itself that is abhorred. It was, we know, a place of anonymous accusations, secret trials, confessions coerced by torture, and black-hooded judges inflicting cruel sentences.[2]

When Parliament abolished the chamber in 1641, it described it as a cancer in the body politic:

The said judges have undertaken to punish where no law doth warrant, and to make decrees for things having no such authority, and to
inflict heavier punishments than by any law is warranted. . . . The
proceedings, censors, and decrees of that Court have by experience
been found to be an intolerable burden to the subject, and the means
to introduce an arbitrary power and government.

An earthier description of the chamber's horrors was given by
a contemporary citizen critic:

When once this Court began to swell big, and was delighted with
blood which sprung out of the ears and shoulders of the punished,
and nothing would satisfy the revenge of some, but cropt ears, slit
noses, branded faces, whipt backs, gag'd mouths, and withal to be
thrown in dungeons . . . then began the English nation to lay to heart
the slavish condition they were like to come unto if this Court continued in its greatness.[3]

For generations after its demise, the Star Chamber was the
favorite scapegoat of legal arguments. It played the same role in
eighteenth-century legal rhetoric that Watergate has played in recent American political rhetoric; it was a giant tar brush that
stained every person and idea that was associated with it. Saying
that a rule of law had been established by the Star Chamber had the
exact opposite effect of saying that it had been established by
Magna Charta. It gave it legal halitosis.

What is to be made, then, of the glowing comments about the
chamber voiced by a multitude of eminent seventeenth-century
lawyers and scholars? They read like the cooings of theater critics
describing an opening night hit. "One of the sagest and noblest institutions of this Kingdom," raved Sir Francis Bacon. "The most
honorable Court (our Parliament excepted) that is in the Christian
world, both in respect of the judges of the Court, and of their proceedings according to their just administration and the ancient just
orders of the Court. . . . It doth keep all England quiet," chimed in
Lord Coke. "[In the Star Chamber] mercy and truth are met together; righteousness and peace have kissed each other," rhapsodized lawyer William Hudson. "[The Star Chamber is the] most
noble and praiseworthy Court, the beams of whose bright justice do

blaze and spread themselves as far as the realm is long or wide," gushed antiquarian William Lambarde.

Were these commentators frightened sycophants trying to survive personally and politically by dishonest praise? Hardly. Give or take a few silly adjectives, they were clear-eyed observers who were telling the truth.

More precisely, Parliament on the one hand and Coke, Hudson, and Bacon on the other each spoke a portion of the truth. During its centuries of existence, the Star Chamber was uniquely noble *and* obscenely oppressive. The fragrance of its youth was obliterated by the stink of its old age.

It seems to have come into being shortly after Magna Charta, perhaps as a council of peers formed to carry out the charter's command that freemen be "destroyed" only by the "judgment of their peers." In the early centuries it was a counterweight to oppressions inflicted by powerful citizens on their inferiors. It created laws against crimes characteristically committed by upper-class villains, such as perjury, subornation of perjury, forgery, and conspiracy. It corrected wrongs done by the corrupt and pusillanimous jury system (its judges being too rich to be bought and too well-connected to be afraid). During these times, it was the place in the English justice system where justice was most consistently found, offering a relative purity of judgment that seemed almost to justify its celestial title.

The chamber was also more civilized in its procedures than other English courts. Most common-law trials resembled "a family quarrel," with the defendant and the prosecutor engaging in angry argument and the judges vigorously joining in, usually on the side of the state. In contrast, Star Chamber proceedings were conducted with a calm and dignity suited to the high rank of its judges.

The common law looked to the Star Chamber for standards of procedural fairness. One of the devastating ways in which the common law crippled a defendant's ability to defend himself was by not disclosing the charges against him until the day of the trial. When Coke repudiated this practice, he used the Star Chamber as a model, saying that "the defendant must have, as in Star Chamber and Chancery, the bill of charges delivered to him, or otherwise he need not answer it."

Rather than a tool of the mighty, the chamber was a poor man's court. It was almost historically unique in making a principle of favoring the poor over the rich. Indigents and peasants were not only fairly heard, they were favored *because* they were poor. The rich and the powerful, on the other hand, were genuinely afraid of the chamber and its humiliating punishments.

One Star Chamber opinion frankly states that a convicted defendant's "punishment would have been far greater but for his base birth, being a peasant and a boy." On the other hand, when the highborn Lord Dudley of Staffordshire was convicted of using an army of six hundred armed men to drive off his neighbor's cattle, the chamber showed him no comparable mercy. When Lord Burroughly objected to the impossible fine imposed upon Dudley, saying that he had no chance of paying it, the Lord Baron muttered coldly: "Let him pay with his body."

The main accusation that history has made against the chamber is that it conducted secret trials. The accusation is probably false.[4] There are no surviving records of, or historical references to, secret Star Chamber trials. Beginning in the sixteenth century, English writers boasted of the openness of English justice, making no exceptions for Star Chamber. The chamber's seventeenth-century enemies charged it with many sins, but not with conducting secret trials. The Petition of Right (1628) and the Bill of Rights (1689) listed Parliment's principal grievances against the Stuart kings but said nothing about secret Star Chamber trials. The long preamble to the act abolishing Star Chamber denounced it for every judicial abuse imaginable—except secret trials. The chamber's reputation for secretiveness probably resulted from its practice of questioning prisoners "in private" *prior* to putting them on trial. There seems to be no other reasonable explanation for it.

Certainly the normal holiday-style mode of the court's operations did not imply a clandestine intent. "People took pride in the Court," according to Catherine Drinker Bowen, "crowding to watch; by three in the morning, there was a line at the door." "Star days," these festive occasions were called. They were evocative of a Harvard-Yale crew race on the Charles River, or a nineteenth-century outdoor political debate. "Coke came up from the City by barge, landing at the watergate and walking up the steps along the causeway. He liked to plead here. The Court was a superb theater for lawyers who knew their business." Theater for whom? Rats crouching in the dark corners of a bolted-door kangaroo court? Obviously not. Secret Star Chamber trials are mostly, if not entirely, a fantasy of history.

It is also said that the chamber's punishments were cruel and excessive. They were by today's standards, but the chamber existed in some amazingly cruel eras and was by no means the worst offender. When the common-law courts convicted a defendant of treason, the judge put on a black cap and advised the unfortunate of his fate, as follows:

> You shall be had from hence to the place whence you came, there to remain until the day of execution; and from thence you shall be drawn upon an Hurdle through the open streets to the place of execution, there to be hanged and cut down alive, and your body shall be opened, your heart and bowels plucked out, and your privy members cut off, and thrown into the fire before your eyes; then your head to be stricken off from your body, and your body shall be divided into four quarters; to be disposed of at the King's pleasure; and God have mercy upon your soul.

Some of the prisoners who heard these terrible words had done nothing worse than engage in barroom conversations about the king. The fearsome Star Chamber, on the other hand, never imposed a death sentence in any form on anyone—it earned its reputation for cruelty by fines, whippings, ear-croppings, and imprisonments.[5]

The allocation of the bizarre punishments of the time among the various courts was almost comically specific. As might be expected, Lord Coke was cognizant of them down to the last ripped fingernail. "[The Star Chamber] may inflict punishment," he enumerated, "by pillory, papers, whipping, losses of ears, tacking of ears [ouch!], *stigmata* in the face, etc." (That "etc." admittedly has an ominous ambiguity about it.) "For it extendeth not to any offense that concerns the life of any man or obtruncation of any member, the ears only excepted, and those rarely and in most heinous and detestable offenses." (Ear-croppings must have been unpleasant, but better an ear than a "privy member.")

The evil side of the Chamber's personality began to emerge in the early 1600s, after James I took the English throne. The chamber became "his" court, to the extent that on occasion—to the amazement of the other judges—he appeared and sat as a member of it. The chamber was a handy political instrument because it created and administered libel law, that most political branch of criminal justice. Its harsh punishments of expressions of opinion gave it a deserved reputation as the king's enforcer.

As the century progressed, the chamber's time-honored procedures became dishonorable in the eyes of the masses, who were attracted to the new constitutional freedoms advocated by its enemies and victims. Particularly obnoxious to the new spirit were the chamber's practice of compelling defendants to testify under oath and its punishment of political and religious expression.

In this climate, the creativity of the chamber began to turn sour. Instead of filling true gaps in the law, it began to invent senseless offenses.

In 1615, John Hollis and John Wentworth were prosecuted for "traducing public justice." The case involved a condemned man named Westin, who had been convicted of poisoning Sir Thomas Overbury. Wentworth and Hollis had attended his execution as interested citizens, and had apparently sought to assist in his salvation. Wentworth had asked him whether he was guilty, in order "that he might pray with him," and Hollis had supported the inquiry, urging Westin "to discharge his conscience and satisfy the world." The Star Chamber thought that these statements implied doubt as to Westin's guilt, thereby "defaming" English justice. It gave the pair stiff fines and one year's imprisonment in the Tower of London.

In 1632, a Mr. Sheffield was prosecuted for breaking a glass window in St. Edmund's Church in Salisbury. He had done so, he said, because he objected to "inaccuracies" in the window's depiction of the Creation. He explained to the court that the window depicted "divers forms of little old men in blue and red coats . . . and Eve being taken whole out of Adam's side, whereas in fact a rib was taken and made into Eve." In protest, he had knocked eleven holes in the glass with his pikestaff. For this piece of foolishness, the devout lunatic was fined what for him must have been the ruinous sum of five hundred pounds.[6]

In the course of an argument with the London customs house, a merchant named Richard Chambers complained "that merchants are in no part of the world so screwed and wrung as in England; in Turkey they have more encouragement." The Star Chamber showed Mr. Chambers the true meaning of "screwed and wrung." It fined him two thousand pounds and ordered him to make a written apology, and when he declined to apologize, it sentenced him to six years' imprisonment. By comparison, Turkey would have been a day at the beach.

Nasty as these proceedings were, they had a zany quality that is not quite what we expect of the Star Chamber. We are looking for the Brothers Grimm, and we get something closer to Lewis Carroll.

The chamber admittedly had no talent for public relations. Its treatment of William Pyrnne was so obscene that it seemed calculated to arouse public disgust. When Pyrnne was convicted of libel in 1632, his counsel said that he was "heartily sorry" for the ill-tempered nature of his libelous publication, *Histrio Mastix*. The chamber made him sorrier by ordering the amputation of his ears. When he was convicted of libel again five years later, the court expressed regret that the prisoner had no ears left to crop and ordered his cheeks branded.

When the chamber convicted John Lilburne of libel in 1637, it first whipped him in front of throngs of people and then left him bleeding in a public stock, to rail against the court to the assembled multitudes. These actions were certainly vicious but, worse from a political standpoint, they were stupid. They became the weapons which the chamber's enemies used to kill it.

The abolishment of the Star Chamber was one part statesmanship and nine parts politics. It was the beginning of a process of usurpation that ended eight years later with the execution of King Charles I. The uprising led by Oliver Cromwell, which established a Puritan government in England after Charles's death, was bent on obliterating every vestige of royalty. As they lowered it into its political grave, Parliament made sure that the king's favorite court was weighted down with all of the sins of the Stuart monarchy. Their purposes required that the evil it had done should live after it and that the good should be interred with its bones. They succeeded magnificently. Harsh though it was in its later years, the Star Chamber would never have become the Black Beast of English justice if its enemies had not survived to write its epitaph.

In years to come the epitaph prevailed. The dark memory of the Star Chamber became a stimulant for better justice, a bogeyman of English law that future generations strained to exorcise. The parliamentary decree of 1641 was what we today would call a "definitive statement." It bundled up an assorted pile of wrongs, wrapped them in their most visible symbol, and ritualistically disposed of them. Abolishing the Star Chamber was to tyranny what closing down Wall Street would be to greed or abandoning the Pentagon would be to war: not an eradication of the targeted evil, but a symbol of abhorrence for it, and of a determination to resist it.

To those who cheered its burial, the Star Chamber represented something in the English law that had never belonged: a king's court, a prerogative court, a foreign sort of court that mimicked the despised justice practiced on the Continent. Not incidentally, it had for generations been the bitter rival of the common-law courts, which—so went the myth—dealt in that muscular guardian of English rights and liberties, the people's common law. Now that the red dragon of anti-justice had been slain, the white dragon of true justice could prevail.

When the Star Chamber was abolished, England was in the midst of passing from the old system of criminal justice to the new. The old had been Coliseumlike. It had offered the defendant a jury, but little other protection, and the jury was largely the puppet of the state. The new would be more theaterlike. It would offer the defendant a lawyer, an independent jury, and a panoply of procedural rights that would give him a major role in the unfolding of a legal drama. This enormous transformation was driven by politics, of course, but it required energizing symbols. The most important of these, by far, was Magna Charta. The second most important may well have been the Star Chamber.

From a trial rights standpoint, the crucial seventeenth-century English event was John Lilburne's treason prosecution in 1649. The brave and loquacious Lilburne demanded every procedural right he could conceive of and was granted quite a few. (See chapter 9, The Privilege Against Self-incrimination.) Like any canny fighter, he began by softening up the opposition. During the first forty minutes of his trial, which was mostly dominated by his civil liberties preaching, he mentioned the Star Chamber no less than nine times (to Magna Charta's three). He reminded his forty judges that the hated chamber had been "totally damned and plucked up by the roots" by parliamentary decree only eight years before. Henceforth, he said, all English prosecutions must be "common trials at ordinary assizes . . . and not in the least to be tried by extraordinary and specially prejudiced, packed and overawing committees of oyer and terminer."

We are no Star Chamber, said the judges, in effect. We are a good old common-law court. Good, said Lilburne, in effect. Then you will want to grant me the trial advantages that are my "inheritance and birthright" according to the "good old laws of England." Anxious to avoid identification with the recently slain Black Beast of English justice, the judges became unwilling participants in a legal revolution.

The same thing happened many times over the ensuing years. The Star Chamber as bogeyman was a major rhetorical factor in the Bill of Rights revolution that occurred in England and America in the latter seventeenth and early eighteenth centuries.

A famous American example occurred in the libel trial of John Peter Zenger, which established truth as a defense against a charge of libel. (See chapter 10, Freedom of the Press.) Zenger's prosecutor argued learnedly—citing many prior decisions—that English law did not accept truth as a defense when a man was tried for criticizing government. Virtually choking on his contempt, Zenger's lawyer, Andrew Hamilton, launched himself to his feet and protested that the cited law was no law because it was the product of the Star Chamber—"The most dangerous Court to the liberties of the people of England that was ever known to that Kingdom." The judge ruled against Hamilton on the legal point, but the jurors got the message. They acquitted Zenger, with the words "Star Chamber" ringing in their ears. Those words had become a folk curse, with the power to eradicate old oppressions and create new law in the blink of a juror's eye.

The first great modern bill of rights decision, *Entick* v. *Carrington* (1765), outlawed "unreasonable" searches and seizures by the king (see chapters 11 and 15). Having little precedent on which to base his ruling, Lord Camden invoked the tyrannical practices of the Star Chamber as the measure of what enlightened government could *not* permit. In Camden's view, the fact that the Star Chamber had indiscriminately confiscated books and papers was in itself a reason for putting such practices to an end. We can make ourselves clean by washing away the filth of our own worst history, his opinion seemed to say.

Of all the contributions the Star Chamber made to justice over the centuries, the revulsion it incited after its demise was perhaps the greatest.

"And he shall cast lots on the two goats. But the goat on which the lot falls to be the scapegoat shall be presented alive before the Lord, to make an atonement with him, and to let him go for a scapegoat into the wilderness" (Leviticus 16:10).

And so, they pulled the rank and aging goat to the sacred place and held him still. Aaron stood over him and, raising his eyes to the heavens, confessed all the sins of the children of Israel and prayed that they be laid upon his back. And when it was done, they sent the beast to wander in the wilderness, bearing away all of their sins with him. When they talked of him in later years, they spoke of the dark burden he had carried away, but never of the loyal services he had performed in the hard years of their passage to the Promised land.

9

THE PRIVILEGE AGAINST SELF-INCRIMINATION

The crooked roads . . . are the roads of genius.
WILLIAM BLAKE

In 1963, Eddie Dean Griffin went on trial in Los Angeles for the murder of his girlfriend, identified in the case report as "Essie Mae." Given the absence of other suspects, Eddie's legal position was precarious. He had been seen with Essie Mae on the evening of the murder, and there was testimony that he had been with her in an alley just before she died. His "rap" sheet listed a number of prior felony convictions. He would have been asked about them had he testified, but he choose not to do so. He sat beside his lawyer in ambiguous silence, while the state produced the evidence it had.

Giving voice to the probable thoughts of the jury, the prosecutor said in final argument:

> The defendant certainly knows whether Essie Mae had this beat up appearance at the time he left her apartment and went down the alley with her. . . . He would know how she got down the alley. He would know how the blood got on the bottom of the concrete steps. . . . He would know whether he beat her or mistreated her. . . .

He would know whether he walked away from that place cool as a cucumber when he saw Mr. Villasenor because he was conscious of his own guilt, and wanted to get away from that damaged or injured woman.

These things he has not seen fit to take the stand and deny or explain. And in the whole world, if *anyone* would know, this defendant would know.

Essie Mae is dead. She *can't* tell you her side of the story. The *defendant won't.*

Eddie Dean Griffin was convicted and sentenced to death. His conviction was appealed to the U.S. Supreme Court on the ground that, by calling the jury's attention to Griffin's failure to testify, the prosecutor had violated his rights under the U.S. Constitution. The Supreme Court agreed. In a 7-2 vote, the Court reversed the conviction and sent the case back to be tried again. If, on retrial, the defendant chose to remain silent again, the prosecution must be careful to refrain from mentioning that palpable fact to the jury.

How odd!

Most of the Bill of Rights provisions have a natural quality about them. An intelligent person who had never heard of the Constitution might list them as basic to a decent civic existence: free speech, free exercise of religion, security from arbitrary intrusion into the home by government, expert assistance in case of prosecution, having neighbors decide one's guilt or innocence, no cruel or unusual punishments for crimes.

The privilege against self-incrimination is something else. The idea that one could say nothing in response to a creditable accusation and not have his silence considered against him is neither obvious nor, many have argued, particularly logical. Some dedicated critics have even said that it is bizarre. Which is appropriate, since it has a bizarre and tortuous history, and was brought to fruition largely through the efforts of a man who was—bizarre.

Passive victims of the legal system such as More and Raleigh, and calculating turf-defenders such as Coke, carry civil liberties forward only so far. What is needed for true progress in human freedom is the services of a madman. John Lilburne provided those services for English law to such a magnificent extent that he deserves—but, because of his very craziness, will never receive—a lion's share of the credit for the emergence of the so-called bill of rights liberties in seventeenth-century England.

He was known throughout his embattled career as "Freeborn" John because of his famous self-description. "I am," he said, "an honest, true-bred and freeborn Englishman that never in his life loved a tyrant nor feared an oppressor." It was certainly true. His spiritual ancestors were men such as John Ball and Wat Tyler, the leaders of the medieval peasants' revolt whose savage loyalty to the rights of the common man made them fearsome to constituted authority. He was inspired by a dream of ancient justice—"the good old laws of England"—that was, in fact, a vision of a more just future that he would help create. His prominent qualities—immense courage, immense energy, a brilliant gift of eloquence—made him a tempting potential ally for government leaders, but he was a disappointment to them all. He was such an *unreasonable* fellow, so bloody *unreliable,* so hard to get *along* with. It was said that if John Lilburne were the last man on earth, John would fight with Lilburne and Lilburne with John.

He first achieved fame as a victim of Bishop William Laud, who ran the Court of High Commission as an attack dog for the Stuart monarchy. When Oliver Cromwell came to Parliament, he made his maiden speech in support of freeing Lilburne from a jail cell where Laud's exertions had placed him. When Charles I was deposed and Cromwell installed in office, the new leader took Lilburne in as a close confidant.

But how sharper than a serpent's tooth was Lilburne's ingratitude! Freeborn John soon discovered that he did not like Puritan intolerance any better than Anglican intolerance, and said so in several public diatribes. In 1649, he wrote a charming little tract called "The Impeachment of High Treason Against Oliver Cromwell and Henry Ireton," which led Cromwell to remark, "The Kingdome can never be settled so long as Lilburne is alive."

In October 1649, Lilburne went on trial for his life on charges of treason. The sullen popular mutterings that had greeted Raleigh's conviction forty-five years earlier resurfaced in Lilburne's case as a full-throated roar. Governmental power had fractured in the intervening years and no longer had the solidity required for true oppression. The myth of the invulnerable leader had been dealt a severe wound by the decapitation of Charles I, who, the people noticed, had bled and died quite humanly. Government retained the power to afflict, but not to dominate, the people.

Throughout Anglo-American history, many trials and executions have been conducted in what is tritely called "a carnival atmosphere." Lilburne's trial was unusual, however, because the carnival-goers were supporters of the *defendant*. They mobbed the courtroom, virtually hanging from the rafters to watch their hero give the court a drubbing.

Which he did. Lilburne was tried by a jury and, in what must have been close to a record, forty judges, including eight common-law judges, the lord mayor of London, the recorder of London, four sergeants at law, and twenty-six "special" judges, among them several London aldermen and members of Parliament. They were badly outnumbered by Freeborn John. Although they were perhaps the most courteous judicial officers ever to preside over a treason trial, Lilburne castigated them from beginning to end, calling them "bloody judges," as oppressive in their rulings as the judges of the Star Chamber itself. Once, when they politely refused one of his novel procedural demands, he theatrically exclaimed: "Oh Lord, was there ever such a pack of unjust and unrighteous judges in the world!"

He routinely demanded from them rights English justice had never thought of granting to defendants. His method, as Leonard Levy put it, was to "challenge every step of procedure, pick to pieces each bit of evidence against him, depict the court as his oppressors, and appeal to the jury over the heads of the judges." Among other things, he demanded:

That the courtroom doors be opened, so he could have a proper "public" trial. Although the court was already packed to overflowing, the meaningless request was granted.

That the attorney general stop whispering with one of the judges—such "hugger-mugger" being inconsistent with the good old laws of England. The attorney general stopped.

That he be granted defense counsel. The court patiently explained that counsel were never allowed in felony and treason trials, but said that it would advise Lilburne on matters of fact and would allow him counsel regarding legal points if the need arose. Lilburne—who was as well-equipped to take care of himself as any defendant who ever appeared in a courtroom—was, of course, outraged at the court's generous offer.

That he be given "eight or nine days" to study the indictment. The court refused this one—most defendants were never even shown a copy of the charges.

That he be given time to call supporting witnesses. The court allowed him an additional day, which was one day longer than other defendants got.

That the jury be instructed that it was the judge of the law as well as the facts, and could reject the court's legal instructions at will. The judges were simply stunned by this request (which most modern American courts would reject out of hand as dangerously radical).

The jury was seeing something no English jury had ever seen before: a defendant on absolutely equal footing with the other trial participants; who actually had a piece of the action; who made demands and sometimes had them granted; who raised more hell and flung more insults than the attorney general raised and flung; who gave his judges better than he got. Raleigh had been a strong presence in his trial, but as a supplicant, not an equal of the prosecution. When he had said of one ruling, "I know not how you conceive of the law," Lord Cecil had cut him dead, replying, "Nay, we do not conceive the law, we *know* it!" When Lilburne's judges ruled against him, and he vilified them for their cruelty and ignorance, they blinked, scolded, muttered—and *took* it. This madman was turning English justice completely on its head, and every person in the courtroom knew it.

When the jury returned its verdict, "the whole multitude of people in the Hall, for joy of the prisoner's acquittal, gave such a loud and unanimous shout, as is believed was never heard in Guildhall, which lasted for about half an hour without intermission."

The crowds that swelled Lilburne's trial must have sensed something of the newness and importance of what they were watching, but it is unlikely that any of them recognized its most important moment. It happened in a short exchange at the outset of the trial when Lilburne announced, "I am not to answer questions against or concerning myself," and Lord Keble replied, "You shall not be compelled." Demanded and granted in a quiet instant! The great, anomalous privilege against self-incrimination had been given its first sure breath of life—and no one seemed to notice.

New and fragile as it was, Lilburne brandished this privilege with confidence. When the prosecutor stuck the treasonous book under his nose, he refused to say whether he had authored it and dared his judges to draw an adverse inference from his silence. His refusal, he said, was "the same ... practiced by Christ and his Apostles," who demanded that their accusers prove the charges against them without their assistance.

When we say today that a defendant has a "right to remain silent," we mean just that, but obviously Lilburne was asserting no such right. Since he was allowed no counsel to speak for him, remaining silent would have been suicidal. Nor was he asserting a right "not to testify against himself," since seventeenth-century defendants had no right to testify at all in their own trials. What he was insisting on was full, but self-edited, participation in the verbal give-and-take that characterized common-law trials; a vigorous debate on the law and facts, in which he could challenge the court but could not be challenged back. No wonder he was acquitted.

Where did this extremely handy right come from? Not, as might be assumed, from Lilburne's fertile and feverish imagination. It had a centuries-old pedigree, which was marked by great cruelty, great courage, and great confusion.

In 1410, an English smith named John Badby died a very bad death. A wooden barrel was thrown into a roaring fire with John nailed up inside, and he was roasted like a sacrificial pig. Present in the watching crowd was young Prince Hal, son of the king of England. When John's agonized screams became unbearable to hear, Hal ordered the barrel removed from the fire and offered the half-dead man his life and three pence a day if he would "repent." John refused, "and so it followed that the foolish man was burnt to ashes and died miserably in his sins."

What was at stake was not the safety of England, or the life and welfare of the king, but a belief, a thought, a point of view. John Badby died horribly because he believed that "it is not the body of Christ which is sacramentally carried in the church, but an inanimate object"; and when, like a schoolyard bully, the church had demanded that John "take it back," he would not do so. He was exterminated like an infectious bug so that he would not contaminate others with what he thought. The fire that burned him to death was not torture, it was a cleansing agent. Or so the theory went.

Such horrendous nonsense was new to England. For almost two hundred years, the English had escaped the Inquisition, which had been loosed upon the Continent in 1215 by a pope with the ironic title of Innocent III. The Inquisition and all of its works had been imported into England just nine years before Badby met his fiery death, by the enactment of the Statute for Burning Heretics of 1401.

The Inquisition had by this time become a sophisticated, well-oiled engine of death. Suspected heretics were brought before a priest, who administered the dread oath *de veritate dicenda,* and questioned the suspect rigorously. If he refused to answer, his silence was taken as an admission of guilt. If he denied having heretical beliefs, he was likely to be punished for perjury. If he admitted heresy and refused to recant, he was, like John Badby, turned over to the secular authorities for "disposition"—the church being too refined to be caught shedding blood.

The horror of this process was that there was no safe and sane way out of it. No acquittals, only death or begged-for mercy. No right to defend, no retorts, no justifications. Suspected heretics were frantic inserts in a bottle with no place to hide and no place to go.

There *was* one tiny crack of light. Nothing substantive, but something to give the illusion of standing one's ground against the crushing pressure of the process, if only for an interval. Over the centuries the power of the inquisitors steadily increased, with every procedural advantage being granted them, but there remained one exception that was never formally withdrawn. Despite all else, it was said that no man could be compelled to "accuse himself."

This was not a privilege to remain silent in the face of questioning. The priest could interrogate a suspect endlessly about his suspected heresies and condemn him if he failed to answer. What he could not do was compel him to originate an accusation against himself. He could not, by general questioning, conduct a fishing expedition into the suspect's soul in the hope of hooking onto some unsuspected sin.

In 1532, a priest named John Lambert became the first accused English heretic to assert this limitation. The archbishop of Canterbury administered the oath to Lambert and asked him if he had been previously suspected of any heresies—a question that by its terms was not addressed to the present charges. Lambert answered that he did not recall, but that, even if he did, "yet were I more than twice a fool to show thereof; for it is written in your own law 'no man is bound to accuse himself.' " Lambert died at the stake five years later, but his words lived after him.

The reign of Bloody Mary (1553–58) was like a scorpion—quick and exceedingly vicious—and for that very reason it was also a seedbed of individual liberty. Twenty years after Henry VIII forced his subjects to renounce the comfort of Holy Mother Church, Mary slammed the process into reverse and crammed Catholicism back down their just-emancipated throats. This entailed, among other measures, the burning of 273 Englishmen at the stake for taking a doctrinal position that had been mandatory a few years earlier.

Far from teaching the people to love the church, this brutal inconsistency taught them to hate arbitrary power. Far from teaching them the hopelessness of resisting governmental whims, it taught them the necessity of doing so. In the long run, it taught many citizens—eventually, a critical mass—to take charge of their own political souls.

Under a despotic regime, subjects can survive by submerging themselves in the personality and goals of the leader. His successes and failures become theirs, and if a few fellow-subjects must be shot, spliced, or barbecued to serve the common good, so be it. Not so in a society that values and promotes individual liberty. Such a society must view government as other than, and a potential adversary of, its citizens. When co-subjects are subjected to the power of the state, there must be a "there but for the grace of God go I" mentality, which suspends collective judgment until guilt is fairly determined.

Governments create optimal conditions for the latter mentality when they act brutally, but inconsistently, about things that matter. The regimes of Henry VIII and Bloody Mary did this to perfection. By the time Mary left the throne, any subject who thought that life, liberty, and happiness could be reliably ensured by identifying with government simply had not been paying attention.

In those dark times, Lambert's brave challenge—"no man can be compelled to accuse himself"—became a rallying cry against official oppression and cruelty. The words had a convenient ambiguity that allowed them to float unmoored from meaning upon the winds of circumstance and passion. They became words of freedom, which meant what they could be made to mean.

In 1568, a lawyer named Thomas Leigh became, by sheer accident, the first defendant to be granted a privilege not to answer questions regarding a preexisting charge. He was indicted for observing Mass at the Spanish ambassador's home and jailed for refusing to answer questions about the charge put to him by the trial judge. Chief Justice Dyer released him from custody, declaring with learned ignorance that "no man can be compelled to produce [i.e., answer questions] against himself."

Leigh's case was a rare, if not unique, exception. The usual process was exemplified by the famous prosecution of John Udall in 1590 for publishing a blasphemous book called *Martin Marprelate*. When he refused either to admit or deny authorship, he was convicted and imprisoned *for his silence,* with nothing in the record "that could by courtesy be called evidence of guilt."

Lilburne himself first attempted to invoke a privilege not to answer during his 1637 prosecution for criminal libel and was whipped, pilloried, and imprisoned for his pains. When he did so again in his 1649 treason trial, he probably acted without much calculation. He was like a street fighter, grabbing every cobblestone he could find and hurling it at the power massed against him. He knew the crowd was with him and that things impossible before might just be possible now. He may have been surprised, however, that the rock that struck most squarely home turned out to be the often-deflected privilege not to answer questioning.

Should he have been surprised? Was it chance or inevitability that made the privilege work? In granting it so readily, did Lord Keble misunderstand history or comprehend the moment?

Consider the circumstances. After centuries of gross inequality, the courtroom was for once a level playing field. It was equal combat, the first rule of which is noncooperation with the enemy. Lilburne's refusal to answer had the logic of warfare—"name, rank, and serial number is all you'll get from me."

Besides, what choice did his judges really have? It was hard enough to get this gibbering maniac to plead to the indictment. How, conceivably, could he be made to answer *questioning*, and what could be done to him, in that hall aglow with popular menace, when he inevitably refused?

No, Keble didn't grant the privilege by mistake. In truth, he didn't really grant it at all—Lilburne took it as a given.

The privilege against self-incrimination has had a hard time of it since Lilburne's trial. It has been, from the beginning, the disliked stepchild of the Bill of Rights provisions. In 1827, the English philosopher and legal commentator Jeremy Bentham sarcastically catalogued the "reasons" for the privilege, including the Old Woman's Reason ("'Tis *hard* upon a man to be obliged to criminate himself") and the Fox Hunter's Reason (like the fox, the defendant "is to have a fair chance for his life . . . leave to run a certain length of way for the express purpose of giving him a chance for escape"). Doddering compassion for the criminal. Sport disguised as justice. And many knowledgeable critics have agreed with Bentham.

Accidental as its birth was, however, the privilege against self-incrimination fits into the logic of our justice system with precision. It is a corollary of the presumption of innocence, and of the state's burden of proving guilt beyond a reasonable doubt. If there is such a presumption and such a burden, it *follows* that an accused can sit in pristine silence and dare the state to do its worst with the evidence it has. If that very silence can be treated as evidence of guilt, how can it be said that *innocence* is presumed?

It has even been suggested that a privilege of testimonial silence is a moral necessity for a legal system.[1] As an experienced investigating officer explained in testimony before the Indian Code Commission: "It is far pleasanter to sit comfortably in the shade rubbing red pepper into some poor devil's eyes, than to go about in the sun looking for evidence."[2]

Even short of outright torture, a judicial process that centers its attention on producing confessions has a threatening, authoritarian cast that is alien to our way of justice. Judge Stephen described with distaste the French inquisitional system, which focuses on the defendant's efforts to "explain himself." "The accused is cross examined with the utmost severity, and with continual rebukes, sarcasms and exhortations, which no counsel in an English court would be permitted by any judge." The result is not only less fairness but less efficiency: "In every one of the English cases [Stephen analyzed] the evidence is fuller, clearer and infinitely more cogent than in any one of the French cases—notwithstanding which, far less time was occupied by the English trials than by the French ones, and not a word was said or a step taken which anyone can represent as cruel or undignified."[3] Fox hunt, indeed!

Despite the scorn that has been heaped upon it, the privilege against self-incrimination seems neither irrational nor silly when viewed objectively. Its essence is a citizen, arms folded, confronting the power of the state and saying, "Prove it." Considering the alternatives, that seems a reasonable enough request.

10

FREEDOM OF THE PRESS

(The Defense of Truth)

Comment is free, but facts are sacred.
C. P. Scott

One Sunday evening in 1981, CBS's "Sixty Minutes" presented a "shocking exposé" that really was shocking. It charged General William Westmoreland—the army commander in Vietnam and a genuine American hero—with actions amounting to treason. According to the grim-faced reporters, Westmoreland had conspired to lie about American and Vietnamese "body counts" in order to maintain public support for his own military failures. Apparently believing that the truth needed help, CBS engaged in some factual creativity of its own, rehearsing witnesses, reshooting unsatisfactory interviews, and presenting statements and pictures in misleading sequences. The general sued for libel.[1]

The press was naturally outraged—at Westmoreland. *New York Times* columnist Anthony Lewis was particularly upset by the spectacle of a national leader seeking to punish a media critic for doing its constitutional duty. To him, Westmoreland's suit was, in its own way, as wrongheaded as the war itself had been.

"From the beginning of the Republic," Lewis wrote in an August 21, 1983, column, "presidents and generals have been subject to uninhibited criticism. Jefferson suffered smears beyond anything published today." Did these great men scurry to the courts for protection and compensation? Absolutely not. "Officials who were criticized had ways to answer, and did. It is only today, in our more legalized society, that anyone would even *think* of turning such debates into libel suits."

Of course, the distinguished columnist was absolutely right. If an eighteenth-century newspaper had charged an American general with "conspiracy"—and, by implication, with treason—it is unlikely that the general would have filed a libel suit. It is highly probable, however, that the printer would have gone to jail.

A professor teaching early American law would find it difficult to discover the subject matter. In its first century, America had no outstanding lawyers or judges, produced no important court decisions, and—unless one counts the crushing underfoot of witches—did not even conduct a memorable trial. All of that began to change in 1735, when John Peter Zenger was prosecuted for criminal libel in New York. If the beginning of an American legal tradition can be identified, Zenger's trial was it. It was a veritable professor's relief act.

It is a deservedly well-known story. An immigrant printer named John Peter Zenger published one of the few independent newspapers in colonial America. He was sponsored by New York governor William Cosby's political enemies, who submitted attacks against the Cosby administration for almost daily publication. They fancied themselves the Gary Trudeaus of their time, lampooning the governor, for example, by depicting him and his allies as various varieties of strayed animals.

The authorities proved to have no sense of humor—and very little sense of any kind. Cosby tried twice to indict Zenger for libel, but Zenger's fellow citizens on the grand jury unsurprisingly refused, both times, to do their imported leader's bidding. Cosby then convinced the attorney general to charge Zenger by information, a maneuver that did not require grand jury action. He would have been smarter and more comfortable if he had inserted his head into an operating butter churn. His unpopular libel case, rebuffed in secret by the grand jury, would now receive a public skewering, and Cosby would live in second-class legal infamy, somewhere behind

King John, Richard Riche, George Jeffries, Richard Nixon, and other anti-luminaries.

Describing the pre-Revolutionary doctrine of freedom of the press to a modern reader is like explaining poverty to a Rockefeller. It simply did not exist in a form recognizable to twentieth-century Americans. It is fitting that the Star Chamber defined the law's power to punish the press in 1603, at about the same time Guy Fawkes was hatching his plot to send the queen and Parliament into eternity with several tons of gunpowder. The English had always treated the press and gunpowder with comparable trepidation. Both were volatile, and either could blow a government sky high.

The Star Chamber's celebrated opinion, *Libelis Famosis* (1603), laid down two principles for libel prosecutions that were exactly opposite to those of modern American libel law. The first was that a libel "against a magistrate or other public person is a greater offense" than a libel against an ordinary person. (In modern America, of course, the press has much greater liberty to criticize public officials than private citizens.) The second was that it "is not material whether the libel be true." (Under present law, the truth of a libel is a complete defense to civil or criminal prosecution.) Indeed, true attacks on government were considered a greater threat than false ones because they were more likely to provoke public unrest. If you called courageous Henry V a coward, you were making a harmless joke, but if you pointed out the cowardice of the cowardly King John, you were making serious trouble. The maxim, therefore, was the anomalous proposition "The *greater* the truth, the *greater* the libel."

This was assumed to be the law in the Colonies, although there were few libel cases to which it could be applied. Most of the presses were under government control and, by definition, did not print antigovernment articles that could result in libel prosecutions. What His Majesty's courts lacked in opportunities for oppression, however, the colonial legislatures more than made up for. Throughout the colonial period, they hauled printers before them to answer for articles relating to legislative proceedings and threw printers into jail, without any thought of inquiring into the substance of what was published—or, indeed, affording the defendants any hearing at all.

Two particularly odious incidents occurred in Pennsylvania in the decade before the Zenger trial. Newspaper publisher Andrew Bradford printed an article in his *Philadelphia American Weekly Mercury* that offended the provincial council. He offered abject apologies, but the council nonetheless demanded that the governor issue a Draconian order:

> That [Bradford] must not for the future presume to publish anything relating to or concerning the affairs of the government or the government of any other of his Majesty's Colonies, without the permission of the governor or secretary of this province.

A prominent lawyer named Andrew Hamilton was a member of the council, and was active in obtaining the repressive order.

Seven years later, Bradford's publications again offended the council, and this time he was jailed after being interrogated by council members. Andrew Hamilton acted as recorder during the interrogation and participated actively in it. He and his colleagues showed no more regard for freedom of the press than the most benighted judges of the Star Chamber had shown one hundred years previously.

It was against the background of this and similar outrages that Zenger went to trial on August 4, 1735. His original defense lawyers had been disbarred for attacking the legitimacy of the chief justice's commission, and a young lawyer named John Chambers had been appointed in their place. When the case was called for trial, however, a portly gentleman of about sixty stood up in the spectator section of the courtroom and walked confidently toward the bench. He was recognized by the judges and spectators as America's most famous trial lawyer. "My name is Andrew Hamilton," he said. "I am concerned in this cause on the part of Mr. Zenger, the defendant."

Dubious that the inexperienced Chambers could mount an effective defense, Zenger's disbarred lawyers had traveled secretly to Philadelphia some weeks earlier to persuade Hamilton to take the case. His sudden courtroom appearance was intended to take the opposition by surprise, and it obviously had that effect.

After the judge and attorney general had collected themselves and duly recognized the eminent intruder, young Chambers stood aside and Hamilton took the helm. The great oppressor was about to become the great liberator. He began by making the surprising concession that Zenger had "printed and published the two newspapers set forth in the information." Assuming that the case was over, the attorney general said, "As Mr. Hamilton has confessed the printing and publishing of these libels, I think the jury must find a verdict for the King." Hamilton then fired the doctrinal shot heard round the legal world: "You will have something more to do before you make my client a libeler; for the words themselves must be libelous, that is *false*, scandalous and seditious, or else we are not guilty."

The chief justice knew better, and reminded Hamilton that truth was irrelevant under the law. "You cannot be admitted, Mr. Hamilton, to give the truth of a libel in evidence," he said. "A libel is not to be justified, for it is nevertheless a libel that is true."

Hamilton persisted, arguing that the law cited by the judge was the product of the wicked Star Chamber and that enlightened legal minds recognized truth as a defense. He had little ammunition insofar as legal precedent was concerned, but he was aided by a strange blunder the attorney general had made in drawing up the information. It charged that Zenger's publications were "scandalous," "seditious," "libelous," and "*false*." In insisting upon truth as a defense, Hamilton was insisting only that the charge be proven as made—the attorney general had said that the articles were false, let him prove it.

There is nothing as vulnerable as a trial lawyer who is sure of his position. Attorney General Bradley must have seen no way at all that he could lose the case, and his response to Hamilton reflected careless arrogance. "Supposing all the words to be true," he said, "yet that will not help them."

When Hamilton persisted in his argument, Judge Delancey grew petulant: "The Court have delivered their opinion, and we expect you will use us with good manners; you are not permitted to argue the opinion of the Court."

"With submission," Hamilton protested, "I have seen the practice in very great courts, and never heard it unmannerly to . . ."

"After the Court have declared their opinion," the judge broke in angrily, "it is not good manners to insist upon a point, in which you have been overruled."

Hamilton abruptly surrendered his hopeless legal argument. He had not been performing for the judge, in any case, but for the twelve good men and true who sat in the crude wooden jury box, and it was to them that he now turned. "The power is in your hands, gentlemen," he said, "to safeguard our liberties."

> If you should be of the opinion that there is no falsehood in Mr. Zenger's papers, you will, nay you ought to say so; because you do not know whether others—I mean the Court—may be of that opinion. It is your right to do so, and there is much depending upon your resolution, as well as upon your integrity.[2]

He spoke to his fellow citizens for a long time, telling them what freedom meant to a proud nation and what it could mean to a courageous one. Then he told them something their countrymen would carry in their hearts, embroider into wall hangings, memorize in school, proclaim on national holidays, and utter at press banquets for generations and generations to come:

> The question before the court and you, gentlemen of the jury, is of no small or private concern; it is not the cause of a poor printer, nor of New York alone, which you are trying. No! It may, in its consequence, affect every free man that lives on the main of America. It is the best cause; it is the cause of liberty, and I make no doubt but your upright conduct this day will not only entitle you to the love and esteem of your fellow citizens, but every man who prefers freedom to a life of slavery will bless and honor you as men who have baffled the attempt of tyranny, and who, by an impartial and incorrupt verdict, have made a noble foundation for securing to ourselves, our posterity and our neighbors that to which nature and the laws of our country have given us a right—the liberty of exposing arbitrary power, in these parts of the world at least, by speaking and writing truth.

To the surprise of probably no one, Zenger was acquitted.

Gouverneur Morris called Hamilton's speech "The Morning Star of the American Revolution." The unfortunate Andrew Bradford had a different opinion. "A single attempt on the side of liberty," he editorialized, could not counterbalance a lifetime of hostility to a free press:

> A person [Hamilton] that has cruelly harassed and imprisoned a printer, and again caused him to be knocked down and assaulted on

the street, merely for copying an English print, or inserting in the newspaper some general invectives against a particular vice . . . can no more merit the character of a sincere advocate for the liberty of the press, than a venal hireling for a fulsome harangue does the name of Cato [the pen name of a free press advocate of the time].

Fair enough. Just what *was* an anti-press activist like Andrew Hamilton doing in that sweltering courtroom, making himself immortal as a defender of truth, justice, and the American newspaper? Was it a miraculous conversion or common cynicism? On the face of it, Andrew Hamilton defending a free press seemed comparable in ethical flexibility to Ralph Nader defending General Motors, or Thurgood Marshall defending the Ku Klux Klan.

Viewed within the context of the time, however, his actions were not inconsistent. What he was defending in Zenger's case was not freedom of the press as we understand it, but rather the "Press of Freedom." What was at stake was not an ecumenical right to publish anything and everything that is factually true, but the right to publish a particular brand of political truth. Zenger had not made factual allegations against Cosby that could be proven true or false by evidence; he had accused a British governor and his allies of being unfit to govern an American colony. He had published expressions of opinion, belief, and patriotic bias that could be argued about but never proven right or wrong. Hamilton agreed with these expressions—thought that they were "true"—and so he spoke for Zenger's right to publish them. The revolution of which his speech was the "Morning Star" was a war, not a search for objective accuracy, and his speech was a first call to arms.

Would he have done the same for Cosby if his role and Zenger's had been reversed? Ask Andrew Bradley.

The *Zenger* case did not usher in an era of free speech and press as we understand those concepts. Quite the contrary, the oppressive tradition brought from England continued to prevail in America for generations after the *Zenger* verdict was returned. When government was criticized, punishment was meted out in accordance with the political strength of the government to do so. Hated British rule continued to be fair game for press critics, but not so its colonial counterparts. The popular view seemed to be that criticism of "legitimate"—i.e., colonial—government *ought* to be punished, and truth in any objective sense had little or nothing to do with it. The eminent legal historian Leonard Levy has described the free press climate in post-*Zenger* colonial America in blunt and startling terms: "The persistent notion of Colonial America as a society where freedom of expression was cherished is an hallucination which ignores history. . . . The American people simply did not believe or understand that freedom of thought and expression means equal freedom for the other person, especially the one with hated ideas."[3]

Some of our more eminent Founding Fathers manifested this limited view of press freedom. In 1758, William Moore, the chief judge of the court of common pleas of Chester County, Pennsylvania, wrote a speech criticizing the Pennsylvania legislature. The house tried him for libel, convicted him, and ordered the public hangman to burn the offending publication and to hold Moore in jail until further notice. Moore later fled to England, where the Privy Council ruled that the colonial legislature had no power to imprison him. Interestingly, the legislature's case against Moore was presented to the council by none other than former newspaperman and Founding Father Benjamin Franklin. Franklin vigorously sought Moore's reimprisonment, describing him as "a common scribbler of libels against publick bodies."

During the period immediately preceding the Revolution, the persecution of minority opinion and criticism moved into the streets. Superpatriot Isaac Sears led a series of attacks on Tory newspaper offices in New York City and initiated riots over pro-Tory handbills. On the eve of the Revolution, Chief Justice Hutchison of Massachusetts complained that Founding Fathers John and Samuel Adams, and their followers, advocated "an unlimited freedom of thought and action, which they would confine wholly to themselves." A Tory writing under the pseudonym Honestes lamented:

Bad as our present ministers are universally represented by the news papers, they still allow us some degree of Freedom; they suffer us to think, to talk and to write as we please, but Patriots allow us no such indulgence. Unless we think, talk and write as they would have us, we are Traitors to the State, we are infamous Hirelings to the Government.

Things did not improve much after the Revolutionary War. In 1800, a Philadelphia printer was convicted for publishing articles stating, among other things, that President John Adams's administration was "in the infancy of its incompetency." In 1804, the state of New York prosecuted Harry Crosswell, the editor of a Federalist paper called *The Wasp,* for libeling President Thomas Jefferson. In 1803, Jefferson wrote a letter to Governor Thomas McKean of Pennsylvania which demonstrated that his ideas for dealing with press critics were not at all what Anthony Lewis had in mind:

> I have . . . long thought that a few prosecutions of the most prominent offenders would have a wholesome effect in restoring the integrity of the presses. Not a general prosecution, for that would look like persecution; but a selected one. The paper I now enclose appears to me to offer as good an instance in every respect to make an example of, as can be selected. . . . If the same thing can be done in some of the other states, it will place the whole band more on its guard.

No modern politician would dream of writing such a letter. The legal climate that produced it has utterly evaporated in the last one hundred and fifty years. For one thing, civil libel actions have replaced criminal libel prosecutions as the means of punishing injurious publications. The lion that had sought John Peter Zenger's hide has been transformed into a litigiously rambunctious but far less potent cub. No doubt CBS found the Westmoreland suit inconvenient and expensive, but at least its executives faced no prospect of a stinking jail cell. Other than the punitive legal expenses it probably incurred, the network's punishment was confined to the issuance of a watered-down, agreed-upon, semi-apology for traducing the general's honor.

Although both are directed at the publication of *damaging words,* criminal and civil libel are different in theory. Criminal libel is a breach of the peace. It is prosecuted, theoretically, because it is a verbal interruption of domestic tranquillity. To qualify as such, the offending publication must contain an accusation that is generally—i.e., culturally—abhorrent. Civil libel actions seek compensation for injury to individual reputation. The scope of liability is, therefore, narrower. That which damages an individual's reputation in his circle of acquaintances may give him a civil right of action but may not be sufficiently obnoxious to people in general to constitute a breach of the peace. Publishing someone's picture in a whiskey ad may, for example, entitle him to damages if he is a teetotaler, but it is not the sort of threat to social harmony that justifies criminal prosecution.[4]

The disappearance of criminal libel prosecutions in modern America has been a silent phenomenon. Like other basic changes in the law, it has been a cultural rather than an intellectual happening that has gone almost unnoticed by legal analysts. The last time the U.S. Supreme Court spoke on the subject, it seemed to say that criminal libel prosecutions were legally viable. The reason for their demise must be looked for in changed conditions of society itself.

There arose, for one thing, a perplexing definitional problem. Physical blows cause tangible injury and are punished by every society. Verbal assaults leave no wounds and are harmful only to the extent that society agrees they are. Libel prosecutions require cultural agreement as to what words are harmful enough to deserve governmental punishment, what values are worthy of governmental protection from verbal attack. If words are to be punished by force, they must themselves be deemed to have the effect of force. Otherwise, the punishment is disproportionate to the wrong.

A nineteenth-century English textbook defined criminal libel with a majestic fog of language that the author and his readers obviously thought meant something: "It may be asserted, generally, that the wilful and unauthorized publication of that which tends to produce mischief and inconvenience to society is a public offense." Such "mischief" and "inconvenience" might, according to the author, consist of "communications which tend to weaken or dissolve religious or moral restraints," "alienate men's minds from the established constitution of the state," "engender hatred and contempt [for the government]," or "in *general* produce *particular* inconvenience or mischief, or to excite individuals to the commission of breaches of the peace or *other acts*." Whew!

Apart from the free speech problems of such a listing, the definitional problems are mind-boggling. What words are "inconvenient" or "mischievous" to society? What sort of utterance tends to "weaken or dissolve religious and moral constraints"? Whose religion and what standards of morality are we talking about? How can strictures against voicing "contempt for government" be enforced when those who hold governmental office are constantly criticized and challenged by those who seek to replace them?

A society enforcing such "standards" of verbal criminality must be either monolithic in its viewpoints or arbitrary in its law enforcement. America ultimately failed to fill either bill. It had too great a multiplicity of tongues, too much splintering in its attitudes, to permit government to choose sides in its citizens' verbal skirmishes. Most of the libel prosecutions brought in the nineteenth and early twentieth centuries looked like silly interventions into personal quarrels, in which no clear governmental interest was at stake. Criminal libel cases went out of style in twentieth-century America, not so much from concern for free expression as for lack of consensus over what words were truly damaging to society's definable interests.

Modern technology abetted this disintegration of consensus. Just as the rise of the printing press in the sixteenth century made public words more dangerous, and more subject to the government's attention, so the sprawling, redundant proliferation of mass communication in our time has had the opposite effect. Public discourse has been devalued by its utter commonality. Tired of listening to G. Gordon Liddy rant about his favorite enemies and scapegoats? Tune in Farakhan and get a rancid earful of *his* brand of free expression. Fearful of the force of "wrong" opinions? Watch them turned to harmless vaudeville on "Crossfire" and its ilk.

Expression cannot be subversive, cannot damage society, unless it has some *force;* and modern communication loses force from its inception, being drowned, smothered, and lost in a thousand competitive utterances. Inundated as we are by rival assertions of fact, opinion, speculation, and rumor, coming from all directions like swarms of gnats, it would be the height of arbitrariness to select a small percentage of them to prosecute as crimes. If Governor Cosby were alive today, he wouldn't charge Zenger with a crime; he would send out spin doctors to give his version of the facts, thus adding to the information overload.

Meanwhile, civil libel suits like General Westmoreland's have burgeoned. But they, too, have met with a countering legal trend: the rise and dominance of the defense of truth, defined as factual accuracy. Contrary to mythology, the *Zenger* case did not establish truth as a defense in American libel cases. Throughout the nineteenth century and into the twentieth, many courts continued to apply the adage of English poet William Blake that "truth that's told with bad intent beats every lie you can invent." They held that truth is *not* a defense, unless published with "good motives" and for "justifiable reasons." Truth was acceptable, in other words, only if "well-intended"—and the jury would be the judge of what *that* meant.

One might think that constitutional guarantees of freedom of speech and press would protect the publication of all brands and forms of truth, but they did not. The First Amendment was held not even to *apply* to libel cases until 1964. Thus, for a century and three-quarters after the Bill of Rights was adopted, American courts were free to impose liability for words, including indisputably true words, without constitutional constraints.

Most American courts allowed the defense of truth in some form, but even they left unsolved the wicked dilemma of libelous *opinion*. It was all well and good to allow a libel defendant to defend himself by proving that the plaintiff had, in fact, done the specific heinous acts the defendant had accused him of; but how does one *prove* that the plaintiff is "incompetent," "crazy," "brutal," or "foolish"? Such unprovable—and undisprovable—generalizations had always been, and remained, the most intractable problem of libel law.

Should judges and juries treat "opinion" statements as true because they could not be proven false, or false because they could not be proven true? The answer given by the courts was a resounding "neither." Judges submitted defamatory opinion statements to juries, accompanied by useless instructions that "truth is a defense." The juries usually followed the lead of *Zenger*'s jury: If they agreed with the defendant's opinions they ruled for him, even though "truth" in any objective sense could not be determined. If they disagreed with him, they found for the plaintiff.

Such a process was more like an election than a fact-finding exercise, but it was not necessarily a bad means of resolving the knotty issue of opinion defamation. Deciding the legal consequences of expressions of opinion is arguably the very sort of logically impossible job the jury was created for. The task may be too subtle and subjective for hard-edged judicial analysis.

In the long run, however, hard-edged analysis won out. By the 1970s, the U.S. Supreme Court had decided that factual accuracy was the be-all, end-all value to be considered in libel cases. To make out a claim, the plaintiff must prove that the defendant had published false *facts* about him. Since statements of opinion are factually neither true nor false, they *cannot* be the basis for a libel suit. The most evilly motivated, unfair, and destructive publisher can obtain salvation in court if he can prove he has printed no lies.

This proposition was given an acid test in *Letter Carriers Branch No. 496* v. *Austin,* which came before the U.S. Supreme Court in 1974. Henry Austin was a letter carrier who had chosen not to join the carriers' union. He was characterized in a union newsletter as a "scab" and therefore imbued with the following characteristics:

> After God had finished the rattlesnake, the toad and the vampire, he had some awful substance left with which he made a scab.
>
> A scab is a two-legged animal with a corkscrew soul, a water brain, a combination backbone of jelly and glue. Where others have hearts, he carries a tumor of rotten principles.
>
> When a scab comes down the street, men turn their backs and angels weep in heaven, and the devil shuts the gates of hell to keep him out.
>
> No man (or woman) has a right to scab so long as there is a pool of water to drown his carcass in, or a rope long enough to hang his body with. Judas was a gentleman compared with a scab. For betraying his master, he had character enough to hang himself. A scab has not.
>
> Esau sold his birthright for a mess of pottage. Judas sold his savior for thirty pieces of silver. Benedict Arnold sold his country for a promise of a commission in the British army. The scab sells his birthright, his country, his wife, his children and his fellow men for an unfulfilled promise from his employer.
>
> Esau was a traitor to himself; Judas was a traitor to his God; Benedict Arnold was a traitor to his country; a scab is a traitor to his God, his country, his family and his class.[5]

Henry was awarded $165,000 in damages by the trial court, but the Supreme Court took it away from him. The Court noted that the publication was factually accurate—the defendant *was,* after all, a non-union member—and held that the union's vile characterization of his non-union status could not be legally harmful, however actually harmful it may have been. "However pernicious an opinion may be," said the Court, "we depend for its correction, not on the conscience of judges and juries, but on the competition of other ideas."

In the 1980s, the Reverend Jerry Falwell sued *Hustler* magazine for publishing a parody about him, accusing him, among other things, of committing incest with his mother in an outhouse. Although factual in form, the parody was intended "merely" as allegorical comment on Falwell's character. No liability, ruled the Supreme Court. However disgusting, upsetting, outrageous, or damaging the article may have been, since it contained nothing that readers would seriously construe as a false *fact,* it had the full protection of the First Amendment.

Writing in the 1840s, Alexis de Tocqueville noted the American obsession with facts. Whereas Continental newspapers and journals dealt preponderantly in ideas and polemics, their American counterparts were crammed with fact—the "what" of the world—and paid little attention to the "why" or the "should." Writing more then a hundred years later, the American critic Dwight Macdonald noted that this obsession had, if anything, accelerated. "We are," he said, "hagridden by Facts, in love with information. . . . Instead of being interested only in useful information, we now tend to the opposite extreme, valuing Facts in themselves, collecting them as boys collect postage stamps, treating them, in short, as objects of consumption rather than as productive tools." Macdonald observed that journalists such as Walter Winchell and John Gunther and publishers of news magazines such as Henry Luce had "made careers out of exploiting the enormous American appetite for Facts." Forty years later, that appetite seems, if anything, even more voracious. Indeed, fortunes have been made publishing books and games which inventory *trivial* facts.

It might be said, and usually is, that the Supreme Court's restriction of libel liability to the publication of false facts reflects the Court's respect for opinion; that the Court considers diversity of opinion too vital to be subjected to legal constraint. Exactly the opposite case can be made, however. The message the Court may well be sending is that only facts are important enough, and potentially damaging enough to society's interests, to justify legal control; that the buzz of opinion that *arises from* fact is the chaff, the fluff, the meringue; that it is protected from legal sanction, not because it is vital, but because it is not.

The judicial attitude at work probably makes little difference at the moment. The reality is that the marketplace of ideas the Court has created *is* vital to a free society, however unnourishing the product sometimes seems. The trick will be to maintain that marketplace in times of peril, when ideas grow large and come to dominate the scene. Whether we have finally learned that trick, time alone will tell.[6]

11

UNREASONABLE SEARCHES AND SEIZURES

[O]ur houses and even our bed chambers are exposed to be ransacked, our boxes chests and trunks broke open ravaged and plundered by wretches, whom no prudent man would venture to employ even as menial servants. . . . By this we are cut off from that domestic security which renders the lives of the most unhappy in some measure agreeable.

INFRINGEMENTS AND VIOLATIONS OF RIGHTS, ENUMERATED BY THE COMMITTEE OF CORRESPONDENCE FOR THE TOWN OF BOSTON, 1772 (THE FIRST ASSERTION BY AN AMERICAN GOVERNMENTAL BODY OF THE PEOPLE'S RIGHT TO BE FREE FROM UNREASONABLE SEARCHES AND SEIZURES)

In Old England, as in the Old West, the most commonly committed felony was cattle stealing and the most sacred individual right was private property. These two realities must have collided often.

The scene is easy to imagine. Hugh of Waltham stumbles through the underbrush, driving his four-footed loot before him, with the din of the hue and cry close behind. The pursuing mob knows where he is headed, and he knows that if they catch him with his bovine booty, "he will have short shrift. . . . He will be brought before some court . . . and without being allowed to say one word in self-defense, he will be promptly hanged, beheaded or precipitated from a cliff."[1]

With the energy of the near-doomed, he makes it to his own crude farmstead and turns the stolen cattle loose to mix with the small herd he claims as his. The pursuers emerge panting from the wood and come to what in future centuries will be called a screeching halt. They don't know what to do. Uninvited entry is a serious offense, and these men have no wish to be charged with hamfare.

On the other hand, there is a vigorously enforced duty to hunt down "hand-having" thieves such as Hugh. On the *other* hand, suppose they intrude and discover that the cattle are not there. The pursuers scratch their lank beards, purse their grim lips . . . and turn away.

A rehearsal of the great prohibition against unreasonable searches and seizures has just taken place. Hugh escapes because the sanctity of the home was given more weight than the apprehension of a criminal. The same hard choice will present itself again and again in the ensuing centuries, and the choices made will show Anglo-American law at its best and at its worst. The ebb and flow of conflict between privacy and law enforcement will reflect the changing face of justice, with a clarity often frightening to behold.

According to John Adams, the American Revolution did not begin at Concord Bridge in 1775 but fourteen years earlier, when James Otis made a stirring courtroom speech in *Paxton*'s case. "Then and there," Adams wrote, "the child Independence was born."

That speech, and Otis himself, have a certain ghostlike quality. Otis is a will-o'-the-wisp of history—almost forgotten today, but an immense presence in his time. He was the Massachusetts counterpart of Virginia's better-remembered patriot-hero, Patrick Henry. He invented the anti-British rallying cry "Taxation without representation is tyranny" to match Henry's equally famous "Give me liberty or give me death."

His public life was short and badly recorded, and had to be recreated by enthusiastic biographers after his death. It is not even certain exactly what he said in the *Paxton* case, since his speech was preserved only in the cryptic notes of John Adams, who later translated them into the version we have today. Adams had every reason to make his fellow colonist sound good, and was no mean speechmaker himself. But even if Otis stuttered, used bad grammar, and put his audience to sleep, he undeniably made history in that memorable case.

He brought to life a basic principle of freedom that had previously been nothing more than an academic abstraction: that government may not arbitrarily invade, and conduct unreasonable searches and seizures within, the homes and shops of citizens. That proposition became the heart of New England's subsequent resistance to English tyranny, and it had a direct connection to the Revolution.

The wonder is not that this principle was advocated in 1761, but that its advocacy came so late in history. The idea that citizens must be free from arbitrary intrusions into their homes is as old as the idea of private property itself. Even the Saxons—who thought that freedom of religion was the road to hell and freedom of speech a license for treason—recognized the sanctity of the hearth. Arbitrary searches and seizures had been an active concern of English legal theorists ever since the printing presses began producing books and other documents in sufficient quantities to stimulate such oppressions. As early as 1589, Robert Beale complained that government agents were violating Magna Charta by "entering into men's houses, breaking into their chests and chambers," and absconding with evidence of supposed crimes. Seventeenth-century constitutionalists such as Edward Coke and Matthew Hale lamented learnedly about the illegality of such practices in their widely circulated treatises.

But none of this affected the real world. No administrative directives were given and no court decisions were rendered to curtail the widespread rape of private property conducted by minions of the king in search of "evidence." Ironically, as Coke himself lay dying, agents of the Privy Council entered and searched his home, carrying off voluminous documents and other personal possessions, including a poem to his children.

Hardly a lawyer arose in court to protest such practices until Otis undertook to do so in *Paxton*'s case.

That extraordinary case was brought into being by the death of King George II in 1760. When a king expired, so-called writs of assistance issued for the term of his reign expired, too. Charles Paxton, the head of customs in Boston, routinely (he thought) petitioned the Massachusetts superior court for a new writ, applicable to the new reign of George III. To his consternation, sixty-three angry Boston merchants went to court to oppose the petition and, worse still, Otis quit his job as Massachusetts attorney general to represent them.

It would be hard to imagine a fatter target for citizen revolt than the English writ of assistance. It was tyranny in its most easily understood form. These writs authorized government agents to enter at will any building owned by a citizen, including his home, in order to search out and seize goods or evidence "believed" to be concealed there. The decision to search was left to the judgment—or whim—of the investigating agent and, as noted, the writ's authority remained in effect until the king in whose name it was issued left the throne.

When Paxton filed his petition, Boston was already in semi-revolt against these super-search warrants. Thirty years earlier, England had enacted the hated Molasses Act, which imposed unrealistically high tariffs on molasses and sugar imported by Massachusetts from West Indies colonies not owned by Britain. Like most patently illogical laws, these tariffs were widely ignored and circumvented. Colonial New Englanders gave them roughly the same respect their twentieth-century descendants gave liquor prohibition laws, with similar results. Smuggling became a burgeoning cottage industry that was supported and condoned by otherwise law-abiding citizens, and the government's efforts to enforce the law, by searching out and seizing smuggled goods wherever they could be found, intensified public resistance.

By applying to the court for authority to continue sending his functionaries across private thresholds, Paxton was turning up the heat on an already boiling political stew.

James Otis was a short, plump, fiery-eyed advocate who had that gift of eloquence that seems to transcend its owner's conscious mind. He was capable of sweeping his opposition before him with a torrent of words and ideas. It is said that there was a violence about his speaking that was "almost frightening, as though he might do or say something monstrous." As he rose in the old State House in Boston to attack writs of assistance, on February 24, 1761, he was at the height of his remarkable powers.

The argument took place in an intimidating setting. On the walls of the elegant courtroom hung portraits of two of the more formidable kings of recent English history, Charles II and James II. Five judges presided. The Boston bar was present in force, as were all sixty-three of Otis's merchant clients.

Otis's adversary was a courtly and gifted lawyer named Jeremiah Gridley, who had taught the law to Otis and his co-counsel, Thatcher.[2] On this occasion the technical law was entirely on Gridley's side, as he proceeded to demonstrate. Writs of assistance were recognized by Parliament, he said, and were particularly authorized in this case. They were contrary to the general privileges of Englishmen, but were justified by the necessity of raising revenues. If they were authorized in the mother country, as they unquestionably were, they were necessarily authorized in the colonies.

Gridley's statement of the law was flawless, but Otis addressed a different law—the law of the unwritten British Constitution, the law of "Right Reason" and "Equity," which took precedence over any specific act of Parliament. The theme of his argument seems commonplace today, but in 1761 it was revolutionary. Taking his text from Lord Coke's opinion in *Bonham*'s case a century and a half earlier, Otis asserted the most fundamental point of constitutional law with force and clarity. That point was, simply, that a law contrary to the British Constitution was no law at all, and that it was the duty of the court to so declare.

Otis was a formidable combination of forces on that day. He had the courage of a revolutionary, which permitted him to perform aggressively under the baleful eye of the mother country. He had the arrogance of an intellectual, which permitted him to brush aside the technicalities of English law and address the broader truths that underlay them. Most of all, he had the passion of a visionary, which permitted him to focus all of his powers upon the task at hand with a full sense of its historic meaning. God had made Otis for this moment, and Otis made the most of it.

He spoke for five hours and was, according to Adams, "a flame of fire." He spoke "with a promptitude of classical allusions, a depth of research, a rapid summary of historical events and dates, a profusion of legal authorities, a prophetic glance of the eye into futurity, and a torrent of impetuous eloquence." He denounced the writs of assistance as "the worst instrument of arbitrary power, the most destructive of English liberty and the fundamental principles of law, that ever was found in an English law book." In a virtual call to revolution he said, "I am determined to sacrifice estate, ease, health, applause, and even life, to the sacred calls of my Country, in opposition to a kind of power, the exercise of which cost one King his head and another his throne."

Most importantly, he said:

> No act of Parliament can establish such a writ. Even though made in the very language of the petition, it would be a nullity. An act of Parliament against the Constitution is void. An act against natural equity is void. The courts must pass such acts into disuse.

Historians identify these words as the foundation stones of American constitutional law.

In the electric silence that followed Otis's speech, truth seemed to hang in the air. But truth got mired in process, as it so often does. The judges put off a decision, sent to England for instructions, heard further argument, and finally, unsurprisingly, came down on the side that had the political weight.

But it turned out to be a Pyrrhic victory for Mr. Paxton and his minions. The echoes of Otis's speech would be heard in the mother country, and before the decade was out, writs of assistance and general warrants would be laid to rest in one of the great constitutional opinions of all time.

John Wilkes was quite a jokester. He once broke up a mock satanic ritual by causing a baboon dressed as a devil to leap out of a box—for a terrifying moment, the worshipers thought their prayers had been answered. Years later, when the earl of Sandwich told Wilkes that he would end up either hanged or with syphilis, Wilkes cheerfully replied: "That depends, My Lord, on whether I embrace your principles or your mistress." On April 30, 1763, he stood in his personal quarters looking at an official document and made another joke—but it was not very funny. "This is a ridiculous warrant against the whole English nation," he roared.

He was referring to what was to become the most famous search warrant in history. On April 23 Wilkes had published *North Britain 45*, an edition of a political journal that he ran. In it he made a blistering attack against a recent speech by King George III, taking it apart with contemptuous sarcasm and labeling much of it false. He tried to give himself some cover by noting that speeches by the king were usually written by his ministers, but it did him no good. George elected to take the article personally and brought the whole weight of the British government down on Wilkes's head.

The king ordered Secretary of State Lord Halifax to take "all necessary measures," and Halifax was nothing loath. He instructed four messengers and a constable to make "strict and diligent search for the authors and publishers of a seditious and treasonous paper known as 'North Britain #45,' to seize all papers relating to the same," and to bring them before Halifax. By the time they got to Wilkes, Halifax's storm troopers had already sacked the homes and shops of dozens of other persons who had, or were reported to have, or might conceivably or theoretically have had, some tangential relationship to the conception, writing, publication, or distribution of the offending article. They found what they were looking for in Wilkes's chambers, and before it was over, he had been convicted of libel, fined five hundred pounds, and sentenced to a year in prison.

This time, however, the bullies had selected the wrong victim. Wilkes was a rogue with principles. He had an instinctive dislike of authority and an over-developed faith in English law as a refuge for the individual. Like John Lilburne one hundred years before him, he was strengthened in his legal battles by a potent ignorance of the limits of his rights—he was much better at making history than studying it.

English gentlemen of the time felt a surge of moral uplift when they read William Pitt's ringing declaration that "every man's home is his castle":

> The poorest man may in his cottage bid defiance to all the forces of the Crown. It may be frail, its roof may shake, the wind may blow through it; the storm may enter it; the rain may enter; but the King of England may not enter; all his force dares not cross the threshold of the ruined tenement.

But only Wilkes was crude and practical enough to give such poetry meaning in the real world. He took hold of Pitt's lyric myth and used it as a battle-ax against the ransackers of his home.

The retaliatory action he took would puzzle a modern lawyer. He did not assert the lawlessness of the search as a defense in his criminal case; it did not occur to him that evidence illegally obtained was tainted and unusable in court. Instead, he took his punishment and administered some of his own. He filed a damages action against Under Secretary of State Robert Woods for his part in instigating the search, charging him with criminal trespass. The suit represented a simple legal idea whose time was long overdue.

The jury returned a verdict in the amount of one thousand pounds, and the court approved it, holding that general warrants are "totally subversive of the liberty of the subject." The decision in *Wilkes* v. *Woods* was a major constitutional beachhead—one of those rare decisions that moves the law appreciably forward—but its impact would not be fully felt until *Entick* v. *Carrington* was decided two years later.

Before they got to Wilkes's house, the king's messengers had spent three days trashing forty-eight other residences. One of these belonged to a printer named John Entick. Entick had printed several copies of the *North Britain,* but not number 45. In their efforts to prove the contrary, the messengers had spent four hours breaking locks and prying open and examining the contents of boxes in Entick's home. They had carried off more than two hundred printed charts and pamphlets, none of which had anything to do with the libel against the king.

Inspired by Wilkes's success, Entick went after chief messenger Nicholas Carrington in similar fashion. His jury awarded him two thousand pounds, and the ruined Carrington appealed to the court of common pleas. In an opinion that ranks as one of the greatest in Anglo-American Bill of Rights history, Chief Justice Camden held that general warrants were illegal six ways from Sunday.

The English Constitution was old, but the personal liberties associated with it were just emerging and had seldom been expounded by judges. The chief justice was plowing a new field on a spring morning; there were no tangled precedents to ensnare his logic. He was able to appeal to first principals and simple rightness in a way that future judges would envy and future lawyers would research for in vain.

Carrington's lawyer made the usual assertion that general warrants were permissible because they had always been permitted. In an argument reminiscent of Gridley's in *Paxton*'s case, he said, "I am not at all alarmed if this power is established to be in the Secretary of State. It has been used in the best of times, often since the Revolution."

Entick's lawyer put a reverse spin on this shopworn bromide: "It is said that this has been done in the best of times, ever since the

Revolution. The conclusion from thence is, that it is the more inexcusable because done in the best of times, in an era when the common law (which had been trampled under the foot of arbitrary power) was revived."

Chief Justice Camden agreed. The longtime acceptance of general search warrants was puzzling, but "it must have been the guilt or poverty of those upon whom such warrants have been executed, that deterred or hindered them . . . or such warrants could never have passed for lawful until this time." In any event, "it would be a strange doctrine to assert that all the people of this land are bound to acknowledge that to be universal law which a few criminal booksellers have been afraid to dispute."

He then stated the proposition that was the backbone of his decision: that the burden was upon those who "rifled the houses" of citizens to prove that their actions were legal, not upon their victims to prove them illegal, and that the absence of authority validating general warrants meant that they were invalid. "By the laws of England, every invasion of private property, be it ever so minute, is a trespass. If no . . . excuse can be found, the silence of the textbooks is authority against the defendant, and the plaintiff must have judgment.' . . . That such a right should have existed from the time whereof the memory of man runneth not to the contrary, and never found a place in any book of law, is incredible."

General warrants had been invented as a weapon against the press, and the chief justice found them especially obnoxious for just that reason. "Papers are their owner's . . . dearest property, and are so far from enduring a seizure, they will hardly bear an inspection; and though the eye cannot by the laws of England be guilty of a trespass, yet where private papers are removed and carried away, the secret nature of these goods will be an aggravation of the trespass. . . ."

This great opinion was an inspiration to the American revolutionaries. The Fourth Amendment to the U.S. Constitution—that most specific of all the Bill of Rights provisions—is tailored to outlaw general warrants of the kind condemned by Chief Justice Camden. It provides that search warrants shall issue only upon "probable cause," stating "the particular place to be searched" and "the particular things to be seized."

Not as poetic as William Pitt's famed elegy, but eminently useful prose.

* * *

It is possible that James Otis never read Chief Justice Camden's vindication of his argument in *Paxton*'s case. The year after Camden's opinion was published, Otis's brilliant mind was almost extinguished by a blow to the head in a coffeehouse altercation with a customs agent. He lived on in a state of recurrent psychosis, a ruined reminder of the springtime of the revolutionary spirit, hardly comprehending the tumult of events that led to the Revolution itself.

In his later years, he gathered together and burned most of his papers and journals (perhaps he had dark visions of being robbed of them at death like Coke), thereby ensuring his ghostlike place in history. Toward the end, he expressed the hope that he would be killed by a bolt of lightning—which, amazingly, is exactly how he died, on May 23, 1783.

John Wilkes was known as England's foremost political eccentric in a time that fairly bristled with that breed. He was unfailingly supportive of the downtrodden, relentlessly vulgar in the "polite" company that he despised, and invariably cynical in manner toward a world he believed to be cynical in fact. It is said that he never did a good thing without giving a bad reason.

He did many good things. During the Revolutionary War, he made ten speeches in Parliament demanding that England set the Americans free, and his efforts in support of press freedom rivaled his resistance to illegal searches. He died alone in 1797, at the age of seventy, utterly insolvent—and blissfully unaware of his insolvency.

Except for the names and dates, these might be biographies of many other constitutional heroes. Such people are like nobody else, but in some generic and indefinable way, they are very much like one another.

The right of sanctuary in one's home is the most ancient conception of individual liberty, and perhaps the most profound. A rifle butt against the door at midnight is not only tyrannical, it is tyranny itself. It tells the people that they belong to the state and may be put into its pocket at any moment. And yet, real world protection against this ultimate form of tyranny came curiously late and was dubiously received by the people when it came. As we will see, the courts have shared the popular ambivalence about it and, as a consequence, the history of the Fourth Amendment has been as volatile as the dispositions of its first two advocates.

Attitudes toward the Fourth Amendment have been the great thermometer for registering the constitutional health of the republic, now warm with passion, now frigid with indifference, now tepid with timidity. Fourth Amendment rights are inherently fragile because they have no broad constituencies. Citizens have their doors kicked in and their belongings seized one at a time, and no one ever assumes it will happen to him. The sanctity of the home has survived J. Edgar Hoover, Watergate, the war on drugs, and, so far, Justice William Rehnquist, but it will not survive forever its most implacable foe—the indifference of the people to its fate.[3]

12

THE BILL OF RIGHTS

The earth belongs always to the living generation.
THOMAS JEFFERSON

During Robert Bork's Supreme Court confirmation hearing in 1987, something called the doctrine of original intent floated for the first time into the general American consciousness. Bork's version of this "doctrine" was more sophisticated, but the popularization of it went like this: When judges interpret the Constitution, and particularly the Bill of Rights, they should search out and follow the intent of the Founding Fathers. All of these modern judges making up constitutional law to suit themselves is a travesty. James Madison, Thomas Jefferson, and the rest of the Framers knew what they were doing, and even if they didn't, it is, after all, *their* Bill of Rights. You give Picasso's paintings his interpretation, not yours.

Many lawyers and legal scholars have argued that it is a bad idea to search out and apply the Framers' original intent in interpreting the Bill of Rights. Before we consider whether such a thing is advisable, however, let us consider whether it is possible.

* * *

The *original* intent of the Founding Fathers was to have no bill of rights at all. A motion to adopt one was presented and summarily rejected on a sweltering September afternoon in 1787, five days before the Constitutional Convention ended. The delegates were droning through a debate on jury trial when the rural Virginia accents of George Mason penetrated the oratorical haze. "I wish," he said laconically, "that a bill of rights had been included in the preface to the plan [Constitution]. It would be a great quiet to the people."

The idea came naturally to Mason, whose reputation rested on his authorship of the Virginia Declaration of Rights eleven years earlier. "It would take but a few hours if we had recourse to the states' declarations," he urged, making a curious appeal to laziness that, in itself, suggests how little passion there was for including the liberties of mankind in the new constitution.

As a great moment in the history of human freedom—which is what it *should* have been—Mason's proposal is a distinct disappointment. From our perspective, the scene is almost comic. After months of arduous labor and strife hammering out a national constitution for a free and revolutionary people, one of the workmen looks up, snaps his fingers, and says, "You know *what?* We forgot a bill of rights!" To put it charitably, the Framers' intent on the subject seems to have been strangely out of focus.

Stranger still, when the focus sharpened the collective intent turned out to be almost entirely negative. Mason offered to second a motion to adopt a bill of rights if one were made. Elbridge Gerry of Massachusetts obliged, Mason seconded, and after a very brief discussion, the motion was buried by a vote of ten states to none. In its historic debut, the American Magna Charta was dead on arrival.

It was not that the delegates were opposed to freedom of the press, freedom of religion, and the rest. As George Washington later said in defending their monumental nonaction, probably every one of them supported the principles later embodied in the first ten amendments to the Constitution. They did not vote against a bill of rights in order to subvert liberty, but from simpler and less sinister motives: (a) They thought a bill of rights was unnecessary; (b) They thought a bill of rights would be more or less useless; (c) They thought a bill of rights might prove to be dangerous; and (d) They were tired and ready to go home.

Looking through our end of the historical telescope, we are

inclined to ask: Why didn't they just *do* it? They couldn't have gone wrong incorporating the great principles of human freedom into their constitution, could they? What would it have hurt? And what was that business about being for a bill of rights *in principle* while voting against one *in fact*? What were they, a bunch of intellectuals?

As a matter of fact they were, and the reasons they gave for voting as they did were intellectually sound. It was only in the real world that they made no sense:

Not necessary. As Roger Sherman explained during the brief discussion of Mason's motion, the proposed new national government—unlike the state governments—would have limited powers, strictly defined by the Constitution. It could not exercise powers it did not have, and it had been given no power to establish religion, abridge a free press, etc. Ergo, there was no need for a bill of rights limiting such (nonexistent) powers.

More or less useless. How would a bill of rights be enforced? While some delegates thought there was an inherent power of judicial review, which would allow courts to enforce individual liberties, many did not and most gave the matter little thought. The popular view was that a bill of rights would be a "parchment fortress," a series of exhortations that governing powers could ignore with impunity.

Might prove dangerous. Expressly limiting governmental powers might imply that the government *had* all the powers that were *not* expressly limited. It might refute the idea that the new government was limited to the powers expressly granted. Would a bill of rights prohibition against abridging freedom of speech, for example, imply that the right of privacy (which was not protected by a similar prohibition) *could* be abridged?

All of this reasoning was obvious to those who had read and understood John Locke's treatises on limited government—a group that included possibly 50 percent of the convention delegates, and perhaps .05 percent of the general population. Most of the public never *did* get the point. When the delegates returned from the convention without a bill of rights to face that public, they were like a husband who comes home without an anniversary present and with three logical excuses. His wife does not want logic, she wants a present, and besides, she doesn't believe the excuses.

Those who opposed ratification of the Constitution—the Anti-Federalists—quickly realized that the absence of a bill of rights was what a modern politician would call a wedge issue, an emotional crowbar that could be used to tear support for the Constitution asunder. Patrick Henry and his allies weighed in with unembarrassed demagoguery. The rejection of a bill of rights was an insult to the people, they orated, and the excuses made for it were an insult to the people's intelligence. The Federalists were stealing liberty from the common man while claiming that the theft was for his own good! What gall they had, attempting to sell the notion that a bill of rights would actually *weaken* popular freedom!

The Federalists tried defensive humor, but it too fell flat. Prohibit a government from doing what it has no power to do? joked James Irdell. "As well might a judge when he condemns a man to be hanged give a strong injunction to the sheriff that he should not be beheaded." "[Is there] in the Constitution . . . the least provision of the privilege of shaving the beard?" quipped Hugh Henry Brackenridge. (Why then should there be one for publishing a newspaper or going to church?) The crucial point is liberal leadership, not liberal law, opined the author of *Letters of a Countryman,* for "no bill of rights ever yet bound the supreme power longer than the honeymoon of a new married couple, unless the rulers were interested in preserving the rights."

When no one laughed, James Madison realized that a preemptive concession was in order. He revised his prior opposition to a bill of rights, declaring, in effect, that adopting one was: (a) important (if not actually necessary), and would be (b) somewhat useful and (c) in no way dangerous. By adopting this position, with the promise that a bill of rights would be added by amendment after the Constitution went into effect, the Federalists managed to squeak ratification by.

Madison grimly set about the task of lashing a bill of rights together, admitting privately, in a letter to Lafayette, that he found the project "nauseous." Following Mason's advice, he gathered together some two hundred proposals from the eight existing state declarations of rights, which he reduced to about one hundred by culling duplications. He then selected the most popular provisions and produced fourteen amendments for submission to Congress, which were later reduced to ten. Although a vital and historic work,

Madison's efforts were the creative equivalent of forging old masterpieces. There was a great accumulation of intent in the collected and culled provisions, but none of it was original with him.

Once in office the first American congressmen, true to the breed, grew tentative about the promise that had gotten them there. They had little time for the sop to the multitudes Madison had prepared. They had important *substantive* issues to consider, such as raising enough revenue to keep the new government functioning. They admired the energy Madison had put into his work, but of what real value was the product itself? "[L]ittle better than whip-syllabub, frothy and full of wind," pronounced Congressman Aedanus Burke of South Carolina, and others were only slightly more polite.

But Madison—who was both more honorable and a better politician than his foot-dragging colleagues—persisted and prevailed. On May 25, 1789, he presented his proposed amendments to Congress in a superb speech that was to be the only comprehensive statement on the Bill of Rights made during the First Congress. Madison did not pretend to be presenting anything new—or debatable—for his colleagues' consideration. He said what all of them well knew: that the proposed provisions embodied "those safeguards which [the people] *have long been accustomed* to have interposed between them and the magistrate who exercises sovereign power."

The legislative process that followed was uninspiring, except possibly to semanticists. Wording was changed, phrases were dropped, a few provisions were added or deleted, but the process was essentially like that of a sculptor or writer putting the finishing touches on another artist's work. Congress was not creating, it was editing. Latter-day scholars have avidly, and sometimes tediously, searched for deep meanings in these legislative adjustments, and certainly they have some meaning, but the basic "intent" of the Bill of Rights provisions—if such a commodity exists—must be sought for elsewhere.

The public debates that preceded the congressional adoption and state ratification of the amendments were equally barren of substance. It was once said that one hundred thousand English yeomen were ready to fight popery to the death, without knowing whether it was a man or a horse. At times, the American people's desire for a bill of rights seemed equally filled with passion and devoid of information. "It is astounding," writes Professor Leonard Levy, "to discover that the debate on a bill of rights was conducted at a level of abstraction so vague as to convey the impression that Americans of 1787, 1788 had only the most nebulous conception of the meanings of the particular rights they sought to ensure. The insistent demands of the 'rights of conscience' or 'trial by jury' or 'liberty of the press' were not accompanied by a reasoned analysis of what those rights meant."

Original intent? *Whose* intent? The fact is that trying to apply the Framers' "intent" is like trying to breathe the atmosphere of the moon. Whether it is a good idea or a bad one is beside the point—the problem is there is nothing of substance to work with.

America had always been the natural home of "parchment fortresses" against arbitrary government. Many of the *ideas*—trial by jury, the privilege against self-incrimination—were English, but the urge to commit them to paper, to form a written contract between the government and the people that required their observance, was distinctively American. The English Constitution was no constitution at all in the American sense. It was an untidy mass of charters, statutes, and celestial emanations (such as Coke's "right reason" of the common law) dating back to the great Charter of 1215. The English Constitution was, itself, virtually an idea.

Colonial American constitutions, on the other hand, tended to be in a form suitable for inclusion in handy pocket almanacs. They were concrete, specific, and comprehensive lists of the rights, powers, and privileges that defined civic existence, in one easy-to-read document. An American might not understand his constitutional rights, but he could at least look them up.

It began with the beginning of the country. The first colonists arrived in a land that, so far as they were concerned, was legally pristine. Unlike the Normans when they came to Saxon England five and one-half centuries earlier, there was no indigenous legal culture waiting to absorb them and their ways of doing things. They brought all of their legal rights and obligations with them in documents called colonial charters. Before John Locke was even born, American colonists had experienced the idea of government as a contract—and a concrete, written one at that.

When the boatload carrying the first permanent English colonists touched ashore in Virginia in 1607, it bore a paper charter guaranteeing that "every the persons . . . which shall dwell and inhabit within [the described colonies] shall have and enjoy all Liberties, Franchises and Immunities . . . as if they had been abiding and born, within this our Realm of England." Thus did America's first written "constitution" incorporate by reference England's own untidy and unwritten one. In the ensuing generations, Americans would give ever-increasing definition to the precious cargo of rights and obligations they had imported from the mother country.

First, there were the Fundamental Orders of Connecticut of 1639, adopted by settlers led by Reverend Thomas Hooker, who left Massachusetts in 1636 to form a colony along the Connecticut River. No bill of rights yet, but a clearly defined structure of government providing the manner of electing and deposing the various officials and entities of government and generally describing their powers. Although limited, it was America's first true constitution.

The Maryland Act for the Liberties of the People in 1639 was the first governmental document that looked like an American bill of rights—a very *short* bill of rights. It stated that (being Christian) all Maryland residents (who were not slaves) had all of the rights of Englishmen, and—in a paraphrase of Article 39 of Magna Charta—it provided that these free Christians "shall not be imprisoned nor disseized nor dispossessed of their freehold goods or chattels, or be out Lawed, Exiled, or otherwise destroyed fore judged or punished according to the Laws of this Province." Thus America's first due process clause.

Two years later came that amazing document known as the Massachusetts Bodie of Liberties. This was Western history's—and probably history's—first comprehensive bill of rights. (England had the Petition of Right of 1628, but it was mostly an enumeration of the privileges of Parliament vis-à-vis the king.) The list of rights legislated by the sober Puritans of Massachusetts included rights for women, children, servants, aliens, and, yes, animals. ("No man shall exercise any tiranny or crueltie toward any bruite creature which are usually kept for man's legal use.") It outlawed slavery. It prevented taking property without just compensation. It guaranteed free speech at public meetings, permitted counsel for criminal defendants, granted jury trial, and prohibited double jeopardy and cruel and unusual punishments. It gave citizens access to public records—a right that was not guaranteed by American federal law until 1966. It was the seedbed for, and inspiration of, all of the colonial bills of rights that came after, including the Charter of Rhode Island of 1663, which contained America's first guarantee of religious freedom. "Noe person," it promised "shall bee any wise molested, punished, disquieted, or called in question, for any differences in opinione in matters of religion" so long as he does "not actually disturb the civil peace of our sayd Colony."

In 1701, "the most famous of all Colonial constitutions"—the Pennsylvania Charter of Privileges—was adopted by William Penn's colony. Penn, a Quaker, had been prosecuted in England for illegal preaching, and the jury's refusal to convict him had resulted in a famous court decision (*Edward Bushell*'s case) that announced the birth of the modern independent jury. As might be expected, Penn's famous charter established, among other things, freedom of religion, the right to jury trial, and the right to defense counsel in ringing and unmistakable terms.

The Revolution accelerated and proliferated constitution-making. The colonists saw their declaration of independence as an opportunity to create a new political society from the ground up. They "thought themselves at full liberty," according to Thomas Hutchinson, lieutenant governor of New Jersey, "to establish such sort of government as they thought proper, and to form a new state as full to all intents and purposes as if they had been in a state of nature, and were making their first entrance into civil society."

The Revolution produced the comprehensive declarations of rights by eight of the twelve colonies—Pennsylvania, Virginia, Delaware, Maryland, North Carolina, Connecticut, Vermont, and Massachusetts—which Madison drew from in drafting the federal bill of rights. All of them drew, in turn, from the colonial antecedents just mentioned.

By 1789, the broth of American liberty had been cooking for a century and a half, having been continually supplemented by a pinch of procedural justice here and a handful of basic freedom there. Did the participants in the constitutional convention *believe* in constitutional guarantees of individual liberties? They were *marinated* in them. Did they invent them? No—did you?

* * *

On the day they were adopted, the Bill of Rights provisions carried whatever complex and contradictory meanings were already associated with them. Asking a 1789 congressman to define them would have produced answers no more precise than asking a twentieth-century congressman to do so. What is an "establishment" of religion? How many members must there be on a jury, and when is jury trial required in a civil case? Should unlawfully seized materials be excluded from evidence, or should the offending government merely be required to pay the owner damages?

Most people never thought about such questions, and those who did tended to disagree with one another. Jefferson believed that freedom of the press primarily meant that publications could not be prevented in advance and that punishing publications that criticized government was appropriate. Madison, on the other hand, thought it "a mockery to say that no laws should be passed preventing publications being made, but that laws might be passed for punishing them in case they should be made." There is no way of telling which version of freedom of the press appears in the Constitution because no one addressed the issue.[1]

The only surprising thing about all of this is that we today are surprised by it. Why on earth *should* the Americans of 1789 have debated the scope and meaning of the liberties they adopted? They were not inventing them, or even purporting to define them. They were, so to speak, hopping on a freight train of history that was already going at full speed and had begun its journey generations and centuries in the past.

The Bill of Rights provisions were different from our other great constitutional documents in that respect. The Declaration of Independence, although a product of the European Enlightenment, had a quintessentially American spirit about it that all the world recognized. The formal, structural parts of the Constitution, which so intelligently distributed power among the branches of government and between and among state and federal government, were the proud work creation of the men of Philadelphia, who sweated through the summer of 1787 to produce them. But the Bill of Rights was another matter altogether. Its roots not only went far back in American history, they largely sprang from foreign soil. The slightly embarrassing fact was that the liberties Congress proposed in 1789 had mostly been created and defined by America's great oppressor, England.

Trial by jury, for example, had been around in one form or another since 829, when Charlemagne's son Louis the Pious invented the Frankish Inquest. By the 1780s, the jury was an ingrained part of the legal system that simply was what it was. The modern independent jury had been established more than a hundred years previously by Chief Justice Vaughn in *Edward Bushell*'s case. When lawyers in the new republic argued about the function and powers of the jury, they did not consult the still-living framers of the Bill of Rights; they consulted Vaughn's great opinion.

It was the same with other provisions of the Bill of Rights. The privilege against self-incrimination was forged in the fires of the English Inquisition by martyrs who thought they were enunciating ancient church doctrine, and was given its modern form in the windy orations of "Freeborn" John Lilburne. The prohibition against unreasonable searches and seizures was first made law in *Wilkes* v. *Wood* and *Entick* v. *Carrington,* both English court decisions. Freedom of the press was more nearly an American creation, but even it had roots in John Milton's famed essay *Areopagitica* and other English writings. When they incorporated these living ideals into their constitution, our forefathers' intent, as nearly as it can be identified, was simply to adopt history.

The doctrine of original intent has a striking historical parallel that the reader may have recognized. It is Lord Coke and Magna Charta all over again. The doctrine of original intent, like Coke's reverence for Magna Charta ("he is such a fellow, he will have no sovereign"), epitomizes the method by which our law moves forward—that is, by pretending to stand still. Twentieth-century "conservatives" (i.e., constitutional minimalists) invoke the intent of the eighteenth-century Founding Fathers, who claimed to be preserving rights they inherited from seventeenth-century Parliamentarians, who said that they were resurrecting the thirteenth-century prerogatives of Magna Charta, which described itself as an instrument for restoring the eleventh-century laws of good King Edward (the Confessor), which were supposedly a compilation of the ancient laws of the Saxons. By this means, the law has moved from King Ine to William Brennan without unduly alarming the people.

*   *   *

Even if the Framers' "original intent" was well-documented, digging it out and applying it today would be an exceptionally bad idea. Why should we, of all generations, penalize ourselves by freezing the evolution of civil liberty? Our forefathers would never have dreamed of doing such a thing to themselves.

Thomas Jefferson himself had the last word on the whole question of seeking original intent. Writing long after the Bill of Rights was adopted, he left no doubt that he considered such inquiries an unworthy pursuit. He was referring to amendment of the Constitution, but he might as well have been referring to interpretation:

> Some men look at constitutions with sanctimonious reverence, and deem them like the Ark of the Covenant—too sacred to be touched. They ascribe to the men of the preceding age a wisdom more than human, and suppose what they did to be beyond amendment. I knew that age well; I belonged to it and labored with it. It deserved well of its country. It was very like the present, but without the experience of the present; and forty years of experience in government is worth a century of book reading; and this they would say themselves were they to rise from the dead.

The search for original intent might be likened to the search for the Holy Grail. It is the process, the search itself, that matters to the true believers. The pursuit of the Founding Fathers' mythical intent represents an attempt to depersonalize and idealize judicial decision-making. Like the doctrines of *stare decisis* and judicial restraint, the doctrine of original intent is a way of resolving a basic paradox of judicial power: that judges, in the final analysis, necessarily control, but cannot be *thought* to control, the outcomes of the cases they decide.[2,3] In order to preserve the image of a government of laws, not men, a greater eminence is invoked—the imagined mental processes of long-dead patriots—from which decisions are said to be derived by a sort of automatic, extra-human process. In this way, the paradox is resolved—at least on paper.

Such myths do little harm—they can do good—so long as they remain mythical; but woe unto the legal system that takes them literally. Like the story of the Grail, they are not meant for that.

13

CONSTRUCTIVE TREASON

To be hanged for nonsense is the very devil.

JOHN DRYDEN

America's most spectacular criminal trial occurred in 1807, in Richmond, Virginia, when its third vice president was prosecuted for treason. The trial inflamed public opinion as no trial has before or since. It pitted a great judge against a great president in mortal political combat. It produced some of the best-remembered courtroom oratory in the nation's history and a profoundly important judicial ruling that swept a fearsome doctrine of English criminal law into the dustbin of history and helped to ensure the stability of America's political future.

What was the "treasonous act" that was the basis for this great prosecution? An uneventful hunting trip on an island in the Ohio River, attended by about twenty young men armed with half a dozen deer rifles and "a few fowling pieces." And the accused "traitor" wasn't even present.

Aaron Burr was prosecuted for "levying war" against the United States, one of the two forms of treason recognized by the Constitution.[1] The case against him was instigated by some nefarious characters with personal axes to grind, and was blown into a

137

national crisis through the bad political judgment of President Thomas Jefferson. The public rage against Burr, caused by the president's assertion that the treason charge was true, was fanned to white heat by the Republican press, and a national tragedy was narrowly averted—thanks mostly to the skill of Burr's lawyers and the brains and guts of Chief Justice John Marshall.

For all of its tragic potential, the *Burr* case was an elaborate farce. The problem was, the prosecution was never able to find any evidence of the war the defendant was supposed to have "levied." How does one misplace a war, Burr's lawyers asked. Yet it was the very silliness of the prosecution that made it so alarming. If Aaron Burr could be put in peril of his life on the basis of the facts presented at his trial, no controversial political figure would ever be safe. The masses, fueled by the presses, threatened to become a greater oppressor of individual liberty than Henry VIII ever dreamed of being.

The *Burr* case had a cast of characters that would do credit to a Russian novel and a plot that John le Carré would envy. Albert Beveridge took 272 pages to tell the story in his magnificent *Life of John Marshall*.[2] For obvious reasons, the version that follows is shorter and necessarily sacrifices some nuance and detail:

In 1805, former vice president Burr departed from Washington an all-but-defeated man. Among other misfortunes, he had killed Alexander Hamilton in a duel, and there were two murder warrants pending against him.

He went into the territories west of the Alleghenies to seek his second fortune, passing through the towns of Cincinnati, Nashville, St. Louis, and New Orleans in what became a triumphal journey. He was feted at all of these stops, and struck up friendships with leaders such as Andrew Jackson and Henry Clay, who found him fascinating.

His main plan was to support an invasion of Mexico in order to "liberate" it from Spain and make it part of the United States. This was a large reason for his popularity in the West, whose residents were very much in favor of such a war. Among the allies he accumulated in his journeys were General James Wilkinson, the commander of the U.S. military forces, and Harman Blennerhassett, an entrepreneur who owned the aforementioned island in the Ohio River. He had communications with Wilkinson about a possible

Mexican invasion, including an infamous—and ambiguous—"cipher letter," which would later be relied on as evidence of a treasonous intent to liberate the western and southern territories from the rest of the Union.

Rumors began to surface that Burr did, in fact, intend to lead a western secession, and they received spectacular coverage in the eastern Republican Press. Not coincidentally, one of the initial sources of these rumors was a paid Spanish spy named Stephen Minor.

In November 1806, General Wilkinson added his considerable weight to the rumor mill in correspondence with Jefferson, in which he stated that Burr had indicated a secessionist intent in his communications with him. Wilkinson's motives were also suspect, to say the least, since—amazingly—he too was a paid agent of the Spanish government.

Jefferson took the news seriously. On November 27, 1806, he made a presidential proclamation announcing that Wilkinson had revealed the existence of a traitorous conspiracy against the United States involving Burr. In a "special message" to Congress the following month, he committed the unforgivable blunder of announcing that "Burr's guilt is placed beyond question." This statement became a tiger whose tail he would not subsequently be able to relinquish.

The caldron of the press now began to bubble poisonously. Denunciations of Burr's "treason" were repeated with the ominous monotony—and factual content—of drum rolls. The specifics that were supplied—for example, that Burr had plans to assassinate Jefferson—were mostly spurious.

Meanwhile, Burr was floating down the Ohio and Mississippi rivers, unaware of the strenuous efforts being made to seal his doom. While in Tennessee, he met briefly with the young men who had attended the deer hunt on Blennerhassett Island, to discuss their future plans. The discussion centered on their prospects for obtaining parcels in a large land grant on the Whitshitz River in Louisiana, which Burr's ally Blennerhassett intended to purchase.

Burr was subsequently arrested in Mississippi and transported under military guard to Richmond, Virginia. When he reached the agitated Virginia capital, he must have felt like a Christian stumbling into daylight in a Coliseum filled with screaming Romans. All of America seemed to want his blood.

On the other hand, America had no case. The Constitution stated that treason could be proven only if two witnesses testified that the defendant had committed an "overt act" in furtherance of a treasonous plan.[3] Burr had done nothing that could be considered an act of war. The government had only suspicion, gossip, and hearsay to the effect that Burr *wished somehow* to promote a western secession.

In order to establish its case, the prosecution would have to overcome two logical hurdles: (1) It would have to convince the court and jury that the deer-hunting party on Blennerhassett Island was somehow an act of war; and (2) It would have to establish that Burr, who was in Kentucky at the time, was a sufficient "participant" in that act to be guilty of it. The motive for making these arguments was obvious. Jefferson had loosed the dogs of popular rage against Burr and dared not try to whistle them back. But why in the name of rationality did the prosecutors believe that the arguments could succeed?

To answer this question, it is necessary to understand a principle of English law known as the doctrine of constructive treason. The legality of Burr's prosecution depended lock, stock, and barrel on whether that very strange doctrine was considered part of American law. It is no exaggeration to say that Burr's life hung in an intellectual balance—he would live or die depending on whether Marshall applied the doctrine of constructive treason to his case.

Punishing traitors had always been a favorite pastime of English monarchs. The reason for this is not hard to find. The life expectancy of an English king or queen was actuarially unimpressive, perhaps slightly better than that of a World War II forward artillery observer. The period from 1307 to 1485 was a particularly bad run. Of the nine kings who reigned during this epoch, five were deposed and, apparently, murdered. (One must say "apparently" because three of the deaths were from mysterious causes while the monarch was residing in the custody of his enemies.) Royal deaths sometimes occurred as a result of unusual "accidents." William Rufus (1087–1100) died in a hunting "mishap," pierced by the arrow of a man who was a much better archer than friend. John (1199–1216) died from consuming "unripe peaches," said by some to be a euphemism for poison administered by an unhappy monk. Some of the killings, on the other hand, were entirely aboveboard and official. Harmless Jane Grey (July 10–19, 1553) and obnoxious Charles I (1625–49) both lost their heads in public courtyards to ax-men who were merely earning a day's pay. The purpose of strong treason laws was, of course, to discourage such occurrences. They were better life insurance than anything Lloyd's of London could provide.

The basic English treason law was always confined to two subjects: "compassing or imagining the King's death" and "levying war against the King." Because kings (and queens) naturally wished to intercept death and war long before it got to their doorsteps, these phrases were given ever-expanding definitions.

Treason was supposed to require an overt, immediately threatening act, but English monarchs had been known to punish unacted-upon expressions of opinion amounting to little more than barroom chatter. In 1213, Peter of Wakefield predicted to his cronies that King John would "not be on the throne come next Ascension Day." John made it to Ascension Day intact, but Peter did not. He was drawn, disemboweled, and quartered for "imagining the death of the King."

Peter's fate was a cruel anomaly in its own time, but a darker future beckoned. In 1399, Henry IV presciently warned Parliament against vague treason laws under which "no man knew, as he ought to know, how to do, speak or say, for doubt of the pains of treason. How dangerous it is by construction and analogy to make treasons where the law has not done it; for such a method admits of no limits or bounds, but runs as far as the wit and invention of accusers, and the odiousness and detestation of persons accused will carry men."

Had he been Merlin himself, Henry could not have better predicted the pain and oppression of the next four centuries. Within a generation, the law had acquired the amorphous viciousness he had warned against, and "reproachful words, idle prophecies, rhymes and ballads, spoken and made of the King, were prosecuted and punished as treason."

During the reign of Edward IV (1461–83) a grocer named Walter Walker jokingly said that he would make his son "heir to the Crown," intending to refer to a commercial establishment he owned called the "Sign of the Crown." The king showed his own sense of humor by having the poor man executed for—"imagining" his death. Such brutal senselessness was still occurring a century and a half later. During the reign of James I (1603–25) a near-lunatic named Williams was executed for predicting, on the basis of the prophecies of Daniel, that the king would be dead within two years.

The main targets of treason prosecutions were not, however, defenseless commoners such as Walker and Williams but powerful leaders who posed real or imagined threats to the throne. Hargrove's *State Trials* contains a partial collection of the major treason cases tried prior to 1680, involving 129 identified defendants, nearly all of whom were convicted and executed. Among them were seven knights (including Sir Walter Raleigh), five earls, three dukes, two archbishops, one bishop, more than a dozen priests, two lord chancellors, a chief justice, a deputy of Ireland, a marquis, a secretary to a king, a king (Charles I), a queen (Mary, Queen of Scots), and the twenty-nine Puritan regicides who were themselves executed for trying and executing Charles I.

Many of these defendants were condemned for conspiratorial words and actions only tenuously related to the health and authority of the king. The most famous of these was, of course, Sir Thomas More, who was beheaded for engaging in a hypothetical discussion, *in his jail cell,* regarding the king's authority over the church.

This arbitrarily inflicted brutality clothed itself in the respectable garb of legal concept. Appropriating the very language of Henry IV's warning against "construction and analogy to make treasons where the law has not done it," seventeenth-century English law developed the infamous doctrine of *constructive* treason.

The word "constructive" is one of the law's most useful frauds. It implies substance where none exists. There can be constructive contracts, constructive trusts, constructive fraud, constructive intent, constructive possession, and constructive anything else the law chooses to baptize as such. "Constructive" in this sense means "treated as." A court can reach a desired result by calling a transaction that doesn't cut the decisional mustard "constructively" a transaction that does. Constructive treason wasn't "real" treason but a vaguely defined, less potent category of conduct that the court deciding the particular case felt should be "treated as" treason. It was the perfect instrument of oppression, being virtually whatever the authorities wanted it to be.

Constructive treason in seventeenth- and eighteenth-century England has been described as "anything whatever which, under any circumstances, may possibly have a *tendency,* however *remote,* to expose the King to personal danger or to forcible deprivation of *part* of the authority *incidental* to his office." The defendant did not have to participate in the "treasonous" action to be guilty, or even be present when it occurred. For example, "any riot excited by an unpopular [governmental] measure" was likely to be branded as treason, and opponents of the measure might be prosecuted, even though they did not instigate the riot and were not on the scene when it erupted. In 1780, Lord George Gordon was prosecuted for treason when a movement he had led to petition the government for legal changes turned into a mob that attempted to burn London down. The prosecution was pressed, even though it was clear that Lord Gordon had nothing to do with the arsonous actions of his followers. Even more infamously, the heads of an organization that had "agitated" for universal suffrage were prosecuted for treason in 1794, although no action amounting to a riot ever took place.

Constructive treason took root in colonial America in the 1701 trial of Nicholas Bayard. This prosecution gave kangaroos a bad name. *Everything* was slanted and fixed, from the biased grand jury to the enemy judge to the confused non-English-speaking trial jury. The offense itself was about as "constructive" as it is possible to get: Bayard was prosecuted for capital treason because he had sent a written petition to the king of England listing various citizen grievances against the English governor of New York. He was convicted and sentenced to a traitor's death but was saved from drawing and quartering by the last-minute arrival of a replacement governor from England.

With all of this background, it was apparent to the Framers of the American Constitution that a loosely applied treason law was potentially the death knell of a democracy. Of all the provisions of the Constitution, Article III, Section 3 was said to have had the most nearly unanimous support. It stated that "no person shall be convicted of treason unless on the testimony of two witnesses to the same overt act, or on confession in open court." Clear as the Framers had tried to be, however, their words were not clear enough to preempt the creative arguments of skilled lawyers. Naturally not.

American prosecutors pointed out that, while the Constitution required strong proof of an "overt act," it did not state what relationship the act must have to the treason (i.e., "levying war"), or what relationship the defendant must have to the act (i.e., whether he must actually have participated in it). The overt acts of arson in Lord Gordon's case had been carefully proved, and then the doctrine of constructive treason had been used to prosecute a man who never saw the flames. Factually proving an overt act was one thing. Establishing legal responsibility for that act was something entirely different. Article III, Section 3 dealt only with proof of the act and left the law free to establish responsibility for it as far as the doctrine of constructive treason would stretch.

Defense lawyers argued that when the Constitution referred to proof of an overt act, it necessarily meant proof of an act *committed by the defendant*. By permitting proof of the act through "confession" in open court, the Constitution necessarily implied that the defendant himself must have committed it—one does not prove the act of another by "confession." Nor would the Framers have worked so diligently to require strict proof of an overt act if they had thought the act could be given an illogically bloated significance by the doctrine of constructive treason. They were not fools, Your Honor.

In the few cases addressing the issue prior to 1807, prosecutors had always won the argument. The doctrine of constructive treason was alive in America when Aaron Burr went to trial.

The Burr trial was held in Richmond's House of Delegates. The spectators, like those in Lilburne's case, must have known they were witnesses to history. During the many weeks of the proceedings, the courtroom was always mobbed to overflowing, mostly by boisterous Republican common folk but also by coldly critical Federalist and Republican gentry. The trial was a festival of rhetoric, sometimes entertaining, sometimes exhilarating, sometimes ludicrous, and in the end exhausting to both participants and the audience. If it had been a movie, critics would have complained that it was overproduced. But it was real, and serious.

The six lawyers who appeared in the case ranged from competent to purely brilliant. Young William Wirt made an argument for the prosecution that would be quoted for generations to come in

American schoolbooks on the art of rhetoric. Burr's chief lawyer, Luther Martin, was—well, we will deal with Martin later. Suffice it to say that there have been few lawyers in the nation's history equal to him, and that he gave an unequaled performance in his penultimate case.

Then there was the great chief justice himself, tall, lanky, careless in his dress, courteous in his manner, and underneath it all, that mind of sheer stainless steel. Winfield Scott, who was a daily spectator, said that Marshall was "the master spirit of the scene." Certainly he needed to be, for he was dealing with unprecedented pressures.

Being a Supreme Court justice in 1807 was not all it was cracked up to be. The federal courts were still the weakest branch of the new government, and the status of judges was shaky. Most of them were Federalists, natural enemies of the popular Republican president, and Jefferson had gone to war with the judiciary on many fronts. It was not yet clear that the courts would survive as a strong independent branch of the federal government. A few years earlier, Congress had impeached and almost convicted Judge Samuel Chase for his conduct of some political libel trials. No one was betting that the same fate might not befall Jefferson's greatest enemy on the bench—Chief Justice John Marshall. The prosecutors' arguments in the *Burr* case were, in fact, laced with clumsily veiled threats that a "wrong" decision might shorten the great career.

The pressure had been greatly magnified by Jefferson's foolish public pronouncement of Burr's guilt. Having personally returned a guilty verdict in the case, Jefferson could not tolerate a contrary result from the real trial in Richmond. Throughout the trial, he was in constant communication with the federal prosecutors, and his manipulative animosity was communicated to Marshall by them and by the courtroom spectators. "Everyone" "knew" that Burr was guilty as hell, and the chief justice had better do his duty. None of the crowd cared a fig about the subtleties of constructive treason or the other pettifogging legalisms that hummed in their ears. What mattered was getting the case to the patriots on the jury, who could be counted on to do justice.

The crowd knew that the jury would do justice because the jurors had announced their biases when they were selected. Almost every juror on the panel had admitted to a belief that Burr was a traitor. They had been seated because their beliefs seemed less obdurate than those of the veniremen who were "excused."

In his opening statement, Chief Prosecutor George Haye imposed an even more specific pressure on Marshall—Marshall's own words. Earlier that year, two couriers who had carried communications between Burr and the other "conspirators" had been arrested for treason and denied bail. They had appealed to the Supreme Court. Marshall discharged them, holding that the evidence against them was insufficient, but his opinion appeared to adopt the doctrine of constructive treason. In order to be guilty of treason, he said, the defendant must "actually levy war." But this, apparently, did not mean that he had to be present where the overt act of treason occurred:

> If a body of men be actually assembled for the purpose of effecting by force a treasonable purpose, all those who perform any part, *however minute, or remote from the scene of the action,* and who are actually leagued in the general conspiracy, are to be considered as traitors.

Haye served these words back to the chief justice with relish, arguing that according to Marshall's own holding, Burr had been "constructively present" on Blennerhassett Island when the overt act occurred. The chief justice merely looked back at him with enigmatic courtesy.

The trial was brought to an early climax by a creative defense tactic. The government had subpoenaed 140 witnesses, the first 7 of whom were supposed to establish the overt act of war. They testified that on December 13, 1806, the Blennerhassett men had "gone a-gunning" in the forest, had later purchased a hundred barrels of pork and fifteen boats for their southward journey, and had engaged in other seemingly innocent actions. The remaining 133 witnesses admittedly knew nothing about the "overt act." The defense therefore moved to exclude the rest of the government's evidence, asserting that the failure to connect Burr to any act on Blennerhassett, and the failure to show that war had been levied by anyone, was fatal to the prosecution. Marshall said that he would hear arguments.

We think of modern trials as being excessively long, but we have no idea what a long legal *argument* is. All six lawyers addressed themselves to Burr's motion, with some of the arguments taking up to two days.

The prosecution team treated Marshall's previous definition of treason as holy writ and made a repetitive sermonette of it: "However minute or remote from the scene of the action . . . however minute or remote from the scene of the action," and so on. It was left to Charles Bot, one of the supposedly lesser lights on the defense side, to define the true danger the prosecution represented to the young republic. "If the law of constructive treason were to be adopted in America, and courts were to execute the will of the people," he said, "alas for any man, however upright and innocent, whom public opinion had been falsely led to condemn."

The last lawyer to argue for Burr was that grizzled barrister with the oddly reversed name of Luther Martin. The fame of this magnificent advocate has become lost in time, but in his prime he was a match for any lawyer on the Continent. He was a notorious boozer and was probably drunk when he rose to defend his friend and client, but drunkenness was a normal condition for him and he acquitted himself with rare distinction.[4]

He truly believed that Burr was the victim of a terrible injustice, and he argued in favor of the motion with a hard bitterness. He thanked "God" and "Heaven" for allowing him to appear in defense of Burr, and for giving him the opportunity to oppose the wicked doctrine of constructive treason. He then bit into the real meat of the problem: Marshall's unfortunate definition of treason in the courier's case and the crushing political pressure Marshall was now under.

He dealt with the first issue with an almost offhanded contempt. Other defense counsel had referred to the Marshall definition in true lawyer fashion, diplomatically suggesting that perhaps His Honor had not meant to say exactly what he had appeared to say. Martin would have no part of such minuets. He told America's greatest judge that, "as a binding legal opinion," his former pronouncement "ought to have no more weight than the ballad of Chevy Chase." The fact that the Court had been wrong before did entitle it to be wrong again. Undoubtedly, His Honor would correct his previous error.

He addressed the political issue even more brazenly. No lawyer likes to refer, even obliquely, to the sufficiency of a judge's courage. The unspoken premise underlying most legal arguments is that the judge is courageous, wise, and beneficent, and needs only to be guided down the path of legal righteousness. Any suggestion that he might not be up to the decision-making task is considered terminal bad taste. Martin knew, however, that the boil had to be lanced. If Marshall was undecided, Martin would invoke the justice's abundant pride to tip his intellectual balance in the right direction.

He minced no words. He told Marshall that the decision he faced was a clear test of his courage, and said—astonishingly—that Marshall would be an accomplice to murder if he decided against Burr:

> I have with pain heard it said that such are the public prejudices against Colonel Burr, that a jury, even should they be satisfied with his innocence, must have considerable firmness of mind to pronounce him not guilty. I have not heard it without horror.
>
> God in heaven! Have we already under our form of government (which we have so often been told is best calculated of all governments to secure all our rights) arrived at a period when a trial in a court of justice, where life is at stake, shall be but . . . a mere idle . . . ceremony to transfer innocence from the gaol to the gibbet, to gratify popular indignation excited by blood-thirsty enemies?

> But if it require in such a situation firmness in a jury, so does it equally require fortitude in judges to perform their duty. . . . [I]f they do not, and the prisoner fall a victim, they are guilty of murder (in fact) whatever their guilt may be (in law). . . . May that God who now looks down upon us, and who has in his infinite wisdom called you into existence and placed you in that seat to dispense justice to your fellow citizens, to preserve and protect innocence against prosecution—may that God so illuminate your understanding that you may know what is right; and may he nerve your soul with firmness and fortitude to act according to that knowledge.

Marshall's lion's gaze did not flicker, but a unique challenge, a virtual threat, had been issued from counsel to Court, and both Court and counsel knew it.

Marshall granted the defendant's motion and instructed the jury accordingly. In a reversal of roles from the *Zenger* case, the prosecution had argued that the issue of guilt or innocence should be left to the jury because they were "the judges of the law as well as the facts." Marshall more or less granted the request, instructing the jury to apply "the law as announced to the facts as proved," but allowing them to "find a verdict of guilty or not guilty as your own consciences shall direct." With obvious reluctance, the jury returned a verdict of not guilty.

The opinion Marshall produced in support of his ruling was the longest and most laborious of his career. It was said that he cited more authority in it than he cited in all of his other major opinions combined. (This was no great feat, since Marshall tended to treat his legal pronouncements as too obvious to require citation of authority.) The most labored part of the opinion consisted of an explanation of his prior definition of treason. He had been misunderstood, he said. He had meant to say that a traitor must "truly and in fact levy war," which meant "performing a part in the prosecution of [a] war." Moreover, the war-levying "assemblage" he had referred to in his prior opinion could not be a mere discussion group but must "be in force," ready and able to "conduct war." None of this, of course, was true in the *Burr* case.

When Marshall departed from Richmond, he left a legal milestone in his wake. Martin went home to his friends, his liquor, and historical obscurity. His angry courage in addressing Marshall so pointedly may have played a role in the result, but that can never be known. One advantage in being an advocate rather than a judge is a pleasant lack of final responsibility for what happens. The great drawback, of course, is in never quite knowing the size of one's contribution.

In 1835, the acute French commentator Alexis de Tocqueville made an observation that was also a prediction. "Scarcely any political question arises in the United States," he said "that is not resolved, sooner or later, into a judicial question." The reverse has also been true: American judicial rulings have had immense political consequences. When a landmark Supreme Court decision is rendered, we are all a little like the English subjects who saw Magna Charta in the hands of royal messengers all those centuries ago. We form new, almost insensible understandings of the relationships between the government and the people.

Marshall's decision in the *Burr* case had that kind of effect. It not only rid American law of a terrible instrument of oppression, it set a lasting foundation for judging individual-state conflicts in this nation. The governmental fear that had bred such cruelty in England would have less force in America. The experiment of "government by the people" would be allowed to be, to some degree at least, the daring experiment our best patriots had hoped for. There would be times when the American legal system would turn mean, but, as Bot obliquely predicted, that meanness would come primarily from the passions of the people themselves.

No one reads the *Burr* opinion anymore. It is not studied in law schools or cited in courtrooms and, in fact, most lawyers have no idea what it says. It nonetheless was and remains an enormous presence in our law. If Marshall had ruled otherwise, something much larger than Aaron Burr would have expired before it truly had a chance to live.

Treason has been a virtually dead issue in America since the *Burr* decision. Attempts at prosecution have been rare, and convictions have been rarer. Only three treason cases have come before the U.S. Supreme Court in its entire history. All three arose during World War II and presented bizarre fact situations, unlikely to be repeated. Absent an uprising in support of an invading foreign army, or some similar ultimate betrayal, it seems unlikely that another American treason case will be brought.

It might have been different. If constructive treason had survived, it might have cut a wide psychological and punitive swath through twentieth-century America. Think of Senator Joseph McCarthy's Red witch-hunts in the 1950s, and the Vietnam protests in the 1960s and 1970s. Who among the "commies" and "peaceniks" would *not* have been constructive traitors? Would Abbie Hoffman have been tried for treason in the manner of Lord Gordon for fomenting the Chicago convention riots? Would Jane Fonda have been unchivalrously executed for going to North Vietnam as Lady Alice Lisle was for similarly nonviolent acts?[5] Would Norman Mailer have written *The Armies of the Night* from death row?

It is impossible to say, but the survival of constructive treason, even as an idea, would have made this country's political climate meaner and more violent. If treason had remained a reality in the public consciousness, if its meaning had retained a threatening fluidity, if protesters could, in acceptable discourse, literally be referred to as "traitors," there would be a smell of fear across the land that none of us—not Rush Limbaugh, not Howard Stern—would want to live with. If Marshall's decision did nothing else, it cleared America's political atmosphere and helped make it fit for a democracy to breathe.

14

EQUALITY AS LAW

I have a dream that one day . . . my four little children will live in a nation where they will not be judged by the color of their skin but by the content of their character.

MARTIN LUTHER KING

Equality was a concept unknown to the English common law—to the contrary, hierarchy and status were its backbone. England was a warrior culture in the beginning, in which land was wealth, might was right, and loyalty was the paramount civic virtue. Until the reign of Henry VIII (1509–47), a national government in the modern sense did not exist. Power radiated downward, person to person, from the king to the nobility to the gentry to the serfs, and loyalty radiated upward through the same layers. These reciprocal hierarchies provided the framework for the law.

Although not as class-ridden as Continental legal systems, English feudal law paid attention to status. The great principle of Magna Charta was not equality under the law but due process of law, which meant that one was entitled to be treated, not like everyone else, but like everyone who occupied the same station in life. Besides the broad categories of royalty, nobility, gentry (non-noble freemen), and serfs (the unfree), there were the monks and nuns (legally dead to the world), the clergy (entitled to special privileges), the Jews (whose property was legally the king's), aliens (whose rights were severely, but vaguely, limited), and outlaws (the legally damned). Women were in a mixed legal position. They had substantial equality in the realm of private law (they could hold land, inherit, and sue) but virtually no public rights or obligations (they could not serve on juries or testify except under extraordinary circumstances, and when representative government arrived, they could not vote).

At the bottom of the heap were the serfs, whose rights could be easily listed: They had none. The criminal law punished physical abuse of serfs by nonowners, just as modern law punishes cruelty to animals, but Cedric the serf had no more right to sue for injuries sustained from such abuse than do Lassie and Tabby today. One was born a serf (when *either* parent was one) and died a serf unless the lord of the manor conferred freedom by a charter of manumission.

Due process was an empty vessel, the content of which was determined by who one was and when one lived. Depending on the century, summarily slicing up a serf for sassing his master might be due process. As we have seen, Magna Charta's most famous promise, that "freemen" were to be punished only by "the judgment of [their] peers," was a guarantee of class-based justice, not the democratic opposite it is commonly mistaken for today.

The equality of mankind was a religious idea, not a legal one. All God's children were equal in *His* eyes, but the law was a biased parent whose favors depended upon accidents of birth, sex, ownership of property, and ancestry. To a nation born in warfare, this seemed not only natural but necessary. Granting a serf the same rights as a nobleman would have been like letting a foot soldier countermand the orders of a warlord.

The American revolutionaries and Constitution makers were caught in a hard conflict between the intellectual ideal of equality and the historical fact of inequality. They proclaimed the brotherhood of man by day and went home to suppers served by slaves. They announced in their Declaration of Independence that "all men are created equal" and then promulgated a constitution that counted each slave as three-fifths of a person for purposes of political representation. And all the while, they seemed not even to notice that their proclamations about "man" and "men" excluded one-half of the adult population of America.

Sooner or later the American Revolution would have to catch up with itself. After government "by the people" had been established, the question became, Who are the people? The answer would inevitably be "Everyone," but the inevitable came hard.

Jefferson had hopes that the American Revolution would be completed, in this sense, by the younger generation that had been bred in the ideals of 1776. He believed that it was possible for the new men of affairs in relatively enlightened states, such as Virginia, to put political altruism above greed and abolish the inequalities whose chief emblem was slavery. It did not happen, of course. Instead, the men of affairs went to war with one another—or, rather, their sons did—and did not accept the concept of legal equality until the battlefields had been soaked with the blood of countless young American soldiers.

The revolutionary concept of legal equality had, however, been quietly brewing in the hearts of the common men—and especially the common women—of America for decades before the bloody conflict came. Equality is an idea of common life. It springs upward from the people, and particularly from the community of women who shoulder the major responsibility for the integrity of ordinary living. It does not overstate the case to say that legal equality is the world's first constitutional principle that speaks in a woman's voice: of community and compassion instead of hierarchy and defiance, of participation in the whole instead of freedom from majority constraints, of the small vital threads that make up the fabric of daily living instead of "great" thoughts and actions on the public stage. It was these values that Margaret Douglas embraced—instinctively and in spite of herself—when the harsh rule of law came crashing unbidden into her small world.

Margaret Douglas was a southern lady in the true and complete sense of the term. She had been born in Washington, D.C., raised and married in Charleston, South Carolina, and had moved to Norfolk, Virginia, in 1845 with her daughter Rosa. She came from a slaveholding family and had owned slaves herself.

In early 1852, she dropped by a Norfolk barbershop to discuss some "business" with the proprietor, who was a free Negro. Looking over the proprietor's shoulder, she noticed two small Negro boys sitting in the back of the shop studying spelling books. The barber said they were his sons and that what Mrs. Douglas was witnessing was the full extent of their educational opportunity. He explained that "there was no one who took interest enough in little colored children to keep a day school for them."

"Without further consideration or hesitation," former slaveholder Douglas offered to teach the barber's children—he turned out to have five—how to read and write. The following week, she welcomed the children into her home, where she and Rosa gave them daily literary instruction at no charge. After several months of successful teaching, she decided to open a school for free Negro children for a fee of three dollars per quarter. They were "overrun with applications" and opened for business in June 1852 with twenty-five students.

On May 9, 1853, at about 8:30 A.M., two city constables—Constable Cherry and Constable Cox—suddenly appeared at Mrs. Douglas's doorstep with an arrest warrant for her and Rosa. The charge was "teaching colored children to read and to write" in violation of the statutes of Virginia. It was an open-and-shut case: If ever two scoundrels were guilty of the offense charged, Margaret and Rosa Douglas were.

The constables brought Mrs. Douglas, her daughter, and the twenty-five frightened children to the office of Mayor Simon S. Stubbs for questioning. Mrs. Douglas was jarred when the mayor explained the charge to her. She had known, of course, that learning was forbidden to slaves as a result of that terrible slave revolt led by Nat Turner in the thirties. But *free* Negroes! Why should it be unlawful to teach intelligent, earnest free Negro children the basic skills of civilization?

Of course, she kept these subversive sentiments to herself. To the mayor she simply said that she had not been aware of the law she had violated, adding that if she had broken the law by her beneficent actions, the mayor should "do [his] duty and put me in prison at once, for I will ask no favors at the hands of any man." Mayor Stubbs nonetheless did her the favor of dismissing the case on the ground that she had been ignorant of the illegality of her conduct.

The local grand jury refused to leave fair enough alone, however, and insisted on returning indictments charging Margaret and Rosa Douglas with unlawfully teaching Negro children to read and write.

On November 12, 1853, Mrs. Douglas went to trial without counsel before Judge Richard H. Baker and a jury of twelve white men (Rosa having fled to New York City). Her lack of defense counsel proved to be no great hardship. After letting the prosecution prove its case without opposition—the facts being undisputed—she rose to make her jury speech. It was not a speech a professional lawyer would or could have made. She spoke not of legal right and wrong, but of everyday life, compassion, and helping. A mediocre lawyer would have scoffed at the speech; a good one would have envied it.

After establishing her orthodox credentials—"I have been a slave-holder. . . . I am no abolitionist, neither am I a fanatic"—she proceeded to reveal herself as a true radical, declaring with unexpectedly fierce conviction: "I am a strong advocate for the religious and moral instruction of the whole human family!" The issue before the jurors was her technical defense of ignorance of the law, but—like an unself-conscious James Otis—she was more interested in a higher and deeper law. "Let it be the welfare of your people and your country that you seek, and I am with you, heart and soul. . . . This is a matter that calls for the consideration of every true and noble heart, the welfare of our people," she challenged them.

True and noble hearts? The welfare of our people? What did such things have to do with whether a violation of the law of the commonwealth had occurred, the jurors wondered.

Douglas told them. If the jurors were to do justice, she said, they must look beyond the letter of the law to the hard facts of life and judge them in unadorned human terms. The technical law could not aid that process, only the jurors' human experience could:

> Let us look into the situation of our colored population in the City of Norfolk, for they are not dumb brutes. If they were, they would be more carefully considered, and their welfare better provided for. For instance, two or three of these people are not allowed to assemble together by themselves, whether in sickness or in health. There is no provision made for them whatever the circumstances may be and such meetings are pronounced unlawful and treasonable. Think you, gentlemen, that there is not misery and distress among these people? Yes, indeed, misery enough, and frequently starvation. Even those

that are called free are heavily taxed, and their privileges greatly limited. . . .

She put it to her twelve male judges straight: Granted that they lacked the moral fiber to alleviate such horrors of inequality themselves, how could they conceivably justify punishing those who undertook to do it for them? It was a dangerous, almost suicidal speech, but it was the only one worthy to be made:

> And when they are sick or in want, on whom does the duty devolve to seek them out and administer to their necessities? Does it fall on you, gentlemen? Oh no, it is not expected that gentlemen will take the trouble to seek out a Negro hut for the purpose of alleviating the wretchedness he may find there. Why then prosecute your benevolent ladies for doing that which you yourselves have so long neglected? Shall we treat our slaves with less compassion than we do the cattle in our fields?

The defendant then made the sacrificial offer committed dissidents always make to their oppressors. Like Thomas More before her and Mahatma Gandhi after her, she tendered her own body as a sacrifice to justice and a rebuke to tyranny:

> But, if otherwise, there are your laws: enforce them to the letter. You may send me, if you so decide, to that cold and gloomy prison. I can be as happy there as I am in my quiet little home; and, in the pursuit of knowledge, and with the resources of a well-stored mind, I shall be, gentlemen, a sufficient companion for myself. Of one consolation you cannot deprive me: I go not as a convicted felon, for I have violated no tittle of any one of the laws that are embodied in the Divine Decalogue; I shall be only a single sufferer under the operation of one of the most inhuman and unjust laws that ever disgraced the statute book of a civilized community.

The jury tried to solve its moral dilemma by declaring the case a tie: It found Margaret Douglas guilty but confined punishment to a meaningless fine of one dollar. Once again, stupidity intervened to rescue the Commonwealth of Virginia from common sense. Judge

Baker refused to brook the jury's impotent foolishness. After delivering a long, bombastic speech on the depravity of making Negro children literate, he gave himself "no choice" but to sentence the defendant to thirty days in jail. (Those who manage to read the judge's speech to completion tend to consider the sentence the lesser of the two evils Douglas was forced to endure.)

Margaret Douglas served her time without complaint, and when she finished, she accepted the invitation of the jailer and his wife to stay an extra two days with them. Then she went home to her little house and her books.

The modern era of Anglo-American law had arrived early, and the principal actor had been, appropriately, a citizen dissident who was also a woman. Her jury speech had, appropriately, employed the female metaphor of the family, in which all of the children deserve equality of treatment. It was a metaphor, and an idea, that would come to dominate the legal discourse of America.

Four years after Margaret Douglas's obscure trial and conviction, a momentous national event occurred. In March 1857, Chief Justice Roger Taney sat in the center of the U.S. Supreme Court bench reading a landmark opinion in a voice that was almost a whisper. The decision in *Dred Scott* v. *Sandford* would tear the country apart and destroy Taney's reputation as a moral and brilliant jurist. It would become known as the worst Supreme Court opinion ever rendered—"a blunder worse than a crime."

Dred Scott was a slave who had traveled to the free territory of Missouri and claimed that he had thereby become an American citizen, with the ability to bring suit in federal court. It fell to Taney and his colleagues to decide whether the promise of equality implicit in the American experiment was reality or rhetoric. Taney, in effect, said that it was rhetoric. When the brave words of the Declaration of Independence were written, he said, slaves "had for more than a century been beings of an inferior order . . . and so far inferior that they had no rights which the white man was bound to respect." Thus, although the phrase "all men are created equal . . . would seem to embrace the whole human family . . . it is too clear for dispute that the enslaved African race was not intended to be included."[1]

There was that word "family" again. Margaret Douglas had used it as a metaphor for a better future; Roger Taney traded it for a maimed past.

Adopted in 1791, the Fifth Amendment to the U.S. Constitution had required of the federal government only the old, chameleon-like promise of due process of law. In 1868, that ancient promise was joined in the Fourteenth Amendment by a brand-new one: that the several state governments of America would henceforth extend to their citizens the content-specific guarantee of "equal protection of the law." More than anything contained in the original Bill of Rights, this provision represented a legal revolution. Unlike "due process," "equal protection" was an external, objective standard that would not change with time and circumstance. It had a mathematical quality that ensured its immutability: One always equals one, regardless of what the "ones" consist of in any given time or place.

It took a male war to bring the equal protection clause into being, but it took female sensibilities to properly implement it. In 1872, Susan B. Anthony of Rochester, New York, looked around and noticed an obvious fact: The promise of the Fourteenth Amendment was proving as empty for women as the promise of the Declaration of Independence had for Negroes one hundred years before. And so, she went to town and cast an illegal vote in the presidential election.

She was prosecuted for voting, just as Margaret Douglas had been prosecuted for the equally heinous crime of teaching, and was of course convicted. Her courtroom speeches dripped with the same contempt for the pretentiousness of male hierarchical justice that Douglas's had carried. When the trial judge took the almost unprecedented—and probably illegal—step of directing a verdict of guilty against her, Anthony rose to make her feelings known. With exquisite sarcasm, she noted that even if the case had been submitted to the jury, she would not have been accorded her constitutional right to a trial by "a jury of [her] peers."

[H]ad Your Honor submitted my case to the jury, as was clearly your duty, even then I should have had just cause of protest, for not one of these men was my peer; but, native or foreign-born, black or white, rich or poor, educated or ignorant, awake or asleep, sober or drunk, each and every man of them was my political superior; and hence, in no sense my peer.

Eighty years later, it all happened again. Although the U.S. Supreme Court had declared legally enforced racial separation unconstitutional, the city fathers of Montgomery, Alabama, continued to enforce segregation in public transportation. Rosa Parks was not a troublemaker or a constitutional scholar. She was just tired, and conscious of her dignity as a human being. Just as Douglas had taught children and Anthony had cast a vote, so Parks refused to surrender her seat to a white man—and changed the world forever.

Rosa Parks's legal ordeal launched the Southern civil rights movement. She was arrested on December 1, 1955, tried in the Montgomery City Court the following Monday, and found guilty of violating Montgomery's segregation laws. In January 1956, her guilt was affirmed by the Montgomery Circuit Court, which, to its everlasting shame, sentenced her to fifty-six days of hard labor. The sentence was stayed pending the outcome of *Browder* v. *Gayle,* a federal court suit challenging the constitutionality of Montgomery's segregation laws. On June 5, 1956, those laws were declared unconstitutional by a 2-1 vote of a three-judge panel, and on November 13, 1956, the U.S. Supreme Court affirmed that decision.

Meanwhile, Parks's prosecution had sparked the famed Montgomery bus boycott, under the leadership of an obscure but brilliant young minister named Martin Luther King. On the day after the Supreme Court decision, King, Mrs. Parks, and several other participants in the boycott boarded a Montgomery bus for the first time in 389 days. The tense silence that greeted them was broken by a soft-spoken white man who turned to Rosa Parks and said, "Looks like it will be a nice day." She smiled and nodded. Today, all races ride Montgomery buses and sit wherever they choose—and some of those buses go past a thoroughfare called Rosa Parks Avenue.

Susan B. Anthony lost her legal battle, but she parlayed that loss into a mighty contribution to the winning of the war. After declaring that she would "never pay a dollar of the unjust [hundred dollar] fine" the judge imposed on her, she walked from the courtroom into history. Already a well-known women's rights activist, she used her conviction as a springboard to even greater notoriety and influence. As president of the Women's Suffrage Association she wrote and lectured tirelessly across the length and breadth of America, a living symbol of the injustice of the anti-suffrage laws.

When she died in 1906, only a handful of states had enacted laws granting the vote to women. But her dream came posthumously true half a generation later, when the male political structure of America finally, acrimoniously and grudgingly, brought forth the Nineteenth Amendment, granting universal suffrage.

Anthony's contribution to the fulfillment of the Constitution's promise of equality was given fitting, if belated, acknowledgment by her countrymen. In 1950, she was elected to the Hall of Fame, and in the 1970s she achieved the ultimate in political recognition when the U.S. Treasury Department issued the Susan B. Anthony silver dollar.

The effects of Mrs. Douglas's heroism are harder to trace. She headed no organizations, started no movements, and gave no lectures. She had no streets named after her, and no coins imprinted with her profile. She sought none of these things, and in fact sought nothing but the right to live her life in quiet decency.

And yet the story of her prosecution has survived. When it is written about, or mentioned, it always strikes a chord. People who think they are not smart or learned enough to understand the Constitution understand profoundly that decent woman who was jailed for teaching Negro children how to read.

It will be noted that these three heroines were all official losers—convicted and jailed, convicted and fined, convicted and saved by another person's lawsuit. Not a word about their prosecutions appears in the official case reports lawyers and judges study. But winning by losing is a common occurrence in the mysterious evolution of the law. Consider Thomas More, consider Walter Raleigh, consider James Otis in the *Paxton* case. Consider Mahatma Gandhi, who used a term in prison to loosen the British Empire's grip upon his nation.

If, as Woody Allen says, most of success in life comes from showing up, so most of constitutional progress comes from *standing* up and making the argument, win or lose. When a big idea comes before a small judge, it is never any contest in the long run—although the run is sometimes very long. Great precedents have their roots in the minds and hearts of ordinary people, and need time to grow. When the Supreme Court decided the school desegregation cases in 1954, the brave, century-old words of Margaret Douglas echoed in its phrases. *Brown* v. *Board of Education* needed *Commonwealth* v. *Douglas* as an oak tree needs a seed.

If an artist were commissioned to paint a portrait of the spirit of the American Constitution, he might paint John Peter Zenger cranking out brave diatribes against the government of New York, or James Otis announcing the dawn of the American Revolution in the old Boston courthouse. If it were left to me, I would commission a painting of a well-dressed, middle-aged lady in a shabby barbershop, watching two young Negro boys intently reading spelling books, and touching one of them on the shoulder. I would caption it *The Family,* and I would hire a woman to paint it.

15

UNREASONABLE SEARCHES AND SEIZURES, CONTINUED

(The Exclusionary Rule)

May I trouble you to tell us what you deem to be the questions before this Court? . . . Are you asking us to overrule the Wolf case[?] . . . I notice it isn't cited in your brief.

JUSTICE FRANKFURTER TO COUNSEL FOR THE PETITIONER DURING ARGUMENT OF THE PRECEDENT-SETTING APPEAL IN *MAPP* V. *OHIO*.

In the sixteenth year of a distinguished career on the Supreme Court bench, Justice Joseph Bradley sat in his dark-paneled office reading the briefs in *Boyd* v. *United States*. He was emphatically unimpressed. The arguments, pro and con, were characterized by crabbed legal reasoning and bogged down in citation and countercitation of dusty precedents. The lawyers seemed not to realize the size of the issues they were addressing. They were like small-time musicians playing a Beethoven symphony on banjos. Well, Justice Bradley would see to it that the appropriate orchestration was provided—he was just the man to do it.

He had been born on a farm near Albany, New York, in 1813, the oldest of twelve children. He came from four generations of colonial stock, and had spent many childhood hours in the home of his grandparents, whose greatest life experience had been the Revolution and whose greatest pleasure was telling stories about it.

Young Joe's other main intellectual companions were the Bible and the Book of Common Prayer.

The Bradleys were the ultimate self-reliant family. They raised all their own food, including the sugar produced by the maple trees on their property, and Joe and his brothers and sisters went to school in homespun clothing, "manufactured" by their mother. As an economic unit they were sovereign, if poor.

They were the very image of the self-sufficient yeomanry Thomas Jefferson had rhapsodized about. "Those who labor in the earth are the chosen people," he had written, "if ever He had a chosen people, whose breasts He has made the peculiar deposit for substantial and genuine virtue." That "virtue," according to Jefferson was produced by economic independence, which bred a spirit of individualism essential to a free republic. "Corruption of morals," on the other hand, was "the mark set on those who, not looking up to heaven, to their soil and industry, as does the husbandman, for their subsistence, depend for it on the casualties and caprice of customers." City folk were corrupt and fatal to a nation's greatness; only farmers could sustain a republic of free and independent people.

True to this agrarian ideal, Bradley was a resolutely independent thinker. All of his life, he had a compulsion to work problems through on his own, with the help of no one but the classical writers whose works he studied. As a Supreme Court justice, he relied far more on a priori reasoning than on case authority. At his funeral, a longtime friend pegged him well when he said that Joseph Bradley "held little or no deference for the opinions of others." He steadfastly—and stubbornly—sought his own truth.

He believed that there was such a thing as truth, in a natural law, humanistic sense. Like many of his contemporaries, he saw America not as a mere heir to English culture, but as a universalist society being constructed from the ground up, with the best the English, Hebrew, Indian, Greek, Roman, and other great cultures had to offer. His legal philosophy was epitomized by his favorite quote, which came from Cicero: "There is a true law, a right reason, conformable to nature, given to all men. . . . [I]t is not one thing today and another tomorrow; but it is one uniform, perpetual, immutable law, comprehending all people, at all times."

He was a true conservative, in a sense that has been almost forgotten today.

* * *

Boyd v. *United States* was an odd little case that occupies a unique place in America's legal history. Decided ninety-five years after the Bill of Rights was adopted, it was the first significant Bill of Rights decision the U.S. Supreme Court ever made. It was also one of the most important—and most controversial—of them all.

Several years previously, the U.S. government had sued Boyd's company, seeking to confiscate thirty-five cases of plate glass that it had illegally smuggled into the country. In the course of the suit, the government had invoked a statutory power to force the company to produce invoices and other documents that established its illegal possession of the glass. After successfully confiscating the glass by this constitutionally dubious means, the government proceeded to prosecute Boyd personally for preparing fraudulent invoices pertaining to the glass and attempted to use the compulsorily produced documents as evidence against him. Boyd's lawyers objected, making (more or less) the following novel arguments:

1. That the documents had been unconstitutionally seized in the forfeiture proceeding in violation of Boyd's Fourth Amendment rights; that they were, therefore, wrongfully in the government's possession—were, in effect, stolen property; and that the government, being obliged to return them to Boyd, had no right to retain and use them in a criminal prosecution against him.
2. That offering into evidence written information taken by compulsion from its owner (Boyd) was tantamount to compelling him to testify against himself and therefore violated his Fifth Amendment privilege against compulsory self-incrimination.

The trial court rejected these arguments, admitted the documents into evidence, and Boyd was convicted. He appealed to the U.S. Supreme Court, and the Bill of Rights took the first bold step on its long march through the center of American life.

Boyd's arguments appealed to Bradley's individualistic instincts. Government use of evidence obtained in violation of the Constitution dishonored the ideals that had brought the government into existence. Admitting such evidence in a criminal prosecution made the Court an accomplice to a constitutional crime. Could such things be permitted in the Land of the Free? The question seemed to answer itself.

And yet it didn't. As Bradley read through the lawyers' briefs, he realized that the "book" answer to the question was surprising. According to the cited law, the documents were perfectly proper evidence, notwithstanding the illegality of the government's acquisition of them. That had always been the law. The courts had never cared *how* evidence was obtained, so long as it was reliable.

If a witness were kidnapped, carried across jurisdictional boundaries, and produced in court, the kidnappers might be punished, but the testimony of the victim would be admissible. A confession beaten out of a defendant was likewise admissible, so long as the court found it "reliable"—the objection to it being scientific rather than moral. So with illegally seized documents. As one judge had laconically put it, "The mere fact of illegally obtaining [documents] does not change that which is written on them."

As Bradley and his colleagues sat in the old Supreme Court Building listening to these well-supported arguments, they were reliving, with eerie similarity, scenes that had played out more than one hundred years earlier, when the Fourth Amendment prohibition was first established. Jeremiah Gridley in *Paxton*'s case, and his British counterparts in the *Wilkes* and *Entick* cases, had also used technically perfect arguments to support government misconduct. But like Lord Camden in *Entick*'s case, Joseph Bradley was looking for something more profound than technical perfection. And like Camden, he found it.

Notwithstanding the universal acceptance of general warrants, Camden had branded them obnoxious to the ideals of a free people and therefore unconstitutional. Bradley responded in the same way to the settled practice of admitting illegally obtained documents into evidence. Whatever custom said, the practice was contrary to the ideals of the nation and therefore not to be tolerated. Bradley needed no authority other than Cicero's "right reason" to support his ruling.[1] Call it a Fourth Amendment violation or a Fifth Amendment violation, he wrote—the two privileges "almost run into one another"—the forcible seizure and evidentiary use of Boyd's papers was detestable governmental action that must not be rewarded.

In reversing Boyd's conviction, Bradley pumped glorious a priori language into American law that would exalt and haunt it for generations to come. "Compelling the production of [a citizen's] private books and papers to convict him of a crime or to forfeit his property, is abhorrent to the instincts of an Englishman; it is abhorrent to the instincts of an American; [i]t cannot abide the pure atmosphere of political liberty and personal freedom."

Powerful as Bradley's words were, doubts lingered as to the true meaning of the *Boyd* decision. *Boyd* was an unusual case that had aspects of both Fourth and Fifth amendments violations. What would the Court hold in a pure search and seizure case? The answer was a generation in coming, but when it came, it was crystal clear.

The two federal agents were behaving like a pair of well-dressed burglars—which, in fact, was exactly what they were. They moved quickly up the front walk at 1834 Penn Street in Kansas City, glancing furtively from side to side. When they got to the door, the short, plump one leaned forward and peered through the glass pane into the darkened house. He nodded to his companion and took a key from his pocket. Ninety seconds later they were both inside. They rummaged through every drawer and closet in the house and carried away a stack of papers and several items of personal property.

The owner of the burglarized house and stolen property was a citizen named Freemont Weeks, who was suspected of having sent illegal lottery tickets through the U.S. mail. The burglars were agents of the U.S. Postal Service, acting upon explicit orders of their superior.

At his trial on the lottery charge, Weeks's lawyer moved to exclude the stolen documents from evidence, relying on Bradley's stirring opinion in the *Boyd* case. The trial judge denied the motion on the ground that the *Boyd* decision was based in part upon the Fifth Amendment privilege not to testify against oneself, whereas Weeks's argument was based solely upon the Fourth Amendment prohibition against unreasonable searches and seizures.

Weeks's conviction was reversed by the U.S. Supreme Court in an opinion by Justice William Day that left no doubt as to the unconstitutionality of using illegally obtained evidence to convict a citizen:

> If letters and private documents can thus be seized and held and used in evidence against a citizen accused of an offense, the protection of

the Fourth Amendment ... is of no value, and ... might as well be stricken from the Constitution. The efforts of the courts and their officials to bring the guilty to punishment, praiseworthy as they are, are not to be aided by the sacrifice of those great principles established by years of endeavor and suffering which have resulted in their embodiment in the fundamental law of the land.

Even as the ink was drying on Day's opinion, a baying sound could be heard in the distance. It was a new sound—the yelping of intellectuals *opposing* civil liberties and remedies for accused persons. Usually in the past it had been intellectuals, representing the "people," who had aligned against oppressive government. That would now change. For the first time in American history, popular rights would not necessarily be a popular cause.

John Wigmore, America's leading authority on the law of evidence, weighed in most viciously. Among the nicer things he said about the *Boyd* and *Weeks* decisions was that they were "ill-starred," that they exercised "an unhealthy influence" upon American law, and that the exclusionary rule represented "misplaced sentimentality" and a "quaint method of enforcing the law." His ultra-logical mind could not fathom how one wrong—an illegal search and seizure—could be made right by a second wrong—preventing the use of relevant evidence in a criminal trial. Punish them both, he exhorted. Punish the cop for violating the Constitution, then use the fruits of his violation to punish the crook he stole them from.

Some of the best judges in the land were equally hostile. In the beginning the exclusionary rule applied only to federal searches, and many state courts refused to adopt it for their own systems of justice. When the New York Court of Appeals was urged to do so, Judge Benjamin Cardozo shook his eminent head and declared himself baffled by the notion that "the criminal goes free because the constable blundered."

Bradley's great principle also had its defenders, some of at least equal eloquence. Supreme Court Justice Louis Brandeis understood the logic of Wigmore's formula—that one police officer's misconduct against one criminal should equal two punishments instead of none. But to him, the exclusionary rule was a great principle of constitutional law precisely because it refused to place the government in the same equation with the criminals it pursued. "The law," he wrote in *Olmstead* v. *United States* (1928), "is the great, the omnipresent teacher. [T]o declare that the Government may commit crimes in order to secure the conviction of a private individual . . . would bring terrible retribution."

That says it as definitively as it can be said. Some accept this premise instinctively, while others never will, which is why the struggle for the soul of American justice begun by Joseph Bradley more than a hundred years ago will last as long as the republic he cherished.

At least we hope it will—for it must be reported that the struggle has of late been going very poorly for the friends of Joseph Bradley.

On a spring morning in 1957, Dollree Mapp was startled by loud knocking on the door of her small home. There was something ominously official and insistent about it. She opened the door wide enough to see two members of the Cleveland police force standing on the porch. "We're conducting an investigation involving a dangerous person," said one of them. "We need to search your residence." "Do you have a warrant?" asked Mapp. "No, but we can get one." "Excuse me, I have to call my lawyer," she said politely, leaving the door ajar. When she explained the situation to her lawyer, he advised her to insist upon a warrant. When she did so, the would-be interlopers grudgingly departed, but only to their squad car, where they kept the house under surveillance and radioed for reinforcements.

Three hours later, Mapp found herself in the middle of a scene straight from the Third Reich. A small platoon of Cleveland's worst descended upon her home and demanded entrance. This time, their leader displayed an official-looking paper that he said was a search warrant. She snatched it from him, but before she could read it, he twisted her arm behind her back, forcing her to return it. The "warrant" never reappeared. In Mapp's subsequent trial, the prosecutors made no reference to it, and no record of its issuance was ever uncovered. It seemed unlikely that there was a warrant, but if there was, it obviously did not authorize the seizures that subsequently took place.

After forcibly retrieving the "warrant" from Mapp's grasp, the police had proceeded to commandeer, rip up, and rummage through every nook and cranny of her household. If they were searching for a "bomb suspect," as they asserted, he must have been a very small man. They examined the contents of every cabinet, drawer, and box on the premises, including a dusty trunk in the basement, but found no midget bombers lurking there. They did carry away a consolation prize, however—a small cachet of photographs and pamphlets that they deemed to be "lewd and lascivious" within the meaning of Ohio's criminal obscenity statutes.

At her trial for possession of pornography, Mapp testified that the photographs and pamphlets were left behind by a recently departed lodger. No matter, ruled the court. As long they were in your household and you knew it, you are guilty. Her lawyer made a half-hearted effort to suppress the unlawfully seized items, but he knew it would be in vain. It was, and his client was convicted.

But what about the exclusionary rule, it might be asked. Excellent question. The answer was that the U.S. Supreme Court had taken a schizophrenic position on that often-maligned protection. In a 1949 case called *Wolf v. Colorado,* the Court had ruled that, although the requirements of the Fourth Amendment applied to the states through the due process clause, the exclusionary rule did not. The exclusionary rule, the Court said, was not part of the Fourth Amendment, and certainly not part of due process. It was simply a federal "rule of evidence" that state courts might ignore if they chose. Ohio had so chosen. When the unlawfully seized materials were offered into evidence, there was literally nothing Mapp's lawyer could do.

Except appeal, which he did all the way to the U.S. Supreme Court. His main argument was that possession of pornography cannot constitutionally be a crime. As an afterthought, he did what 165 other Supreme Court petitioners had futilely done over the prior eleven years: He argued that the Court should overrule *Wolf* v. *Colorado* and apply the exclusionary rule to state searches and seizures.

The justices listened to the arguments, which focused on the constitutionality of the possession charge, and retired to discuss the case. During the Court conference, it became apparent to a minority of the justices that five of their brethren were engaged in an arcane legal maneuver known as "sandbagging the opposition." A nice little argument on the possession issue, said the five, but let's talk about the *real* issue—extending the exclusionary rule to state criminal trials. But that issue was hardly argued, protested the minority. We can't decide a major question of constitutional law without full-dress briefing and argument. It has been argued, and argued, and argued for eleven years, replied the five. Now, it is time to *do* something.

The result was an expected reversal of Mapp's conviction by an unexpected nationalization of the exclusionary rule. The Court ruled that unconstitutionally seized evidence would henceforth be inadmissible in every American court. From the day *Mapp* was decided, every constable, sheriff, investigator, process server, and police officer in the land was subject to the same standard of constitutional uprightness, enforceable by the exclusion of tainted evidence, that had applied to FBI agents, Treasury agents, Secret Service agents, Internal Revenue agents, and U.S. marshals for generations. The howls from the public and private sectors of America were deafening. As usual, the people were for constitutional principles in theory, but—as with the principles of Christianity—they were horrified to see them put into actual practice.

The effect of the *Mapp* decision on criminal justice will be forever debated, but its effect on defense lawyers, law book publishers, and pulpwood processors is indisputable. Defense counsel whose intellectual endeavors had been limited to making the presumption of innocence sound reasonable to juries, suddenly found themselves engaged in hypertechnical debates over "probable cause," "limits of curtilage," "standing," and "reasonable expectations of privacy."

A 1990 annotated listing of search and seizure cases, most of them decided since 1970, takes up more than eleven hundred pages and contains more than twenty thousand paragraphed references to reported decisions. Whole forests have been felled providing paper for search and seizure opinions, and for the texts and articles that learnedly dissect them. Distinguished jurists have debated such issues as whether, and to what extent, public restroom stalls and adult bookstore viewing booths are subject to Fourth Amendment protection; whether an airplane overflight of a marijuana field constitutes a "search" and whether taking a urine sample constitutes a "seizure"; and they have pondered the constitutional implications of turning over a stereo to check the serial number or of poking through a garbage can in a suspect's yard.

All of this is deadly serious stuff—the drawing of the lines of

sanctuary around the private lives of citizens—but the very specificity of the process makes it look foolish and renders it vulnerable
to easy criticism. After *Mapp*, Fourth Amendment values paradoxically lost much force and favor among the people and leaders of
America—until, eventually, this most vital of constitutional principles was permitted to suffer grievous injury at the hands of men
elected to preserve and enforce it.

The senator from Georgia hunched forward on his elbows,
leaning into the question: "Now, if the president could authorize a
covert break-in, and you do not know exactly what that power
would be limited to, you do not think it could include murder or
other crimes beyond covert break-in, do you?"

Looking like a tough, balding CPA, John Erlichman gave a
chilling answer. "I don't know where the line is, Senator," he said.

Senator Herman Talmadge continued leaning in, but his voice
became folksy and confidential. "Do you remember when we were
in law school, we studied a famous principle of law that came from
England and also is well known in this country, that no matter how
humble a man's cottage is, that even the King of England cannot enter without his consent?"

Erlichman's smile was tight and condescending. "I am afraid
that has been considerably eroded over the years, has it not?"

Talmadge did not return the smile. "Down in my country," he
drawled,"we still think it is a pretty legitimate principle of law."
(Applause from the audience, which sounded more like relief than
triumph.)

The "erosion" had been far greater than Talmadge could possibly have guessed. The subject under discussion was, of course, history's most famous "third-rate burglary"—the June 1972 break-in
of the Democratic headquarters at the Watergate complex in Washington. That bit of official lawlessness was bad enough, but what
Erlichman knew and Talmadge did not was that it constituted
merely the unpleasant tip of a horridly proportioned iceberg.

If Talmadge and his fellow senators could have unraveled the
skein of lawlessness far enough, they would have discovered a five-
day period in July 1970 when the president of the United States authorized the effective repeal of the Fourth Amendment to the U.S.
Constitution. It was called the "Huston Plan."

Tom Charles Huston, a tall, gangling White House staffer, all of twenty-nine years of age, had decided, more or less on his own, that the government must smoke out and eradicate the traitors who were undermining the president by protesting the Vietnam war—and the Constitution be damned. The procedure authorized by his plan made Lord Halifax's general warrants look like parking summonses. In order to combat the heretical and traitorous activities of the protestors, it provided that:

The National Security Agency would be authorized to intercept and read overseas cables and correspondence to and from American citizens.

Agencies of the United States would be authorized to read the private domestic mail of American citizens.

Agencies of the United States would be authorized to burglarize American homes and seize what needed to be seized.

This emasculation of the Constitution was to be presided over by—you guessed it—Tom Charles Huston. He was to wield control over the privacy of the nation that the court of high commission never dreamed of.

Astoundingly, the plan was quickly approved by the CIA, the Defense Intelligence Agency, and the National Security Agency. The only barrier between Huston and his dark dream of power was a crusty, seventy-five-year-old federal cop named J. Edgar Hoover. No friend of civil liberties, Hoover opposed the plan as a matter of turf-protective reflex.

Huston was exasperated. Hoover's objections, he said, were "frivolous," "unreasonable," and "detrimental to our domestic intelligence operations." The old man must be brought to the Oval Office and "told who is president." (He should be forced to kneel and kiss thy ring, my Liege, for the realm is not safe so long as such men are allowed to prattle.)

Nixon liked the plan but not the suggestion for effectuating it. He decided to bypass Hoover and proceeded to immediate implementation. His top aide, Bob Haldeman, addressed a brief memo to Huston saying, "The recommendations you have proposed as a result of the review have been approved by the President. He does not, however, want to follow the procedure you have outlined. . . . He would prefer that the thing simply be put in motion on the basis of this approval."

On July 23, 1970, the "thing" became official policy by the secret issuance of copies of the plan to all American intelligence agencies. The rule of law in America suffered a great humiliation that was mitigated only by its shameful secrecy.

The plan lasted all of five days, after which Attorney General John Mitchell, responding to pressure from Hoover, convinced the president that trashing the Constitution in such flagrant fashion was not the politic thing to do. All copies of the plan were recalled, and the republic survived. But Nixon had given a wink and a nod to his underlings that were an implicit authorization of all the clandestine illegalities that followed.

America's George III was ultimately forced to resign, and he took a few Halifaxes with him. But the vision of that tough face, with its tight, condescending smile, lingered. As did the fear, half-submerged in the consciousness of many Americans, that it might conceivably be the face of the future.

In 1984, a pair of California dopesters known as "Patsy" and "Armando" were convicted on a cocaine rap. Their convictions were reversed because there was insufficient cause for issuing the search warrant, and the reversal was appealed to the U.S. Supreme Court.

The increasingly conservative and drug-conscious Court took the opportunity, once again, to throw Fourth Amendment protections into reverse.[2] Its opinion in *United States* v. *Leon* decided, in effect, that property seized in an unconstitutional search could be used in evidence if the search was not *too* unconstitutional. The evidence was admissible, the Court held, if the officers who made the search *reasonably believed* that they were acting constitutionally. (Imagine asking Nicholas Carrington what he "reasonably believed" about the search of Entick's quarters. Imagine thinking that it made any difference.)

The Supreme Court ruled that the evidence seized from Patsy and Armando was admissible under this new principle. The search may have been unconstitutional, but—hey—the Court had seen much *worse* searches. Sorry, Patsy and Armando. You were born about a generation too late.

"In case after case, I have witnessed the Court's gradual but determined strangulation of the [Exclusionary] Rule," raged octogenarian Justice William Brennan in a dissenting opinion. "It now appears that the Court's victory over the Fourth Amendment is complete."

Following the tortuous path of the Fourth Amendment and the exclusionary rule from *Boyd* to *Weeks* to *Watergate* to *Leon* tends to reverse commonly held assumptions. There is a myth abroad that constitutional liberalism is modern; that American history has marched in a straight line toward ever more humane law enforcement; that a return to the past would produce rock-ribbed, minimalist Bill of Rights' applications that would protect the "people" more and would worry about defendants' rights less; that our forefathers were more fearful of granting civil liberties than we are. If you believe that, conjure up two images in your mind. Imagine the face and words of Joseph Bradley. Then imagine John Erlichman's.

16

THE RIGHT OF PRIVACY

*If everyone minded their own business . . . the world
would go round a deal faster than it does.*

LEWIS CARROLL

Joseph Pulitzer couldn't wait to get to the promised land. When his
ship entered Boston Harbor in 1864, the young Hungarian immigrant dove from the rail and swam ashore. He reached the army
paymaster ahead of his fellow foreign recruits and collected his en-
listment bounty, which might have been pilfered by the shipping
agent if Pulitzer had waited for the ship to dock. Skinny, weak-eyed,
and apparently ill-suited to commercial combat, Pulitzer continued
to arrive ahead of his rivals for the rest of his life.

After a tough year in the Union cavalry, he moved to St.
Louis, where he had a brilliant career as a newspaper reporter spe-
cializing in local politics. He eventually scraped together enough
money to purchase two newspapers, which he merged into the
St. Louis Post-Dispatch in 1878. In 1883, he purchased a dull, conservative New York City paper called *The World* and inaugurated a
new era in American social history.

He sprang his innovation on an unsuspecting nation in his first
edition of *The World*. "There is room in this great and growing
city," he editorialized, "for a journal that is not only cheap but

bright, not only bright but large, not only large but truly democratic. . . ." Not only democratic, he might have added, but grossly sensationalized. The first edition gave promise of an interesting future, carrying not one, but two front-page stories detailing the agonized final moments on earth of two convicted killers facing execution in New York and Pittsburgh. One had reacted in abject terror when his death warrant was read to him, and the other—according to *The World* headline—had "SHOUT[ED] FROM UNDER THE BLACK CAP THAT HIS EXECUTIONERS [WERE] MURDERERS."

Pulitzer's new "democratic" journalism was facilitated by new technology: cheap pulpwood paper, which was just beginning to replace the more expensive rag paper publishers had always used; improvements in photoengraving techniques that allowed disasters and monstrosities to be seen, as well as imagined, by readers; and linotype machines that streamlined and improved the printing process. These innovations permitted Pulitzer to sell a visually attractive and broadly appealing paper at a price anyone could afford. At two cents a copy, the newly sensationalized *World* increased its circulation from 15,000 to 1.5 million readers within an amazingly short period of time. Using every available technological resource and his unromanticized knowledge of human nature, Pulitzer had invented the beast and master of modern life: the mass communications medium.

What he created was not merely bigger, but different. American journalism had always loved sensationalism, but the dirt had always been dished on a relatively small scale. When newspapers began to grow exponentially, and to vie for growth by publishing ever more lurid and gossipy information, a new form of human injury came into being. Private citizens became overnight anti-celebrities, whose real and asserted shortcomings, sins, and secrets were suddenly public property on a scale never previously known. A demeaning indiscretion by a businessman, or the lament of a mother whose children had died in a fire, might be read about by the sinner or lamenter on the pages of a newspaper they knew was simultaneously being read with prurient curiosity by hundreds of thousands of their fellow citizens. It was a painful form of psychological torment, which a world with a talent for inflicting pain and torment was just beginning to master.

Years later, a newspaper editor vividly described the depredations of this new monster of American life:

Careers, reputations, friendships, lifelong labors; the sanctity of homes; confidences in business; errors long atoned for; feuds long buried; the guarded secrets of the heart; innocent pleasures; loyalties—all the things that hitherto were respected and honored in the society of men, this creature (the press) violated, ripped up, disgorged, blasted, and threw, mangled and bleeding, to the scavenging rabble, that fed ravenously on it, and clamored always for more.[1]

If there was a new form of injury, there must be a new legal remedy. So reasoned Samuel Warren and Louis Brandeis, two prominent Boston lawyers who had been stung by the excesses of the popular press. Warren in particular was outraged by what Boston gossip columns had done to his dignity and peace of mind, and that of his wife and friends. Most of the new journalism was not outright false or damaging enough to be libelous, but it was embarrassing and insolent, and in Warren's opinion, none of the public's business. Americans frustrated by circumstance are wont to exclaim, "There oughta be a law," but these fellows were prepared to do something about it. They set about inventing a new legal right to combat the wrongs produced by Pulitzer's subversive invention.

The "right of privacy" is the only common-law right with a specific, known birth date. Warren and Brandeis brought it to life in Volume 4 of the *Harvard Law Review* on December 15, 1890. Necessity was, they insisted, the mother of their invention. Society faced conflicting realities that made a right of privacy imperative. On the one hand, nineteenth-century people were more vulnerable to the kind of pain inflicted by the popular press than their ancestors had been. "[M]an, under the refining influence of culture, has become more sensitive to publicity. . . ." On the other hand, the press had become vastly more proficient in inflicting such pain, "overstepping in every direction the obvious bounds of propriety and of decency."

It was an era that believed in progress through the exercise of human intelligence. Within the last decade, telephone service had been established between New York and Chicago; the Brooklyn Bridge—more than five football fields in length and half again as long as any existing suspension bridge—had been completed; and New York City had been set aglow with electric lights. By comparison, inventing a legal remedy for the barbarisms of the press looked easy.

Warren and Brandeis saw it as a matter of natural evolution. In the dark ages of the law, they wrote, there had been legal protection only from direct physical force. Later the concept of assault evolved, which protected citizens from fear produced by the *threat* of force. Still later, the law created remedies for injuries to reputation and other intangible interests. "Now," they wrote, "the right to life has come to mean the right to *enjoy life*—the right to be *let alone.*" Like one of Darwin's embattled species, the law must grow a new appendage to deal with advancing civilization—a right that would allow people to sue and recover damages when their private lives were subjected to unwanted public exposure.

The main target of privacy suits would be the scandal-mongering press. Plaintiffs would recover damages for publications that exposed facts decent people would regard as confidential. "Idle gossip" and "prurient" journalistic eavesdropping would be curtailed, news coverage would be devoted to serious subjects, and the intellects and morals of the readers would be improved. The authors obviously hoped that the new "right to be let alone" would raise the general quality of American life, as had the mechanical inventions of Alexander Graham Bell and Thomas Alva Edison.

The authors claimed merely to be following the tradition of the "ever youthful" common law, which had always expanded to meet changing needs. In the past, however, the common law had denied its own progress. Rights were not invented, they were "discovered," in the immemorial customs of the people, in an ancient charter, in remote and inaccessible court records no one but the "discoverer" was likely to read. If Lord Coke had written that *Harvard Law Review* article, he would have claimed to have discovered the right of privacy in old pipe roll cases, now safely beyond the reach of prying scholarship. Warren and Brandeis did not indulge in such frauds. They were honest about the fact of their invention, thereby launching—for good and ill—a new, frank way of looking at the evolution of the law.

They employed the inductive reasoning of a scientist. Like a chemist who derives a general theory from individual experiments, they combed existing case law to see whether it afforded "a principle which can properly be invoked to protect the privacy of the individual." Their researches disclosed instances in which the law had applied a "principle of inviolate personality." There were cases, for example, that allowed the authors of personal letters to sue persons who published them, or passed them on, without permission. From these cases, Warren and Brandeis derived a legal theorem: "The common law secures to each individual the right of determining, *ordinarily,* to what extent his thoughts, sentiments and emotions shall be conveyed to others."

They set about defining this "right of privacy," conferring upon it the following attributes: (1) It would not be violated if the published matter was of "legitimate general or public concern"; (2) It would not apply to reports regarding "public or quasi-public" conduct; (3) It would not apply to communications in a privileged setting, such as courtroom testimony or legislative oratory; (4) It would apply to oral statements only when "special damages" (i.e., specific monetary loss) could be proven; (5) It would apply to true as well as false statements; and (6) It would apply to statements published in good faith as well as to "malicious" publications (i.e., those made for the purpose of causing harm).

A scientist who derived such specific conclusions from so general a theory might be denounced as a fraud. But in the less-demanding world of legal scholarship, Warren and Brandeis were hailed as geniuses. Their right to be "let alone" became the darling of legal scholars, who liked not only the idea of such a right but the idea that *any* legal right could be brought to life in a law journal.

The courts were less hospitable. The right of privacy was accepted in principle by most of them, but the principle was seldom applied in favor of plaintiffs. The "right to be let alone" ran into a more powerful phenomenon of twentieth-century American law—the "right to know." As the century progressed, courts increasingly recognized freedom to impart and receive information as the most nearly absolute civil liberty, and it became difficult to carve out a niche for the right of privacy. The courts indulged in a form of circular reasoning. The right of privacy did not apply to information that was a matter of public interest, and if information was interesting enough to the public to sell newspapers, it was by definition "of public interest."

The flaccidity of the new right was vividly exposed by the sad case of William James Sidis. Sidis had been a remarkable child prodigy. At the age of eleven, he had lectured to mathematicians on the subject of "four dimensional bodies," and at sixteen he had graduated from Harvard College. He had then deliberately withdrawn from the public spotlight, spending the rest of his life in obscurity as "an insignificant clerk" leading the most ordinary of existences. On August 14, 1937, *The New Yorker* magazine chose to yank him from obscurity, featuring him in an article titled "Where Are They Now?"

There could not have been a more calculated violation of the "right to be let alone." The very point of the article was the secluded nature of Sidis's existence and his dislike of publicity. The author reported an interview with Sidis at his lodgings, "a hall bedroom of Boston's shabby south end," describing the untidiness of his room, his "curious laugh," his "odd manner of speech," and other "unusual personal habits" with barely concealed derision. The article ended by quoting Sidis as saying "with a grin" that it was strange, "but, you know, I was born on April Fool's Day."

If a right of privacy existed, surely *The New Yorker* had violated it. But when Sidis brought suit in the Federal District Court for New York City, the court dismissed the complaint. He appealed to the court of appeals, arguing that he was at least entitled to have a jury hear his case. The court of appeals readily conceded that

> the article is merciless in its dissection of intimate details of its subject's personal life, and this in company with elaborate accounts of Sidis' passion for privacy and the pitiable lengths to which he has gone in order to avoid public scrutiny. The work possesses great reader interest, for it is both amusing and instructive; but it may be fairly described as a ruthless exposure of a once-public character, who has since sought and has now been deprived of the seclusion of private life.

But the court ruled that Sidis's lawsuit had properly been dismissed, holding, in effect, that the very fact of public interest made him subject to public exposure. The judges declined to apply the civilized standard of *legitimate* public interest suggested by Warren and Brandeis, concluding instead that what the public was *entitled* to read was defined by what it *wanted* to read:

> Regrettably or not, the misfortunes and frailties of neighbors and "public figures" are subjects of considerable interest and discussion to the rest of the population. And when such are the mores of the community, it would be unwise for a court to bar their expression in the newspapers, books and magazines of the day.

It was, of course, these very community "mores" that Brandeis and Warren had hoped to improve with their invented right. Nonetheless, most other decisions adopted a similar approach. Despite the enthusiastic boosterism of legal academics, the common-law "right to be let alone" more or less died on the judicial vine.

It was born again, as a constitutional right, seventy-five years after its original birth, in a remarkable opinion by the U.S. Supreme Court. If Warren and Brandeis's invention of a common-law right of privacy had been pseudo-chemistry, Justice Douglas's invention of its constitutional counterpart in *Griswold* v. *Connecticut* (1965) was pure alchemy.

Connecticut had a statute making it a crime to use, or advise the use of, contraceptives, and the head of a Planned Parenthood organization had been prosecuted for violating it. There was no doubting the offensiveness of the law. It intruded government into private bedrooms and punished citizens for intensely intimate conduct that—even to some who opposed contraception—seemed to be none of the government's business. If the possibility of such crass public interference in private affairs had been suggested to James Madison, he might have outlawed it. But it wasn't, and his Bill of Rights contains nothing directed at such forms of governmental officiousness.

In a dissenting opinion, Justice Hugo Black, who took a back seat to no one in protecting individual liberties, put the matter as simply as it can be put: "I like my privacy as well as the next one, but I am compelled to admit that government has a right to invade it unless prohibited by some specific constitutional provision."

To Justice William O. Douglas and a majority of the Court, the issue was not so simple. While it was true that the Bill of Rights *said* nothing about a right of privacy, they thought Black's conclusion that it therefore did not *provide* for one simplistic. Bill of Rights provisions have *penumbras,* Douglas declared, idea-emanations that are *suggested* by that which is specifically provided for.[2] The First and Fourth amendments *by their terms* refer to freedom of speech and protection from unreasonable searches and seizures, but these protections are evidence of a commitment to a broader idea—individual privacy—that can be implemented on its own.

It was the Warren/Brandeis law-as-science methodology all over again: Induct a general theory from specific instances and find new applications for it. What the Court was saying, in fancy language, was: Because the Constitution prevents the government from searching your bedroom without probable cause, we can deduce that it *intends* to prevent the government from prosecuting you for using contraceptives in your bedroom.

In subsequent decisions, the Court used the constitutional right of privacy to strike down state abortion laws and to aid in its analysis of search and seizure cases. In 1987, Supreme Court nominee Robert Bork was denied Senate confirmation partly because he was unable to detect a right of privacy in the Bill of Rights' penumbra, as the vast majority of American lawyers and judges were by then able to do.

If the invention of the right of privacy had been typically American in its honest optimism, its progress through the years has been typically American in its zany flexibility. A legal concept created to protect nineteenth-century Boston sensibilities has brought about the legalization of contraception and abortion. Meanwhile, *The National Enquirer* and its ilk are making 1890s' gossip columns look like a nun's diary.

The scientific style of legal reasoning pioneered by Warren and Brandeis has been responsible for much legal progress over the last hundred years, but it has exacted a price in perceptions of the law. It has, to a large extent, been responsible for the generally held view that the law is whatever the judges want it to be.

When judges *admit* that they are making law, the people shudder. It is like a priest admitting he is making up religion. The people prefer the comforting myth that the law is already *there,* and merely being discovered and interpreted by its servants.

Public alienation is exacerbated by the specificity of invented rights. Warren and Brandeis did not merely present the *idea* of a right of privacy, they announced a *specific law* of privacy, as detailed as a complicated statute. They described the privileges, exemptions, and elements of proof applicable to the new right as though they were modern Moseses who had received it from on high—word-for-word.

The same troubling specificity marked the evolution of the right of privacy as a constitutional principle. The Supreme Court concluded not only that it protected abortions, but that it conferred different degrees of protection depending upon the trimester of pregnancy in which the abortion was conducted.

Other constitutional rights explicitly discovered and defined by the Court in the 1960s and thereafter were similarly specific. In reapportionment cases, the Court ruled that the Fourteenth Amendment required not only fairness in legislative representation, but a rule of "one person, one vote." It decided that the Sixth Amendment permitted six-member juries in criminal cases, but not five-member juries. It decided that the First Amendment required a "public figure" such as Frank Sinatra or Mickey Mantle to prove deliberate falsehood in a libel case, but "private figures" such as you and I to prove only negligence. Small wonder that the plaintive cry went up from laymen and experts, from liberals and conservatives, alike: Where do these judges *get* this stuff? How do they derive such detail from the general commands of the Bill of Rights?

Of course, the old method of law creation, with its myths and frauds, had exacted its own costs in public confidence. It had hardly inspired trust among knowledgeable observers when judges invented the myth that the right to jury trial was created in an age when juries were not even thought of, or that the power to declare laws unconstitutional was conferred by precedents that involved nothing of the sort. But, of course, most observers were *not* knowledgeable and believed the pleasant lies. Like successful con men, the judges had retained the public trust by employing methods that demonstrated that they didn't deserve it. When they adopted the inductive method of law creation, they made a Faustian bargain with the people, giving them the truth and the misgivings that went with it.

There is an old saying that "those who love the law and good sausages should never watch either being made." The discovery of the quintessential twentieth-century right gave rise to a quintessential twentieth-century judicial method, which illustrated that old saying to the core. Beginning with the Warren/Brandeis article, the doors of the legal sausage factory have been opened wide by overt, "scientific" lawmaking, and the public has not enjoyed the view one bit. Such is the exorbitant price of maturity.

17

NATIONALIZING AMERICAN JUSTICE

(The Due Process Clause)

Our dual form of government has its perplexities.
JUSTICE JOSEPH McKENNA

When Lizzie Borden went to trial for the ax murder of her father and stepmother in Fall River, Massachusetts, in 1892, it was a civilized affair. The five lawyers who participated (three for the defendant and two for the prosecution) were refined, highly skilled professionals, and the three judges who presided were courteous and well-grounded in the law. The examinations of witnesses and arguments of counsel were artful and occasionally artistic. The local citizens, for their part, seemed remarkably unperturbed that their little town had produced the crime of the century. They provided Lizzie with a calm, thoughtful jury that actually acquitted her, and a crowd of townspeople greeted her with a sporting "tempest of applause" when she emerged victorious from the courthouse.

Lizzie's constitutional rights were protected throughout the trial with a tenderness that would have made Earl Warren proud. Indeed, she was afforded one crucial protection that the U.S. Supreme Court itself did not apply for another seventy-four years. She had appeared as a witness at the coroner's inquest and had more or less testified herself into prison. In describing her whereabouts in the Borden house at the time of the murders, she had contradicted herself and then contradicted the contradictions. If her prosecutors had been allowed to offer her inquest testimony at the criminal trial, her conviction would have been virtually assured; but miraculously, her lawyers prevented its use, arguing that it had been obtained in violation of her constitutional rights, because she had not been represented by counsel when she gave it, or warned that it might later be used against her.

When the U.S. Supreme Court applied a similar rule to pretrial interrogation in *Miranda* v. *Arizona* in 1966, the country almost expired in apoplexy. When it was applied in Lizzie's case, Chief Prosecutor Josiah Knowlton merely sighed and shrugged, and the sophisticated spectators merely nodded. They knew due process of law when they saw it.

Nineteenth-century justice was a bit rougher in other parts of the republic. When settlers left the East and traveled into the emptiness of the American continent, they entered a state of nature. They were farmers and herders, not lawyers, and they thought of law as self-defense and self-defense as law. The practice of "taking the law into your own hands" was romanticized as an expression of the democratic spirit, but it was more a matter of mundane practicality. The prevailing down-home legal "philosophy" was well expressed in a Golden, Colorado, newspaper account of an 1879 lynching: "The popular verdict seemed to be that the hanging was not only well-merited, but a positive gain for the county, saving at least five or six thousand dollars."

Lynch mobs tended to make mistakes, of course. A man would be hanged for a crime, and damned if it wouldn't later turn out that someone else had done it. Such things were regrettable, but violence was too much of an everyday reality and swift justice too valuable a commodity for folks to brood over hanging a few thugs and drifters for the wrong crimes. "The safety of the people is above any law," is how a San Francisco newspaper put it, and most people agreed.

The quality of justice practiced in Western courtrooms was often only slightly more refined than the lynchings. While that learned trio of jurists was presiding punctiliously over the Borden trial in Massachusetts, Judge Isaac Parker was running roughshod over the Bill of Rights, doing what "he had to do" in the District Court for Western Arkansas. He, not the unjustly maligned Charles Lynch, was America's true hanging judge. During his tenure on the bench, he condemned no fewer than seventy-nine defendants to death in the sparsely settled territory over which he reigned. Many of them probably deserved their fates but, given the crudeness of the process which visited it upon them, *how* many will never be known.[1]

Southern lynch law was, of course, the worst of all. It did not have the excuse of necessity, and because its perpetrators knew in some unadmitted way that their conduct was unjust, they acted—as such people always do—with double ferocity. Their homemade justice filled no legal vacuum. It subverted and supplanted existing legal institutions, ostensibly because they dealt with newly emancipated Negroes inefficiently, but in reality for the pleasure of punishing a powerless people who symbolized the humiliation the South had suffered.

Lynch law tended to be cloaked in sanctimony. When four Columbia, South Carolina, Negroes were lynched on suspicion of murder in 1876, the *Daily Register* waxed poetically indignant in support of the atrocity: "Civilization is in banishment, a thing apart, cowering in a corner. . . . There is a need for the equity of Judge Lynch." Things got worse before they got better. Between 1888 and 1903—the same period in which Easterners were being edified and enthralled by the nuances of that gentile courtroom joust in Fall River, Massachusetts—241 Negro citizens were subjected to such poetic justice, some by burning, some by drowning, some by beating, but most by a good piece of hemp over the bough of a tree.

At the end of the nineteenth century, the quality of justice in America was, to say the least, uneven. The definition of due process depended, as always, on who you were, but even more on *where* you were. This would have to change. As the new century dawned, it was time to begin the nationalization of justice—time to spread a unitary peace upon the land.

The catalyst was the murder prosecution of Leo Frank. Frank was a Northern-born and -educated Jew who was employed as the manager of the National Pencil Company in Atlanta, Georgia. He was working in his office on Saturday, April 26, 1913, when thirteen-year-old Mary Phagan dropped by to collect $1.20 in wages due her. The next day, her strangled body was found in the basement of the factory with a cord around her neck.

Two people knew how she had died: her killer, a twenty-seven-year-old Negro named Jim Conley who worked in the factory as a sweeper, and a fourteen-year-old named Alonzo Mann, who was employed there as an office boy. Lonnie Mann had a terrifying encounter with Conley on the main floor of the factory on that Saturday, which might have had a large effect on American legal history if he had been a little braver. The stocky Negro was on his way to the basement, carrying an unconscious but still alive Mary in his arms. He stopped and glared at the boy for a full ten seconds before muttering drunkenly, "If you ever mention this, I'll kill you." Lonnie never did—until it was far too late.

Both Frank and Conley were questioned vigorously by police. As so often happens, the guilty man accused the innocent one who, being moral, did not retaliate, and justice turned upon itself. Lonnie Mann lost his chance to avert a great injustice through fear of the dark forces that were gathering around him. On the advice of his frightened mother, he "kept quiet" about his knowledge of the crime, answering only the innocuous general questions the authorities asked him about his whereabouts on April 26.

What followed can be compared to the popular eruptions that fueled the Salem witch trials. As described in a letter written thirty years later by Mary Phagan's own pastor, Reverend L. O. Bricker:

> When the police arrested a Jew, and a Yankee Jew at that, all of the inborn prejudice against the Jews rose up in a feeling of satisfaction, that here would be a victim worthy to pay for the crime. From that day on, the newspapers were filled with the most awful stories, affidavits, and testimonies, which proved the guilt of Leo M. Frank beyond a shadow of a doubt.
>
> The police got prostitutes and criminals, on whom they had something, to swear anything and everything they wanted them to swear to. In reading these stories in the paper day by day, there was no doubt left in the mind of the general public but that Frank was guilty. And the whole city was in a frenzy. We were all mad crazy, and in a blood frenzy. Frank was brought to trial in mob spirit. One could feel the waves of madness which swept us all.[2]

The fragile shell of liberalism Georgia had acquired in the first decade of the century shattered with the *Frank* case, and the poisoned flood of bigotry poured forth again.

The evidence against Frank was pathetically weak and palpably false, but that was the least of the injustice. What removed the trial from the realm of due process were the mobs that dominated it. They filled the streets, choked the halls, and overflowed the courtroom. They formed an ugly Greek chorus as the trial proceeded applauding the prosecutors, jeering and laughing at the defense, and muttering at any suggestion that their reactions threatened the fairness of the proceedings. Their power was demonstrated at the outset, when the defense requested that the courtroom be cleared so that judge and jury would not be intimidated by their presence. Already intimidated, Judge L. S. Roan rejected the request, let the hostile mob stay, and doomed Leo Frank.

When the evidence was all presented and final arguments had been made, Frank's lawyers made a last hopeless stab at justice, moving for a new trial on the ground that the "disgraceful" conduct of the courtroom spectators and the shouting and ovations of giant crowds in the streets had made it psychologically impossible for the jurors to render an honest verdict. The lawyer who argued the motion noted that his point was being proved even as he spoke: "Why, Your Honor! You can't even keep them quiet now, here in the courtroom." Judge Roan stated he would "certify" to that but denied the motion nonetheless.

By agreement with defense counsel, Judge Roan then entered an extraordinary order requiring that Frank be absent from the courtroom when the jury announced its verdict. The concern was that the spectators might kill or injure him in the unlikely event of an acquittal. Presumably, the jurors would have to fend for themselves.

After the conviction was returned and the death sentence imposed, Frank's lawyers filed an appeal citing 103 errors in the record, most of which boiled down to the fact that Frank had been convicted by a mob. In affirming the conviction, the Georgia Supreme Court reacted to the horrendous trial conditions as though a few guests had belched at a dinner party. "The *applause* of the spectators," the court stated, "is but an irregularity not calculated to be substantially harmful to the defendant."

Frank's lawyers then filed a writ of *habeas corpus* in the U.S. district court, asserting that the state of Georgia had denied Frank due process of law as guaranteed by the Fourteenth Amendment to the U.S. Constitution because it had convicted and sentenced him under circumstances in which no actual trial could be conducted.

The mob domination of the trial proceedings, his lawyers argued, had been so complete and continuous as to effectively deprive the trial court of jurisdiction over the case. The district court denied the petition without even allowing Frank to present evidence that the facts stated in it were true.

When the case reached the U.S. Supreme Court, American justice had arrived at an important crossroads. The issue was not whether Frank had in fact been denied due process of law, but the far more profound issue of whether he was *entitled to present evidence in federal court* that he had been denied due process. The answer to that question would determine whether there would be a uniform national standard of justice, and ultimately whether the Bill of Rights would have significant meaning across the land.

The nine justices who reviewed Frank's conviction stood at this vital crossroads for an instant of history—and then seven of them wandered off in the wrong direction.

The second most important question to ask about a legal system is, What is the law? The most important question is, How is the law applied? The precise definition of first-degree murder is less important to the rights of an accused, for example, than the requirement that it be proven beyond a reasonable doubt before a jury of his peers.

In Frank's case, there was no definitional problem. The entire Court agreed that if a mob had in fact dominated the trial, intimidating judge, jurors, and witnesses, a due process violation *would have* taken place and Frank *would be* entitled to a new trial. They split over an apparently mundane, but actually immense, issue of procedure: In determining whether a due process violation had taken place, who was to determine the facts—the state court system, which was accused of the violation, or the federal court system, which had been asked to redress it?

As Supreme Court Justice Charles Evans Hughes put it some years later, "Let me find the facts, and I care little who lays down the general principles."[3] The power to find facts is the power to decide cases. The evidence presented at trials and hearings is perceived subjectively, and therefore differently, by different observers. Judge Jerome Frank believed that it was "misleading to talk . . . of a trial court 'finding' facts at all." More accurately, he said, facts "are processed by the trial court—are, so to speak, made by it, on the basis of its subjective reactions to witnesses' stories."[4] A federal judge who accepts the factual findings of his state court brethren in a habeas corpus case, therefore, has largely abdicated his power to decide. There can be no federal justice without federal fact-finding.

Achieving the intellectual equivalent of making water run up-hill, Justice Mahlon Pitney's majority opinion nonetheless said that there could be—and there was: "We hold that . . . a determination of the facts as thus made by the court of last resort of Georgia respecting the alleged disorder and manifestations of hostile sentiment cannot, in this collateral inquiry, be treated as a nullity, but must be taken as setting forth the truth of the matter." Thus, Leo Frank was stuck with the "truth" of the Georgia Supreme Court's finding that the mob dominance of his trial actually consisted of "an irregularity not calculated to be substantially harmful to the defendant."

Although the Constitution required states to assure defendants due process of law, according to Pitney, federal courts were required to accept the assurances of state courts that they had done so. In the words of an old Georgia saying, Pitney had "put the fox in charge of the henhouse." In doing so, he had gutted the federal due process clause and ensured the continuation of regional standards of justice in America.

The road chosen by dissenting justices Oliver Wendell Holmes and Charles Evans Hughes was harder to travel but promised to lead to better justice for America. Holmes and Hughes saw that there could be no federal due process without federal fact-finding and, more specifically, that the *Frank* trial record fairly screamed out for independent factual review. Holmes could not muster a majority of the Court's votes, but his words would be heard in the land and would set the Court on the proper path in years to come. "Mob law does not become due process of law by securing the assent of a terrorized jury," he wrote.

We are not speaking of mere disorder, or mere irregularities in procedure, but of a case where the processes of justice were actually subverted.

If the trial and the later hearing before the Supreme Court had taken place in the presence of an armed force known to be ready to shoot if the result was not the one desired, we do not suppose that this Court would allow itself to be silenced by the suggestion that the record showed no flaw. . . .

When we find the judgment of the expert on the spot—of the judge whose business it was to preserve not only form, but substance—to have been that if one juryman yielded to the reasonable doubt that he himself later expressed in court as the result of most anxious deliberation, neither prisoner nor counsel would be safe from the rage of the crowd, we think the presumption overwhelming that the jury responded to the passions of the mob. . . .

[I]t is our duty . . . to declare lynch law as little valid when practiced by a regularly drawn jury as when administered by one elected by a mob intent on death.

Holmes's reference to a "mob intent on death" turned out to be hideously prophetic. On June 21, 1915, two months after the Supreme Court confirmed Frank's death sentence, Georgia governor John Slayton commuted it to a term of life in prison. "It may mean death or worse," he told his wife—and it very nearly did. Small armies of armed thugs surrounded the governor's mansion, carrying placards saying, "Slayton, King of the Jews," and threatening the governor with death, but state police managed to drive them off.

The lawless element then turned its attention back to Frank. After the commutation was announced, a group of about seventy-five men calling themselves the Knights of Mary Phagan met at her grave and swore to avenge her death. On August 16, 1915, they invaded the prison farm at Milledgeville, Georgia, dragged Frank from his bed, threw him into the backseat of a car in handcuffs, and drove him to Marietta, Georgia. He was taken from the car in an oak grove near Mary's home, butchered, and hanged from a tree with his face turned toward the Phagan house.

According to one newspaper account, the vengeful mob "seemed to rise up out of the ground" at the site of the lynching. There were a number of women in the crowd, some with babies in their arms. Several of them turned their heads away upon seeing the frail, dangling corpse with the "red gaping wound" in its neck, but many stared at it in apparent satisfaction. A gaunt, wild-eyed lunatic began to scream that the corpse should be burned, but a stocky former judge named Newton Morris prevented this final atrocity. After quieting the crowd, he said, "God bless whoever did this, but we must concede that he has left us nothing to do." He reminded them that Frank had a mother and was entitled to a burial, and then asked for a show of hands as to whether the corpse should be surrendered to an undertaker. Only the lunatic dissented—ranting that the Jew should be reduced to pieces "no bigger than a cigar."[5]

In 1923, a quiet rerun of the *Frank* case was conducted before the U.S. Supreme Court. Five Arkansas Negroes had been convicted and sentenced to death in a trial attended by "an adverse crowd" that "threatened the most dangerous consequences to anyone interfering with the desired result." The condemned prisoners' lawyers filed a federal habeas corpus petition, making the same argument Frank's lawyers had made without success eight years earlier: that mob dominance had prevented an actual trial from taking place, thus depriving the defendants of due process of law under the Fourteenth Amendment. Following the precedent of the *Frank* decision, the federal district judge had dismissed the complaint without hearing evidence, noting that the Arkansas state courts had made factual findings that validated the trial.

The Supreme Court reversed, in a unanimous opinion authored by—Justice Oliver Wendell Holmes. Much troubled water had flowed over the dam of American public opinion in the previous eight years, and the justices—many of whom had been elevated to the Court after the *Frank* decision—felt the pressure of it. Making no reference at all to Pitney's abject deference to state factual findings in the *Frank* case, Holmes's opinion rejected the prosecutors' reliance on it out of hand, blandly stating: "We shall not say more concerning the corrective process afforded to the petitioners than that it does not seem to us sufficient to allow a judge of the United States to escape the duty of examining facts for himself, when, if true, as alleged, they make the trial absolutely void." One would never have guessed that the same Court had sealed the fate of another human being by an exactly contrary statement only a few years previously.

* * *

The revolution that was to make America a truly constitutional nation was thus quietly begun. Requiring federal determination of the facts of due process violations was the vital first step. Next came the systematic incorporation of the Bill of Rights provisions into the concept of "due process." When the due process clauses were first incorporated into the Constitution in the eighteenth and nineteenth centuries, "process" meant "process." The clauses were held to guarantee defendants procedural rights—grand jury indictment, jury trial, and so on—but had nothing to do with the substance of the law. In the twentieth century, however, it began to be argued that there was such a thing as "substantive due process," which included basic constitutional freedoms. After some initial resistance, the Supreme Court finally began to accept these arguments, eventually holding that "due process" includes all rights and freedoms that are "implicit in the concept of ordered liberty."

In 1925, the Court decided that "due process" included the First Amendment guarantee of freedom of speech. This meant that federal courts could require the states to grant freedom of speech to their citizens by invoking the due process clause. Most of the other Bill of Rights provisions—freedom of religion, the right to counsel, the prohibition against unreasonable searches and seizures, the right to jury trial, the privilege against self-incrimination, and the prohibition of cruel and unusual punishments—eventually followed. By the early 1960s, criminal justice standards had become truly national. Insofar as the courts could ensure it, a Lizzie Borden would have received as fair a trial in western Arkansas as in Fall River, Massachusetts.

In 1982, Lonnie Mann finally revealed his dread secret. In an interview with two reporters for Nashville's morning newspaper, *The Tennessean,* he told what he knew about the murder of Mary Phagan and the innocence of Leo Frank. On March 11, 1986, the Georgia parole board granted Frank a posthumous pardon. It was a commendable action, but no believer in the rule of law could take much satisfaction in it—all things considered.

* * *

In a 1990 statement to Congress, Chief Judge Gilbert Merritt of the Sixth Circuit Court of Appeals broke some grim news. "In *habeas corpus* cases," he said, "the Bill of Rights is now a relic to be encased in its present shroud and frozen in time, no longer a living document to be applied to new situations."

The judge was referring to the Supreme Court's decision in *Teague* v. *Lane,* which had been announced the previous year. Teague was a black Alabamian who had been convicted of attempted murder, robbery, and aggravated assault. The prosecutor had systematically used all ten of his peremptory challenges to exclude blacks from the jury panel, and Teague had been convicted by an all-white jury. Several years later he had filed a habeas corpus petition from his jail cell, alleging that the systematic exclusion of jurors of his own race had violated his constitutional right to equal protection of the law. When the case came before the Supreme Court, the justices (a) agreed that Teague's rights had indeed been violated, but (b) noted that they had not been violated according to the law in existence at the time of his conviction, and therefore (c) denied him a retrial.

Henceforth, said the Court, defendants in habeas corpus cases will not be given the benefit of new principles of constitutional law, or of expansions of existing principles. Their rights will be determined strictly by the law on the books at the time of their convictions. Enhancements in constitutional rights that subsequently occur will not be "retroactively" applied to their cases on writ of habeas corpus.

Merritt's response to the new rule was unambiguous. "We cannot live with *Teague,*" he said.

The effect of *Teague* on the proper functioning of Merritt's court and all other federal courts was indeed devastating, if not quite terminal. States are the great laboratories for defining and evolving due process. State criminal prosecutions outnumber federal prosecutions many times over, and injustice, in all of its infinite variety, is most predominately represented there. The federal courts review the due process validity of state convictions by only two procedures. One is the relatively rare grant of discretionary review, or writ of certiorari, issued directly from the U.S. Supreme Court to the state court involved. The other is by writ of habeas corpus, in which the entire federal judicial system, from district courts to courts of appeals to the Supreme Court, participates. By eliminating the role of federal habeas corpus in the evolution of due process principles, *Teague* cut a major sinew in the musculature of American justice. The federal courts may literally be able to "live with it," but they have been severely crippled.

Worse was *Teague*'s effect on Teague himself, and on all the other Teagues who will come after him. For, what the High Court had said to Citizen Teague was something no American citizen should ever have to hear from any court: *We know you are being punished in fundamental violation of the United States Constitution, but we nonetheless turn our backs on you and leave you to your fate.* From Thomas More to Sacco and Vanzetti, English and American courts had administered their share of rank injustice, but this particular dose had an especially vile taste. For a court to deny the existence of a patent wrong is bad—and common—enough, but to acknowledge wrong and refuse to remedy it is close to judicial nihilism. A court that could, but will not, relieve a perceived injustice is, to common sense, like a surgeon who will not remove an operable cancer or a soldier who will not attack a vulnerable enemy.

The Court justified its decision by what it thought was obvious logic. Since habeas corpus petitions attack the validity of convictions, Justice Sandra Day O'Connor's opinion said, they must logically rely upon the law that existed at the time of conviction. A defendant cannot logically claim that he was unconstitutionally convicted if the conviction was valid according to the law that existed at the time it was entered.

But when the Supreme Court said that Teague had been denied equal protection of the law by the systematic exclusion of blacks from his jury panel, it was not inventing a right. It was *detecting* a right that had been withheld from him because it had not been recognized at the time he appealed his conviction. To deny him the belated benefit of that right, on writ of habeas corpus, because of previous judicial obtuseness, was to make a game of due process and a viciously *illogical* one.

The true source of the *Teague* rule is to be found not in considerations of common justice, or even in law books, but in newspapers and television news reports. Everyone, not excluding Supreme Court justices, knows that "the public" is "fed up" with the "inefficient, slovenly, ineffective" mechanisms of criminal justice, and probably most of all, with the "unforgivable procrastinations" of a habeas corpus process that leaves condemnees on death row for decades, watching television.

Something must be done, it is said, to assuage this public disquiet, and *Teague* was part of that something. If constitutional rights could be frozen at the moment of final judgment, the endless clamor for posttrial justice might be reduced. Would such a rule destroy the hopes of a few individuals seeking deserved constitutional relief? Would it give the lie to the Court's essential function of doing justice case by case? Never mind, both the harm and the abdication of function would be trivial compared to the countervailing interests of "the people."

We have seen all this before, many times. Defendants have no constituencies but courts, and when the public heat turns up, courts melt—just a bit, just around the edges—and then later melt some more. The Bill of Rights principles are for the protection of individuals and minorities, but they are applied by judges who hear the majority's angry voices, loud and clear.

The popular pressures that produced the *Teague* rule were different only in intensity and proximity from those that doomed poor Leo Frank. And the placid legalisms of Justice O'Connor's opinion were a disturbing distant echo of Justice Pitney's tranquil prose.

The wheel had turned a half turn back again, and Justice Holmes was gone.

18

THE RIGHT TO COUNSEL

What defending counsel learns . . . is to refrain from judgment.
There are plenty of people whose business it is to perform that
unpleasant function. Judges, juries and, perhaps, God.

JOHN MORTIMER

There was a little best-seller out a few years ago called *Lawyer Abuse and Other Good Ideas*. The author had previously written *One Hundred and One Uses for a Dead Cat*. The appeal of the two books was similar, except that no one actually hates dead cats. The animosity toward lawyers, on the other hand, is both sincere and specific—*Doctor Abuse and Other Good Ideas* would not get laughs. It is more than the arrogance and the money. It is the perception of moral flexibility, as conveyed in the frequent cocktail party comment "You guys will represent *anybody*." Well, isn't that what we are *supposed* to do?

Not that lawyers don't richly deserve criticism. There are plenty of slobs and rhinos out there who use their law licenses as permits to dump garbage on people and to defeat justice by sleazy maneuvering. But they are not the root of the problem. What truly rouses the public to fury is not the outrageous excesses but the logic of the job itself. The irony is that, where criminal defense lawyers are concerned, the public sees as bad that which is good and positively despises that which is superb.

* * *

He had a full black moustache, and was quite handsome in a foreign sort of way. When he walked into the mobbed courtroom on the morning of November 9, 1942, one of the spectators asked a friend who he was. "I believe he represents the German government," she said. He conducted his case during the morning session with the practiced grace of a professional, showing signs that he would be brilliant when things got tough. The more sophisticated of the spectators knew him as one of the best and most successful trial lawyers in New York City, and it was clear to them that he intended to earn his fee with the full measure of his talent. As he was returning to the counsel table after the morning recess, a spectator spit in his face.

And no wonder, thought many in the crowd. The day before, Allied troops had begun to reverse the fearful string of defeats they had suffered at the hands of the Germans by invading North Africa en route to a victorious encounter with Rommel's famed tank corps. While brave soldiers were dying on foreign soil to protect freedom, this adroit sleazeball was making big money in comfortable surroundings—defending a German-born national on charges of treason against the United States.

It is hard to fathom such men, the spectators thought. Harold Medina had grown rich and famous on the American way of life, and here he was, giving aid and comfort to its enemies. Either he had been paid a very large fee—under the table by the Third Reich, perhaps—or he was a closet Nazi sympathizer. In either case, he was reprehensible.

Medina had not sought out his client Anthony Cramer, and was, in fact, paid nothing for representing him. District Judge Henry Goddard had asked him to defend the penniless and despised man without fee, "as a patriotic duty." "Of course, I accepted," Medina later said. "It was just wonderful to be in there pitching for justice, without any thought of fee and without the prospect of any benefit to myself."

He soon realized that he had been handed no bouquet of roses. "[P]eople in general and my friends in particular . . . began to treat me with a certain coolness," he said, and "when we actually got on trial, this hostile attitude became more pronounced. The general public which thronged into the courtroom every day of the trial indicated to us very plainly that they thought perhaps we were in some way involved."

Cramer was accused of giving traitorous assistance to eight German spies who had been arrested in New York City and Chicago in June 1942. All eight had been convicted, and six of them had been put to death. Cramer had been charged with "aiding and harboring" two of the spies.

The trial testimony showed that one of the spies had been a friend of Cramer's when he had lived in Germany several years previously. The men had looked Cramer up after reaching America and had met with him several times in public places. Cramer testified that he did not know his friend was in America to commit acts of espionage. It had been his impression, he said, that he had come merely "to spread stories and spread rumors to create unrest."

It was never entirely clear what Cramer was supposed to have done to aid and harbor his friend, other than fail to turn him in to the authorities. The two old friends had talked, of course, but not secretly and not about anything that might have facilitated espionage.

A remarkable incident occurred in the courtroom after final arguments to the jury had been completed. The judge turned to Medina and expressed his heartfelt thanks to him "for having accepted the assignment by the Court to represent this defendant." Medina's neck reddened: The well-meaning judge had thoughtlessly implied that the defense lawyer was not "for" his client. He had made it appear that Medina was an involuntary champion, who had been commandeered to defend an outcast and was only doing what he had to do. Medina was barely able to control his anger. "I do not think the jury should have been told that," he scolded Judge Goddard. "I have tried to keep it from them myself, and I have not mentioned it." The startled Goddard could only blink and say he did not think that "any harm had been done."

Something had obviously done harm. The jury returned with a conviction after considering the flimsy evidence for only two hours. The prosecutor vigorously argued for the death penalty, but Judge Goddard demonstrated that the quality of mercy was only somewhat strained in wartime America by sentencing Cramer to forty-five years in the Atlanta penitentiary.

Three years later, Medina appeared for his client before the U.S. Supreme Court and got the conviction reversed on the ground that there was no evidence that Cramer had engaged in treasonous acts. The Court held there was "no showing that Cramer gave [the spies] any information whatever of value to their mission or indeed that he had any to give." The author of the opinion that freed Cramer was none other than Justice Robert Jackson, who later served as the chief Allied prosecutor at the Nazi war crimes trials in Nuremberg, Germany. Interestingly, no one seems to have questioned *his* patriotism in the affair.

There was a close historical precedent for Harold Medina's defense of Anthony Cramer. One hundred and seventy-two years earlier, a prominent Boston lawyer had defended eight British soldiers on charges that they had murdered five American citizens in cold blood. Great Britain and America were virtually at war at the time, and soon would actually be at war. The lawyer had defended his foreign clients with what many thought was excessive zeal, calling his slain countrymen part of "a motley rabble of saucy boys, Negroes and Mulattos, Irish Teagues and outlandish Jacktars" who had essentially deserved what they had gotten. He had parlayed his skill as an advocate and his personal popularity into verdicts of acquittal for six of his clients, and of manslaughter rather than murder for the other two.

Many Bostonians were outraged at his lack of patriotism. The backlash was, in fact, so strong that the ambitious young man retired from public life three years later. The harm was not permanent, however: John Adams eventually became the second president of the United States.

Adams had agreed to accept representation of the "Boston Massacre" defendants, with the assistance of young Josiah Quincy, because no other experienced lawyer would. "The bar seems to me," he said, "to behave like a flock of shot pigeons. The net seems to be thrown over them, and they have scarcely courage left to flounce and flutter."

Unlike Medina, Adams did not go uncompensated for his efforts. He received the princely sum of nineteen guineas—about one week's wages for a working man—for his prodigious efforts and for the personal and political pain he endured. "At this time," he later wrote, "I had more business at the bar than any man in the Province. My health was feeble; I was throwing away as bright prospects as any man ever had before him and . . . devoted myself to endless labor and anxiety, if not to infamy and death, and that for nothing, except, what indeed was and ought to be in all, a sense of duty."

His countrymen hated him for his sacrifice. When he got up to make his final argument to the jury, he could feel the hostility of the courtroom crowd on his back and could hear it in their muttered grumblings. "I am for the prisoners of the bar," he began, "and shall apologize for it only in the words of the Marquis Beccaria: 'If I can but be the instrument of preserving one life, his blessing and tears of transport shall be a sufficient consolation to me for the contempt of all mankind.' "

According to Page Smith, "Blessings and tears of transport" were both conferred. After the verdicts of not guilty and manslaughter were returned, "the men crowded about [Adams], some weeping openly to express their gratitude. Rough, simple men, most of them little more than boys, they hardly understood the nature of the ordeal through which they had passed, but they were convinced that they owed their lives to the two Colonial lawyers who had defended them so ably."

As previously noted, Adams's fellow Americans were—less impressed.

Always a tiny, generally despised minority in any age, defense lawyers have unusual psychological makeups. They take special pride in being warriors for the underdog, the despised, and—yes—the probably guilty. They are peculiarly constructed to believe that there is more of truth in honest doubt and second chances than in all the judgments sanctimonious mankind can impose.

Where on earth did this peculiar species come from?

In the formative period of the English legal system, there was no need for—or possibility of—defense lawyers. Trials were personal, physical tests of the accused. The defendant might be taken before a church congregation, to have his hands blistered by boiling water or hot iron, his guilt or innocence to be determined by whether the burns festered or healed after three days. Such trials by ordeal were matters between the accused, his God, and his king. Retaining a lawyer to assist would have made as little sense as employing a consultant for a baptism.

The same was true of trial by battle, which was imported by William the Conqueror when he took the English throne in 1066. Like the ordeals, this hideous innovation was a physical test of unaided defendants. In noncriminal cases defendants were eventually allowed to hire champions to fight for them, but not so accused criminals. They were required to face their armed and mounted accusers—often hired killers who were working off their own debts to society—personally and alone. There were elaborate preliminary pleadings, but once the issue was joined and battle loomed, the method of establishing guilt became simple: "If the [defendant] is defeated before the stars come out, he is hanged." As with the ordeals, God was imposing judgment on a wrongdoer who had been weakened by his own guilt. Expert defensive help was limited to the smith and the stable boy.

By the middle of the thirteenth century, trials had become nonphysical, rational investigations of the facts, in which men were making the decisions rather than relying on God to do so. The rationality and complexity of the trial process were beginning to make expert legal advice necessary, but it continued to be forbidden at least in serious cases. One hundred and fifty years earlier, a compilation of English law called *Leges Henrici* (*Laws of Henry I*) had stated that in felony cases "the accused is allowed no counsel but must answer at once," and that ancient rule still prevailed. Strangely, in cases of less serious crimes and in noncriminal cases, the defendant could have the advice of counsel.

The curious prohibition against defense counsel in felony cases remained in effect in England until 1836. In the intervening centuries, countless prisoners stood friendless in court, tricked and hounded by prosecutors, bullied by judges, confused by the rules, and overwhelmed by the alien environment in which they found themselves. Elaborate justifications were invented for denying them professional assistance, but the actual reasons were sheer inertia and conservatism. The system stubbornly clung to the image of a criminal trial as an individual performance test, like an ordeal or a joust.

The idea of providing *some* assistance to helpless defendants was, nonetheless, entertained in a few isolated instances over the years. In 1303, a knight named Hugo was accused of rape and brought before the king's court for jury trial. He brought his friends Brian and Nicholas with him to act as counsel. The justice told Brian and Nicholas to "stand back as the prisoner may have no counsel against the King."

Hugo was then launched solo into a procedural quagmire. "How do you say against the charge," asked the justice. "I am a clerk [and entitled to benefit of clergy]," responded Hugo. "But," said the justice, "you married a widow, are therefore a bigamist and have therefore lost your [benefit of clergy] privilege." Hugo denied this, and the justice asked the jurors whether it was true. They said that Hugo had not married a widow and was not a bigamist.

As the process moved on, Hugo ungratefully objected to having these same jurors decide his case because he was a knight and they were of a lower rank. The court agreed to hear specific name-by-name juror challenges. Hugo said that he could not read and needed the assistance of counsel. The justice wondered aloud how Hugo could claim benefit of clergy if he could not read but granted the request to the extent of allowing him to be prompted by a person who could read. With this limited "assistance of counsel," Hugo prevailed in his challenges and was ultimately acquitted.

This obscure man had made a tiny crack in a great wall of prohibition: He had obtained *some* advisory assistance in a felony case. It was severely limited, but it was exactly the assistance he required. The judge allowed it because he recognized that Hugo was completely disabled from conducting part of his defense. Over the centuries, as criminal trials became progressively sophisticated, the helplessness of the unaided defendant became ever more apparent, until even the most loutish judges began to see it. But the process of recognition was slow.

In 1518, an eminent barrister named Christopher St. Germain published a book called *Doctor and Student,* which discussed points of English law in dialogue form. One of the tougher questions asked by "Student" was this:

How the law of England may be said reasonable, that prohibits them that be arraigned upon an indictment of felony or murder to have counsel.

"Doctor" gave an astonishing answer. The defendant, it seemed, had a friend in court—namely, the judge—who provided all the counsel he needed:

> The law is as thou sayest, that he shall have no counsel: but then the law is further, that in all things that pertain to the order of pleading, the judges shall so instruct him and order him, that he shall run into no jeopardy by his mispleading.

English judges had been called many names behind their backs, but counsel for the defendant had seldom been one of them. Whatever they gave defendants by way of technical advice, they more than took away with their bullying efforts to secure convictions. The pro-prosecution tactics of judges were, in fact, one of the main reasons the absence of defense counsel was so crippling to defendants.

In 1590, a Puritan preacher named John Udall was put to trial for publishing a blasphemous pamphlet. The crosscurrents of public emotions aroused by the case made the selection of the jury crucial, and the prisoner was naturally unfamiliar with the rules of jury selection. He tested "Doctor's" counsel for the defendant theory by asking the presiding judge, Baron Clarke, how many jurors he was entitled to challenge and get rid of. "Nay," replied the judge pleasantly, "I am not to tell you that: I sit to judge, and not to give you counsel."

By the end of the sixteenth century, criminal assize courts had been conducted in the outlying counties of England for more than 250 years, but they had made little progress in their mode of dispensing justice over that quarter of a millennium. The visiting judges put the contents of the local jail to trial, crowding as many cases into as little time as possible, and then moved on to the next stop on their circuits. The assizes were mainly poor peoples' courts, where the dirtiest laundry of British society was washed. They did the bulk of England's day-to-day criminal trial business.

The courtrooms were crowded, dilapidated, sometimes physically dangerous places. The trials were verbal free-for-alls, featuring heated exchanges between prisoner and prosecutor that focused sharply on the points at issue. The judges occasionally intervened, usually on the side of the prosecution, like truculent bartenders breaking up an argument between two drunks.

There was almost no limit to what could be said on either side, as a matter of fact or argument, but defense lawyers were still nowhere to be seen. Even if there had been no legal prohibition, there would probably still be few of them. First, there was the matter of money. Few of this class of defendants had any, and we know how quickly that can empty a courtroom full of lawyers. In any event, trial lawyers in the modern sense would have functioned poorly in this pell-mell process. The law was still conducting ordeals, albeit verbal ones, and there was no place—or time—for set theater pieces produced and directed by legal professionals.

What lawyers were especially needed for was advice and argument in attacking the wording of indictments. Grammatical purity in stating charges was the one procedural protection offered defendants, but a man must know what he was looking for. A good lawyer could have gotten an additional 20 percent of the defendants off on grammar alone, but this possibility was unknown to most of the rough and ignorant defendants, and beyond their economic reach in any case.

On very rare occasions, the potential for injustice was strong enough, or the judge softhearted enough, to produce an exception to the prohibition against counsel. In 1633, a Hampshire man was indicted in a particularly emotional murder case and outlawed when he attempted to flee. Chief Justice Richardson appointed not one but two counsel to advise him. In 1636, Chief Justice Finch went Richardson two better, assigning the *four* most eminent junior barristers on the western circuit to advise a poor woman accused of witchcraft. Why four for her and none for others charged with capital crimes? No one could say, but such whimsicality made the general prohibition against counsel seem even more unjust.

Early America's "blessings of liberty" definitely did *not* include the assistance of professional counsel. The issue seldom came up because, basically, there were no lawyers. Virginia and Connecticut had statutes that barred them from courtrooms, and Massachusetts and the Carolinas achieved the same result by prohibiting the payment of legal fees. The colonists were not shy about expressing the feelings behind these enactments. The Carolina Constitution said that it was a "base and vile thing to plead for money or reward," and in Massachusetts they called the practice of law "a dark and knavish business."

The general colonial attitude was summed up in a seventeenth-century account of life in Pennsylvania: "They have no lawyers. Everyone is to tell his own case, or some friend for him. . . . Tis a happy country." It was not clear whether this happiness was shared by those who were convicted and punished because of their own legal ineptitude.

The Massachusetts Bodie of Liberties of 1641 provided the first Anglo-American authorization of defense counsel in *all* criminal cases. There was an all-important hitch, however—the counsel could not be paid:

> 26. Every man that findeth himselfe unfit to plead his owne cause in any Court shall have Liberty to employ any man against whom the Court doth not except, to help him, Provided he give him no fee or reward for his paines.

This provision represented a step forward—if it had been in effect 338 years earlier, Brian and Nicholas could have helped Hugo in his rape case—but, on the face of it, it was hardly rampant progress. How effective, after all, was amateur assistance against the entrenched machinery of the state?

In 1688, England experienced the Glorious Revolution as the despotic James II was displaced by the liberal William and Mary. The horrors of the Popish Plot cases, and the subsequent Bloody Assizes, had produced momentum for reform. Laws were enacted giving some scattered trial rights to defendants, including the right to counsel in treason (but not felony) cases.

Some of the early counsel were understandably reluctant warriors. Being asked to stand up in court with an accused traitor was a little like being asked to join a hunt as an ally of the fox.

Two appointed lawyers named Wallop and Sanders had set the tone in their "defense" of Lord Stafford in a parliamentary treason trial several years previously, making it abundantly clear that they would have preferred to be elsewhere. The presiding judge, Lord Nottingham, had finally been obliged to assure the cowering duo that they were safe from guilt by association. "Speak up," he had commanded, "you have the protection of the counsel you give in matters of law."

The first treason prosecution under the new legislation produced a similarly abject profile in cowardice. An obsequious hack named Bartholomew Shower appeared as counsel on behalf of a defendant named Rockwood. Like Wallop and Sanders, Shower was obviously terrified that the judge would visit the sins of his client upon him. His opening speech was painful to hear.

"My Lord," he began with a deep bow, "we are assigned of counsel in pursuance of an act of Parliament, and we hope that nothing we shall say in defense of our client shall be imputed to ourselves. I thought it would have been a reflection upon the Government and your Lordship's justice if, being assigned, we should have refused to appear. . . . But, my Lord, there can be no reason for . . . fear; I am sure I have none; for we must acknowledge, we who have been practitioners at this bar especially, that there has never been a reign of government within the memory of man, wherein such indulgence, such easiness of temper, hath been shown from the Court to counsel, as there always hath been in this."

The presiding justice, Lord Holt, who *was* a remarkably fair and humane judge looked down at Shower like a housewife inspecting a bug and said sharply, "Look ye, Sir Bartholomew Shower, go on with your objections; let us hear what you have to *say*." Sir Bartholomew said little, and his undoubtedly guilty client was duly sentenced to death.

Such judicial encouragement soon ceased to be necessary, as the new breed of lawyers got the hang of their craft. They learned that defending was safe—even fun—and it became hard to shut them up, much less discourage them. In a 1704 libel prosecution, Sir James Montague appeared as counsel for the defendant, a publisher named John Tutchin. Accurately described as a "low class party scribbler," Tutchin was not the sort of client to give inspiration to his lawyer. He gave Sir James no help at all in preparing his defense, refusing even to communicate with him until the morning of the trial. Sir James nonetheless identified himself completely with his disreputable client, turning Tutchin's recalcitrance into evidence of innocence in a graceful opening speech:

"I can hardly say I am counsel with Mr. Tutchin because I have never seen him [before today]. . . . And he has not thought fit to send us any instructions til this morning, when we were just going down to Westminster. But I do suppose this remissness in his temper does proceed from the innocency of the accusations against him, and he has a mind to let the world see how easy it is to make his defense, since he has pitched upon me for his advocate, and given me so little time to prepare myself for it." The all-out defense advocate had definitely arrived.

The progress was still inch by inch, however. The prohibition against full-service defense counsel in felony cases remained in effect throughout the eighteenth century, although lawyers were allowed to accompany their clients to trial and provide limited assistance. They were given leave to stand close enough to their clients to prompt them, and began to take advantage of this indulgence by sneaking in cross-examinations of prosecution witnesses. By the time felons were officially allowed full representation of counsel in 1836, all of the elements of professional defense were part of English practice except for final argument. The rhetorical excesses of some nineteenth-century lawyers may have caused judges and jurors to question whether legalizing this final element was necessarily a good thing.

Meanwhile, the colonies were excising the old rule more surgically. Being less entangled in history than the English, they were taking the radical approach of doing what seemed sensible. The English justification for denying defense counsel was that "counsel are not needed in felony cases because, in order to convict under English law, the proof must be so clear that no counsel could contend against it." The colonists saw through this veil of sophistry to the stack of judicially murdered corpses behind it. If the proof in English felony cases seemed so clear that "no counsel could contend against it," it was usually because no counsel had been allowed to do so. The English were using the effects of their unfair prohibition of counsel to justify the prohibition itself.

William Penn was particularly unimpressed with this logic. He had experienced the butt end of English justice in his own prosecution for "tumultuous assembly" thirty years earlier, and was resolved that his colony of Pennsylvania would do better. The Pennsylvania Charter of Liberties of 1701 reflected his determination. Its simply worded fifth article commanded that the prosecution and defense in future criminal cases would perform on a level playing field: "All criminals shall have the same privileges of witnesses and council as their prosecutors."

Later in the century other colonies followed suit. By the time the federal Bill of Rights was drafted eighty-eight years later, the right to counsel in all criminal cases was among the least debated of that famous document's scarcely debated provisions.

On November 24, 1778, almost a century after Shower's humiliating debacle, a young English lawyer named Thomas Erskine appeared before the Court of the King's Bench to make his first argument. He was one of several barristers who represented an old sea captain named Thomas Baillie, charged with libeling the earl of Sandwich, the first lord of the admiralty of Britain. He had accused the earl of corruption and favoritism in the provision of medical services in the royal hospital for Superannuated Seamen, at Greenwich.

As he warmed to his task, young Erskine became somewhat overheated in his references to the earl. The presiding judge was Lord Mansfield, the most famous English judge of the era. His Lordship suggested that perhaps young Erskine was being a bit personal in his references, considering that the earl was not before the court.

Without missing a beat, Erskine replied: "I know that he is not formally before the Court, but, for that very reason, I will bring him before the Court!" He then returned to his diatribe with renewed vigor: "I will drag him to light, who is the dark mover behind this scene of iniquity. . . . I assert that, the Earl of Sandwich has but one road to escape out of this business without pollution and disgrace; and that is, by publicly disavowing the acts of the prosecutors, and restoring Captain Baillie to his command."

With the arrival of Erskine and his generation of defense lawyers, the center of gravity of the judicial system had dramatically altered. A new figure had entered the arena, demanding and occupying a place. Nothing so fundamental had occurred to the process of judging guilt and innocence since the arrival of the modern jury system one hundred years earlier.

Nine defendants were charged with a heinous crime that had aroused the community to a fever pitch of anger and hatred. Six days after they were indicted they were arraigned before the court, without counsel. Six days later they were put to trial in bunches of three, still essentially without counsel. The prosecution's proof was met with almost no defensive resistance, and guilty verdicts were returned in each case in less than fifteen minutes. All nine defendants were sentenced to death. Later investigation revealed that the defendants were clearly innocent. They had been convicted by the blatant perjury of a malicious prosecution witness, abetted by the jurors' thirst to punish the defendants as members of a hated class. The perjury might have been exposed by effective cross-examination, but there was none. London, England, 1679? No. Scottsboro, Alabama, 1931.

The Scottsboro defendants were denied effective counsel not because of any legal principle, but simply because no one wanted them to have it. They had been charged with raping two white women on a train from Chattanooga, and it was the vigorously expressed consensus of the community that the Constitution did not apply to such vermin. The nine stumbled through their arraignment without any mention of the present absence of lawyers or the possibility of future ones. On their trial day an alcoholic Chattanooga lawyer named Stephen Roddy appeared in court and went into an Alphonse-Gaston act with a "doddering and senile" Scottsboro lawyer named Milo Moody. Each expressed a willingness to assist the other in defending the cases, but neither expressed a willingness to take the lead: "After you, Mr. Moody." "No, after *you*, Mr. Roddy." With a straight face, the trial judge expressed confidence that effective counsel would emerge from the mishmash and ordered the games to begin. They began, and soon came to their inevitable end.

After the death sentences had been imposed, the Constitution's promise of a right to counsel in criminal cases finally began to be met. The nation's conscience had been pricked by news of the legal lynchings, and some gifted New York lawyers intervened to appeal the Scottsboro convictions. They argued that the convictions were void and without effect because they had been obtained without effective assistance of counsel.

An elderly, conservative Supreme Court listened to this argument in ambiguous silence. The lawyers for the state called up all of the old English ghosts to support their thesis that defense counsel was not a due process necessity, even in a capital case. Counsel were not even *allowed* in English felony cases until 1836, they argued. How can we say that they are *necessary* a mere ninety-five years later? No one prevented these Negroes from hiring lawyers. If they couldn't afford one, that was not the court's fault.

The majority opinion was written by the conservative George Sutherland, who eschewed politics and stated the obvious:

> The right to be heard would be, in many cases, of little avail if it did not comprehend the right to be heard by counsel. Even the intelligent and educated layman has small or sometimes no skill in the science of law. ... [An innocent defendant who is unrepresented] faces the danger of conviction because he does not know how to establish his innocence.

The convictions were reversed.

Unfortunately, this was not a fairy tale with a happy ending. It was a sadder thing called life. Four of the Scottsboro "boys" were tried again, represented by some of the best lawyers in America. And they were convicted again, by jurors determined to exercise *their* right to do injustice.[1] The integrity of the system is, after all, a matter of intent, and the final expression of that intent resides with the people, not the lawyers.

Despite his classy name, Clarence Earl Gideon was a bum, with a lengthy small-time police record to prove it. That record was about to lengthen another notch. The Bar Harbour Pool Hall in Panama City, Florida, had been broken into in the early morning hours of June 3, 1961, and Gideon had committed the age-old crime of being in the vicinity. He was indicted and brought to trial on a charge of breaking and entering a commercial establishment with the intent to commit a misdemeanor. This was a felony charge under Florida law, and Gideon badly needed a lawyer.

He did not get one. The trial judge apologetically informed him that Florida furnished lawyers only to accused murderers. "The Supreme Court says I am entitled to a lawyer," he responded doggedly. It was another case of aggressive ignorance—like old Hugo before him, Clarence Earl simply did not understand the rules and so did not accept them. And because he did not accept them, he eventually changed them.

He did his best to defend himself, but he was Clarence Gideon, not Clarence Darrow. He cross-examined the prosecution witnesses, presented some of his own, and argued his innocence earnestly—although, strangely, he did not testify. He was convicted and sentenced to five years in prison.

His judicial conviction did not erase his moral conviction that he had been deprived of a constitutional right. In his prison cell he composed a short, blunt, pencil-written petition to the U.S. Supreme Court asking for a review of his case. Gideon's petition bore a superficial resemblance to many others the Court received that month—just another few scraps of paper in a very large pile. His crude cry for justice turned out to have the mark of destiny on it, however. The Court plucked it from the pile, made constitutional history with it, and made Gideon a minor folk hero in the process.

The Court began by giving Gideon a sure 'nuff defense lawyer at last. It appointed Abe Fortas—believed by many to be the ablest appellate advocate in the country and soon to be a Supreme Court justice himself—to brief and argue the case on Gideon's behalf. Fortas argued that "a criminal court is *not properly constituted* . . . under our adversary system of law, unless there is judge and unless there is a counsel for the prosecution and unless there is a counsel for the defense." To remove the defense counsel from the trial was to remove an essential leg of the due process tripod.

It was a logically powerful argument, but the coup de grace to the prosecution's position was administered from the bench. In the midst of the ACLU's "friend of the court" argument in support of Gideon's petition, Justice Potter Stewart penetrated the flow of learned rhetoric with a simple, unanswerable question: "Florida wouldn't let Gideon represent anyone *else* on trial in that state, would it?" A wave of knowing laughter swept the courtroom, which said: "Of course not." "How ridiculous." Then, how ridiculous to *require* Gideon to represent *himself*.

Stewart's witty inquiry effectively ended the argument and forecast the result. The justices had obviously already decided to overturn existing law, which made appointed counsel mandatory only in capital cases, and to replace it with a rule requiring counsel in all felony cases. They did so 9-0, and Gideon was given a second trial, armed with a competent court-appointed lawyer.

This time, there was a happy ending: Gideon won his case; the brilliant *New York Times* columnist Anthony Lewis told his story in a book called *Gideon's Trumpet;* the brilliant actor Henry Fonda played him in a movie of the same name; and a grossly unfair tilt in the criminal trial system at long, long last got fixed.

To borrow Willie Loman's favorite phrase, defense lawyers "are liked, but not *well* liked." They are liked in the abstract. They play well on television and in the movies, where their clients are usually innocent and they can be excused for their noble fervor.

It is different in the concrete. We see them wrangling and bargaining in and out of court to get the best verdict or the best deal, the slightest edge, for seedy characters who are usually, face it, guilty. We see them quoted in newspapers complaining that some antisocial, havoc-causing troll they represent has been denied his "rights." We see them performing mostly as specialists in delay and obfuscation: obtaining endless trial postponements, grousing about obviously just rulings and verdicts, threatening to appeal their richly deserved losses. Most of all, we see them helping the people we least wish to see helped; arguing for the lives and freedom of the least competent and most destructive among us, thereby threatening the rest of us with the continued depredations of such people.

These are caricatures, of course, that ignore the essence of the story. You do not have to like defense lawyers, but it is only intelligent to recognize what they have meant to our civilization. They have been a vital force in our courtrooms that has kept our criminal justice system from being something to be ashamed of.

Think of it on the retail level. No one knows how many innocent people suffered imprisonment, mutilation, or death between 1300 and 1700 because they were crushed by a judicial system they could not understand, much less master. But they must have been legion. We know this because every time we get a glimpse of the trial process during those four hundred years we see terribly one-sided contests—bullfights in which doomed citizens are harassed, played with, and destroyed by governmental matadors. How many innocents could have been saved, to what degree could criminal punishment have been equalized, had there been competent defense lawyers available for the unjustly accused during those years? Certainly enough to change the essential quality of justice in England and America.

Now think of it on a wholesale level. Defense lawyers not only save individuals, they change laws. There was little improvement in criminal justice from 1400 to 1700. There was significant improvement in the 1700s and more in the 1800s. In the 1900s, the avalanche of due process development occurred. It is a safe guess that very little of this movement would have taken place without defense lawyers—it is hard to progress when no one is arguing for progress.

Take the defense lawyer out of the lawmaking equation, and there would have been a continuation of the poisonous stagnation that plagued the English system for so many centuries. In a real sense, the Sixth Amendment right of counsel has been the key to preserving and realizing the other Bill of Rights liberties. Without the engine, the glorious vehicle would not have moved forward very far.

19

EQUALITY AS LAW, CONTINUED

(The Eclipse of Judicial Restraint)

The Law is the true embodiment of everything that's excellent.
It has no kind of fault or flaw, and I, my lords, embody the Law.
                                                            W. S. GILBERT

The announcement of the decision in America's great school desegregation case, *Brown* v. *Board of Education* (1954), was coming to a climax. Reading from the text of the opinion, Chief Justice Earl Warren said, "[W]e conclude," and then paused to interject the immense word "unanimously." It was the interjected word, not the decision itself, that sent shock waves through the silent courtroom audience.

One did not have to be a Benjamin Cardozo to anticipate that the opinion would outlaw segregation in public schools. Everyone from the *New York Times* to the Ku Klux Klan had been predicting that certain result for months. But possibly no one in the land, beyond the precincts of the Court itself, had dreamed that the result would be arrived at without dissent. When Warren said "unanimously," those who feared that racism was the original sin that would ultimately damn America felt a miracle happening.

In theory, all Supreme Court decisions are created equal—they all represent law, and are therefore identical in force. It is *just* a theory, of course. The Court's decisions bind the parties to them by the power of the state but bind the nation only by consent. A decision that is doubted becomes diluted in its general effect, and one that is hated can be all but nullified. Nine unarmed men in robes cannot coerce a hundred million people. They can only declare the law and count on the good instincts of a law-respecting public to accept it.

When the nation is passionately divided over a constitutional issue, the division on the Court becomes crucial. Whatever its formal effect, a closely divided vote signals that the justices aren't quite sure; that they concede some wiggle-room for noncompliance; that foot-dragging may be in order, because a change in the Court's personnel might mean a change in what the law requires. One or two dissenting votes is less supportive to resisters but makes resistance at least respectable. When, as in the *Brown* case, vast popular opposition is certain, unanimity becomes essential. Unanimity says that the decision is the law, and that there will be no prospect of change and no breathing room for the recalcitrant.

To a degree unprecedented in the Court's long history, *Brown v. Board of Education* called for the Court to speak with one voice. Outlawing segregation would shake one-third of the country to its roots and send powerful vibrations into the other two-thirds. It would be a flat-out repudiation of the Court's own firm precedents stretching back for almost sixty years. The Court would be accused of crossing a threshold it had always said it wouldn't cross, from objective logic into subjective notions of fairness, from rendering analytic judgments into rendering moral ones. Not since the *Dred Scott* decision one hundred years before had justices confronted an issue so morally and regionally divisive as this one—and every justice knew what *Dred Scott* had done to the Court and to the country. Even one dissenting vote would have invited resistance to the decision, and a closely divided Court might have led to something like a second Civil War. Only unanimity could provide decent prospects for ultimate compliance with the order to desegregate.

As an institution, the Court had itself to blame for the racist mess that confronted it. Fifty-seven years earlier, in *Plessy* v. *Ferguson* (1896), eight predecessor justices had told the nation that the Constitution was no obstacle to the forced separation of races in public places; that the law could isolate Negroes in their own train cars so long as their facilities were physically equal to those provided for whites. If the cushions were soft and the toilets flushed, they had no cause for legal complaint, however humiliating the compelled herding together may have been.

The idea that physical equivalency was legal equality was, of course, a breathtakingly simpleminded one. Justice John Marshall Harlan had said as much, and more, in dissenting from the *Plessy* decision itself. "The destinies of the two races in this country are indissolubly linked together, and the interests of both require that the common government of all shall not permit the seeds of race hate to be planted under the sanction of law," he had written. "What can more certainly arouse race hate, what more certainly create and perpetuate a feeling of distrust between these races, than state enactments which in fact proceed on the ground that colored citizens are so inferior and degraded that they cannot be allowed to sit in public coaches occupied by white citizens?"

Harlan's warning turned out to be a distressingly accurate prediction. "Separate but equal" became a respectable concept, not only in law but in society, and was directly responsible for much of the domestic injustice that plagued America throughout the first half of the twentieth century.

As Justice Brandeis would later write, the law is "the great, the omnipresent teacher," and it never taught a more damaging lesson than in *Plessy*. The justices had not intended to say that racial segregation was right, merely that it was not prohibited by the equal protection clause of the Fourteenth Amendment. They were employing a technique called judicial restraint, by which they told themselves that they were applying the Constitution according to its "actual intent" rather than their personal moral judgments of what ought to be. As men they might or might not have considered forced racial separation abhorrent, but, *they thought,* that had nothing to do with their judicial duty. A law may be unwise or immoral and still be constitutional.

The public did not read it that way. As *Plessy*'s message spread through American society, it made a simple, powerful point: Segregation is okay. The Court had forfeited its opportunity to nurture the tender shoots of racial justice that were trying to grow in post–Civil War America. By the time the school desegregation case came before the Court in 1953, the legal and, hence, human inferiority of Negroes had been so reenforced in the American—and particularly the Southern—mentality that it had largely sunk below the level of conscious thought. In the South, even the water fountains were separate—and the ones reserved for Negroes were usually brown.

If the school desegregation cases had been decided when they first came before the Court, a shaky, dangerous 5-4 decision for the plaintiffs would have been likely. The justices were divided largely by the degrees of their fears. They all knew that it might be very bad in the South if they outlawed the segregation of races in public schools. *Plessy* had fostered the belief that racial apartheid was not only right but was a sacred duty owed by white people to themselves. There would be resistance, there might be violence, and the greatest fear of all was that the Court's orders might prove unenforceable. Such impotence, once displayed, might be ultimately lethal to the Court. Successful disobedience to its most sweeping decree would surely diminish the nation's respect for its decrees in general, and perhaps for the rule of law itself.

The strongest holdouts, accordingly, were Justices Stanley Reed and Tom Clark, both Southerners with a vivid awareness of the hell a desegregation mandate might produce in their home territories. They were joined by Robert Jackson, an elegant and often brave jurist who saw the issue as essentially a political one with no traction in the law. When he read the brief of NAACP counsel Thurgood Marshall, he professed to see only an exercise in "sociology." The fourth likely negative vote belonged to Frederick Vinson, the Court's inept chief justice. An amiable back-slapper of shallow intellect and outlook, he seems to have regarded the reversal of legalized segregation as simply too serious a prospect to contemplate. These doubts were in danger of becoming self-fulfilling. By withholding their votes, the four potential dissenters threatened to deprive the Court's decision of the force it would need to quell dangerous opposition to it.

The four potential voters for desegregation included Southern apostate and former Ku Klux Klan member Hugo Black, belligerent liberal William O. Douglas, and their two quiet allies, Harold Burton and Sherman Minton, both Northern born and bred. The remaining justice, Felix Frankfurter, was a voluble enigma.

More than any other Supreme Court justice we have had, Frankfurter was obsessed by the paradox of judicial power. To him, the act of judging was antithetical to the exercise of power in any personal sense. Since the source of judicial authority is objective law, he thought, its exercise should be unsullied by the judge's personal moral and political views. But how could law exist divorced from moral and political considerations, and if it could not, how could a judge get outside himself in applying such considerations?

Frankfurter insisted that it could and must be done. He was the preeminent advocate of the doctrine of judicial restraint, believing profoundly that personal preferences can have no place in judging because to let them in produces a rule of men, not laws. Before becoming a justice he had been the Red Professor, a Jewish radical from Harvard who battled the establishment fiercely and famously on behalf of America's underdogs. When he ascended the bench, his adherence to the doctrine of judicial restraint created the illusion that he had undergone a profound reactionary metamorphosis. It was said that he took an almost masochistic pleasure in ruling contrary to his most powerful libertarian beliefs.

If so, he earned all of the punishment his psyche could conceivably have craved. Liberals considered him a traitor, conservatives never trusted him, and on a subjective level he was forced to struggle painfully with his conflicting philosophical and personal impulses.

His most visible judicial performances featured Frankfurter the judge at war with Frankfurter the man. The most painful and notorious of these conflicts came in 1943, when the Court decided *West Virginia Board of Education* v. *Barnette,* the second of the "flag-salute" cases. Three years earlier, Frankfurter had written the 8-1 majority opinion in *Minersville School District* v. *Gobitis,* upholding a law compelling children raised as Jehovah's Witnesses to salute the American flag. His former liberal constituency was horrified, denouncing the opinion as a carrying of against-the-grain judicial restraint to the level of lunacy. Here was a Jewish judge, who had spent his adult life fighting for civil liberties, approving prosecutions that did not differ in principle from some of the things that were happening to the Jews in Germany. To Frankfurter, it was simply a matter of doing what his position required of him. "Judges," he told his outraged liberal friends, "move within a framework of duty very different from that in which you happily are free to move."

Again, as after *Plessy,* the people did not understand the philosophical rationale for the decision. Again, they thought the Court had approved that which it had merely declined to prohibit. In particular, those willing to sacrifice individual conscience on the altar of forced patriotism thought the Court had given them a green light. A short but vicious chapter in the history of American intolerance ensued. Vigilantism threatening Jehovah's Witnesses with violence broke out across the country. In Maine a child was wounded in an anti–Jehovah's Witness riot, and the governor threatened to call out the National Guard. In Illinois sixty-one Jehovah's Witnesses were attacked and had to be given refuge in a jail. In California thirty people who refused to salute the flag for religious reasons were escorted from town with an enraged mob virtually on their heels.

Sickened by the ugliness their decision had helped produce, most of the justices resolved to change it—but not the obdurate Felix Frankfurter. The decision in *Barnette* reversed *Gobitis* by an 8-1 vote, this time with Frankfurter as a lone and embattled dissenter. In perhaps the most personal paragraphs ever written by a Supreme Court justice, he tried to justify his position to his perplexed countrymen:

> One who belongs to the most vilified and persecuted minority in history is not likely to be insensible to the freedoms guaranteed by our Constitution. Were my purely personal attitude relevant, I should whole-heartedly associate myself with the general libertarian views of the Court's opinion, representing as they do the thought and action of a lifetime. But as judges we are neither Jew nor Gentile, neither Catholic nor agnostic.
>
> As a member of this Court I am not justified in writing my private notions of policy into the Constitution, no matter how deeply I may cherish them or how mischievous I may deem their disregard. The duty of a judge who must decide which of two claims before the Court shall prevail, that of a state to enact and enforce laws within its general competence or that of an individual to refuse obedience because of the demands of his conscience, is not that of the ordinary person.

The people still did not get it. After *Barnette,* Frankfurter was popularly considered—depending on one's viewpoint—either a fallen liberal or a born-again conservative. That he was merely an intellectual attempting to do his duty as he abstractly saw it was too subtle an idea for popular consumption.

The school desegregation cases afforded Frankfurter the opportunity to replay the tragedy and farce of his flag-salute performance on an even larger stage. Once again, the Court was confronted with a precedent of its own (*Plessy* in place of *Gobitis*) that had allowed, and thereby seemed to sanctify, governmental oppression of a minority group. Once again, the form of that oppression (racial segregation in place of religious intolerance) was personally abhorrent to Frankfurter. Once again, the very strength of his personal feelings seemed to be pushing him, perversely, in the opposite decisional direction. "However passionately any of us may hold egalitarian views," he wrote in an intra-court memorandum, "however fiercely any of us may believe that such a policy of segregation as undoubtedly expresses the tenacious conviction of Southern states is both unjust and short-sighted, he travels outside his judicial authority if for this reason alone he declares unconstitutional the policy of segregation." The memo read for all the world like a warm-up for a reprise of the *Barnette* dissent.

Still, there were signs that this time it would be different. True, Frankfurter had engaged in certain Hamlet-like behavior while the desegregation cases were pending, expressing doubt and anguish over the difficulty of the decision, engaging in philosophical ruminations that gave hints of leaning in both directions, and making requests for reargument and delay. But these were probably smokescreens, intended to give him room to maneuver and his colleagues time to move toward unanimity.[1] The clearest early sign of his real intentions came in September 1953, when he was informed of the unexpected death of the ineffectual, pro-*Plessy* chief justice, Fred Vinson. "This is the first indication I have ever had that there is a God," he said.

Vinson's replacement, Earl Warren, hardly seemed much of an improvement to most observers. He had no experience on the bench. He had been a district attorney, a state attorney general, and a Republican governor of California for a rare three terms, and had compiled records of competent moderation. He had the best conviction percentage of any district attorney in California, and had been a plainspoken, pragmatic governor who had displayed few illusions about the shortcomings of human nature and a fine instinct for the political common denominator. There was even a taint of racial oppression in his history: As attorney general he had taken a position of forceful leadership in the compulsory "resettlement" of Japanese-American citizens in wartime concentration camps. By any reasonable calculus, he seemed most unlikely to solve for the fierce desegregation dilemma in which the Court was entangled.

And yet, that is precisely what he did. In a supreme irony, it was the moderate pragmatist Warren who set in motion the freight train of liberal decision-making that rumbled through the next twenty years of American life and the radical intellectual Frankfurter who went along as a reluctant passenger, when he went along at all—and it started with *Brown* v. *Board of Education*.

Those who had predicted that Warren would bring little change to the Court had, in truth, failed to do their homework. He had been a notably effective prosecutor, but a notably fair one too. With the awful exception of the Japanese concentration camps—which could be blamed on, if not justified by, wartime hysteria—he had refused to tolerate prosecutorial oppression of the kind he later condemned as chief justice. His pragmatism may have looked like anti-intellectual good-old-boyism when he was a politician, but as chief justice it made him result-oriented and determined to do justice regardless of technical legal constraints. His feel for the average person, which had produced vast support for him as an elected official, translated into sympathy for oppressed individuals and minorities when he became a judge charged with enforcing constitutional guarantees.

Warren's approach to judging was, in an absolute sense, the opposite of Frankfurter's. Those "personal" moral and political considerations that Frankfurter tried to remove from the decision-making process were the motivating forces in every important decision Warren ever made. On the other hand, the established precedents and principles Frankfurter thought should dominate judging were to Warren verbal technicalities to be manipulated in the service of common sense, where justice truly lay.

Frankfurter had written that even a fierce belief in the injustice of forced segregation could not, by itself, justify declaring it invalid. In his first Court conference on the school cases, Warren bluntly expressed the precise opposite view:

[T]he more I've read and heard and thought, the more I've come to conclude that the basis of segregation and "separate but equal" rests upon a concept of the inherent inferiority of the colored race. I don't see how *Plessy* and the cases following it can be sustained on any other theory. If we are to sustain segregation, we also must do it on this basis.[2]

In somewhat politer English, the chief justice was saying that a vote for legalized segregation could logically be cast only by a racist. Other members of the Court were ultimately unwilling to dispute this idea, and even less willing to vote in favor of racism. The dynamics that produced a unanimous decision outlawing school segregation were complex, but at the center was Warren's insistence that he and his colleagues could not permit as judges what they abhorred as men.

Frankfurter's apparent departure from his usual policy of judicial restraint in *Brown* may have been, in part, a product of his ethnic background. Like many Jewish immigrants who prospered in America, Frankfurter believed profoundly in the benefits of the American educational system, which he thought went far beyond the mere imparting of knowledge. In a 1948 opinion, he had described American schools as "perhaps the most powerful agency for promoting cohesion among a heterogenous democratic people." One of his file notes in a 1950 case states that "if the Negro is to make his due contribution to the Commonwealth, he must have the knowledge, training and skills which only good schools can vouchsafe."[3] It seems probable that in *Brown,* Frankfurter—just that once—permitted a powerful personal belief to overcome his stern professional code.

And so, two generations late, the Supreme Court found the courage to take back the cowardly lesson *Plessy* had taught. Familiar history has recorded the violent ill-will with which the South received the Court's new pedagogy. Almost immediately, a block of Southern congressmen signed a "manifesto" denouncing and defying the school desegregation decision. Billboards from Atlanta to San Diego solemnly instructed no one in particular to "Impeach Earl Warren." When six black children made a court-ordered entrance into Little Rock's Central High School in 1957, it took a national guard unit to get them in, while a thousand yahoos screamed incredulously from the street, "They're *in*, the niggers are in *our* school."

It was much worse in later times and other places, but only for a while. Eventually, most of respectable America came to see that racial degradation through racial isolation was a loathsome business, in which the government could have no part. Despite America's towering racial problems, the rightness of *Brown* v. *Board of Education* is no longer subject to debate by most people. By acting with courage and unanimity, the Court helped create the moral base for acceptance of its own decision.

If *Brown* v. *Board of Education* gave black citizens a new sense of themselves, it did the same thing for the Court. Not since *Marbury* v. *Madison* had the justices conferred upon themselves such a psychological power surge. Once the barrier of judicial restraint was crossed in *Brown*, there seemed to be no turning back. Under Warren's common-sense leadership, a majority of the justices found "doing right as they saw the right" quite addictive, and for a giddy decade and a half it seemed to their supporters that power and morality had met in a miraculous embrace.

The Court had previously played a central role in the constitutional history of the Country, but essentially as a negative force. It had exercised veto power over constitutional abuses by other branches, within more or less clear lines of doctrinal demarcation. Now it became an affirmative force as well, filling in gaps created by other branches' failures to act, and in so doing, frankly creating new governmental policy.

The most aggressive judicial invasion of territory previously occupied by the "political" branches of government was in the reapportionment cases. Having declared as recently as 1946 that legislative reapportionment was a "political thicket" that it would never enter, the Court proceeded to wade into it throughout the 1960s. If legislatures would not reapportion, the Court would do it for them. By the end of the decade, the Court had adopted a previously unheard-of "one person, one vote" rule of apportionment, which legislators across the land were required to apply with something approaching mathematical precision.

Before Warren, the Court had also repeatedly refused to constitutionalize libel law and other categories of traditionally regulated "speech," such as advertising. Now it used the First Amendment to rewrite the centuries-old common law of libel in unprecedented ways and to force bar associations to permit lawyer advertising—thereby altering the fabric of the legal profession. A few months before Warren joined the Court in 1953, the justices declined to apply the Fifth Amendment self-incrimination privilege to the nontestimonial act of filing a gambling tax return. Now they made revolutionary use of the privilege to invalidate a host of nontestimonial acts and processes—*including* the filing of gambling tax returns, pretrial confessions, and gun registration laws.

Schools were a particular target of the new judicial largesse. One court appointed a magistrate who decided, among other details, that inner-city high school basketball teams should include more whites. The length of students' hair and their right to wear black armbands to class were the subjects of adjudication. Institutions of higher learning were judicially ordered to merge with one another in order to reduce the possibility of race-based enrollment choices.

By the end of Warren's tenure, federal courts had their hands on almost every important phase of American life. Everything desirable was becoming a right, and Americans strove to be members of an injured class. The Supreme Court case reports became a burgeoning set of regulatory manuals that applied to almost every aspect of social existence.

Despite much public grumbling, many Americans rather liked the Court's new role. Life's most intractable problems became, by definition, constitutional ones, to be resolved by the High Court's special wisdom. Court decisions were so much less *trouble* than political ones, so much more antiseptic and definitive. No marching in the streets, or employing lobbyists, no writing or voting for politicians who didn't do one's bidding anyway. When the Court resolved an issue, there might be anger and frustration, but it was all blessedly beyond the people's responsibility. Having been granted control over their political destinies two hundred years before, many people were glad to give the more burdensome portions of it back.

More than two thousand years ago, Plato wrote: "Until philosophers are kings, or the kings and princes of this world have the spirit and power of philosophy, and political greatness and wisdom meet in one . . . cities will never have rest from their evils—no, nor the human race, as I believe—and then only will this our state have a possibility of life and behold the light of day." America had acquired philosopher-kings; it would now see whether Plato was right.

20

FREEDOM OF THE PRESS, CONTINUED

(The Public Official Rule)

If you shut your doors to errors, truth will be shut out.
R. TAGORE

It was the confiscation of the ministers' cars that best exemplified the meanness of the whole affair. They were not, God knows, worth much as security for a half-million-dollar libel judgment, although that was the excuse for taking them. The state of Alabama seized them from the Reverends Ralph Abernathy, Joseph Lowery, and Fred Shuttlesworth, sold them at auction, and held the proceeds to be applied against the judgment in the very likely event it was upheld on appeal.

"Let 'em walk to the church." The good old boys chuckled. "Let 'em *hitchhike* to the next nigger demonstration."

There were, of course, much bigger things at stake. All across the South, segregationist public officials were learning that libel actions were effective weapons against newspapers that were reporting their oppressions. Coverage of violent police clashes with citizen protesters was bound to contain inaccuracies—or, at least, disputed facts—that could be converted into punishing judgments against the press and its allies. It was a creative way to neutralize dissent.

On the day judgment was entered against the ministers and

their codefendant, the *New York Times*, in favor of Montgomery Police Commissioner L. B. Sullivan, the *Montgomery Advertiser* carried the chilling headline: "State Finds Formidable Club to Swing at Out-of-State Press." Within the next eighteen months, Southern public officials had filed a multitude of libel actions involving news coverage of desegregation battles, claiming a total of three hundred million dollars in damages. If the trend begun with the Sullivan trial continued, the segregationists would *own* the *New York Times*, and liberal Southern owners and editors, like Hodding Carter in Greenville and John Seigenthaler in Nashville, would be walking around in barrels.

The Sullivan case did not even involve the reporting of news. It arose out of a paid political advertisement run in the *Times* on March 29, 1960. Titled "Heed Their Rising Voices," the ad described an "unprecedented wave of terror, that is sweeping the South in response to desegregation efforts." According to the ad, a student protest at Alabama State College in Montgomery had been quelled by police, who "padlocked [the] dining halls . . . in an effort to starve [the students] into submission."

The *Times* and the sixty-four named sponsors of the ad had been caught with their collective pants down. There had been police oppression but no padlocking of the dining hall, and no attempt— so far as was known—to starve anyone.

Out of a total circulation of 650,000, exactly 394 copies of the *New York Times* made their way into the state of Alabama on a daily basis. No names were mentioned in the ad, but the sensitive Mr. Sullivan felt that he had been sufficiently identified as a perpetrator of the alleged outrage. As commissioner, he was, after all, the man supposedly in charge of police actions. He felt certain that the ad had harmed his reputation in Alabama to the tune of half a million dollars by suggesting that his police force had dealt less than fairly with civil rights protesters on a Negro college campus. And he felt even *more* certain that a Montgomery jury would accept that somewhat dubious proposition.

When the jury returned a verdict granting every nickel sued for, the *Times* lawyers knew their client was in deep trouble. The verdict was impeccably correct under Alabama law and the law of every other state in the Union. The common law of libel favored reputation and was hard on those who, intentionally or otherwise sullied it. If a published statement was defamatory (i.e., abstractly damaging to reputation)—which this one was—it was *presumed* to be false. The publisher was required to prove it true, a burden which the *Times* could not sustain. A false and defamatory statement was presumed to have caused actual damage, and in reaching its verdict the jury was free to guess just how much damage it had caused. Sullivan's jury guessed that his reputation had sustained the entire five hundred thousand dollars in damages he claimed as a result of the offending published sentence. It was all quite outrageous, but—as lawyers are inclined to say—there it was.

Moved by desperation, the *Times* made a somewhat novel argument on appeal. It asserted that the verdict, under all the circumstances, violated the First Amendment's free press provision. By requiring newspapers to guarantee the truth of everything they published, the *Times* argued, on pain of being subjected to exorbitant judgments, the Alabama common law inhibited that free discussion of public issues that was at the very heart of the First Amendment. A five-hundred-thousand-dollar civil "fine" for publishing a regrettable, but not actually harmful, factual error regarding a matter of profound public concern was an "abridgement" of "freedom of the press" in its worst conceivable form. Wasn't it?

The legendary legal commentator William Blackstone had answered that question to the satisfaction of the Alabama Supreme Court two centuries earlier. "Where blasphemous, immoral, treasonable, schismatical, seditious, or scandalous libels are punished by English law . . . the liberty of the press, properly understood, is by no means infringed or violated." The Alabama Supreme Court responded to the *Times'* First Amendment argument less elaborately, but no less definitively. "The First Amendment of the United States Constitution does not protect libelous publications," it said. And the Court was absolutely right, according to the then-existing law.

Toleration of criticism of government came slowly to the English-speaking world. During most of English history, words directed at government had the capacity to kill—their authors.

In medieval England, all forms of scandal and gossip about government officials were feared and punished. As early as 1275, the statute *Scandalum Magatum* was enacted, providing that persons caught repeating "false news or scandal" regarding the "great men of the realm" were to be thrown into prison and kept there until they identified the originator of the tale. It is not known whether the bizarre remedy was ever effectively used.

In a famous incident during the reign of Richard III, two English dissidents named William Collingbourne and John Tuberville went around London poking fun at the king and his ministers— William Catesby, Richard Radcliffe, and Francis Lovell—by scrawling the following rhyme in public places:

> The Catt, the Ratt, and Lovell our Dog
> Rullen all England under an Hog

The prank came back to haunt them two years later, when they were tried, convicted, and executed largely because of their ill-advised critique. The little verse was certainly not great satire, but it hardly seemed worthy of drawing and quartering. A truly dedicated critic would have been boiled in oil by such a regime (a refinement, incidentally, that was introduced into English jurisprudence in the succeeding century by Henry VIII).

Truly systematic punishment of governmental criticism came with the printing press. In 1603, the Star Chamber began four decades of political oppression by publishing an opinion called *Libelous Famosis,* which defined the elements of antigovernment, or seditious, libel. The chamber made it clear that its main business would be protection of the ruling classes. "If [a libel] be against a Magistrate, or other public person," the Court warned, "it is a greater offense; for it concerns not only breach of the peace, but scandal of government; for what greater scandal can there be than to have corrupt or wicked Magistrates to be appointed and constituted by the King to govern his subjects under him." The point was, of course, that the "scandal" consisted not in the corruptness or wickedness of the Magistrate, but in the reporting of it by the press. Such was the working of the seventeenth-century governmental mind.

It increasingly ceased to represent the working of the popular mind, however. Throughout the eighteenth century, criticism of government was both a crime and a cherished pastime of the English people. It was clear during that period, Judge Stephen later wrote, that any "written censor upon public men for their conduct as such" was a criminal offense; that "the practical enforcement of this doctrine was wholly inconsistent with any serious public discussion of political affairs"; but that, nonetheless, "all through the Eighteenth Century political controversy was common and ardent, and on all occasions the freedom of the press was made the subject of boasts and applauses inferior only to those which were connected to trial by jury."[1] As usual, the people were ahead of their leaders.

Colonial America was hardly more hospitable to criticism of government than was the mother country. The main prosecutors of political critics during the colonial period were not the British but the popularly elected American legislatures. A historian who conducted a careful study of the subject found that "literally scores of persons, probably hundreds, throughout the Colonies, were tracked down by various messengers and sergeants and brought into the house to make inglorious submission for words spoken in the heat of anger or for writings which intentionally or otherwise had given offense."[2]

The more prominent cases on the docket of eighteenth-century American press prosecutions make depressing reading:

In 1723, Boston printer James Franklin stated in the *New England Courant* that the government was preparing a ship to chase coastal pirates "sometime this month, wind and weather permitting." Interpreting this as a criticism of the pace at which the government was moving, the house ordered Franklin imprisoned for the remainder of its session.

In 1754, Daniel Fowle of Boston was suspected of having printed an anonymous pamphlet entitled *The Monster of Monsters,* which satirized an excise bill enacted by the house. The house ordered the public hangman to burn a copy of the pamphlet and had Fowle jailed in a "stinking and unheated" cell on a charge of being "*suspected* of being guilty" of printing the pamphlet.

In 1756, James Parker published in the *New York Gazette* an article describing the distressed condition of citizens in Orange and Oster counties. The house charged him with a "high misdemeanor and contempt." He confessed his guilt and apologized but the house nonetheless threw him in jail for a week.

In 1758, Samuel Townsend, a justice of the peace for Queens

County, New York, asked for legislative relief for refugees on Long Island. The legislature decided that this request constituted "a high misdemeanor and a most daring insult." Off to jail went Mr. Townsend until he bought his release with an abject apology.

In 1767, James Pride made the mistake of writing a letter to the Virginia House of Burgesses advising that he could not attend a hearing because of illness. Terming the letter "scandalous," the house jailed Pride without a hearing. While in jail, he wrote an unpublished account of his ordeal, for which action the house subjected him to "close confinement without use of pen, ink or paper and that he be fed on bread only and allowed no liquor whatever."

In 1770, Herman Husband, himself a member of the North Carolina Assembly, was suspected of being the author of an article in the *North Carolina Gazette* that criticized the assembly for not relieving conditions for debtor farmers. His colleagues expelled him and sentenced him to jail for two months.

In 1773, Thomas Pyle published an unlicensed account of the proceedings of the South Carolina Council. The legislature tried him and committed him to jail, from which he was released by a writ of habeas corpus issued by two politically sympathetic judges.

The founding of the new republic eventually reversed this tide of tyranny. The birth of government by the people inevitably meant the death of governmental criticism as a crime. "If the ruler is regarded as the superior of the subject . . . it must necessarily follow that it is wrong to censor him openly," noted Judge Stephen. "If, on the other hand, the ruler is regarded as the agent and servant, and the subject as the wise and good master who is obliged to delegate his power to the so-called ruler, because being a multitude he cannot use it himself, it is obvious that this sentiment must be reversed." Quite so.

It took two terms of a Federalist administration before "the sentiment" was reversed, however. Until governmental power changed hands, Federalist to Republican, Judge Stephen's point was not permitted to prevail. There continued to be a number of prosecutions for criticism of government under state law and under the widely abhorred Federal Sedition Act.

The Sedition Act of 1798 was a bad idea. It was based on a misconception of how American democracy would work. Many of the Founding Fathers hoped that the new nation would have no political parties and no blood disputes between candidates for public office. They hoped that after electoral ballots had been cast, the country would unite in more or less monolithic support of the government and that verbal fidelity to its leaders would prevail until the next election.

The clearest evidence of this early ecumenical vision was the method adopted for selecting vice presidents. Until the Constitution was amended in 1814, the presidential candidate who received the second highest vote total—*the chief rival of the man elected president*—was declared vice president and placed in governmental harness with his victorious adversary.

There was, of course, never any chance that this arrangement would work. Think of it. Vice President Herbert Hoover helping FDR ram his New Deal program through the U.S. Congress. Vice President Jimmy Carter marching with soldiers of the Reagan revolution. And imagine President John F. Kennedy and Vice President Richard M. Nixon touring Dallas, Texas, on November 22, 1963. The Warren Commission would still be in session.

Ongoing struggle between contending political forces was to be the birthright of the new government, and criticism of those in power was to be a matter, not merely of right, but of inescapable fact. Once political choice was conferred upon the people, the disputatious process by which choice was exercised also had to be conferred. Choice required discussion, discussion implied criticism, and criticism of candidates was indivisible from criticism of officeholders. Sedition in a democratic country was a political oxymoron that could not long endure. Either sedition would kill democracy or democracy would banish sedition—and it would happen very quickly.

The Sedition Act was honest enough in motive. The French Revolution had shown what havoc popular rage could cause and had put the fear of citizen uprisings back into the spines of politicians. To its supporters, the act dealt with real threats to domestic tranquillity in a carefully circumscribed way. Its provisions were narrowly directed at speech that was both corrupt and dangerous, declaring it a federal felony to "write, print, utter or publish . . . any false, scandalous and malicious writing . . . against the government of the United States, or either house of the Congress, or the President . . . with intent to defame . . . or bring them . . . into contempt or disrepute; or to excite against them . . . the hatred of the good people of the United States." In prosecutions under the act, juries were to decide both the law and the facts, and the maximum penalties were a mere two years in prison and a fine of two thousand dollars. Compared to seventeenth-century sedition prosecutions—in which judges redefined the offense from case to case, cared nothing for the truth, and sent some defendants to prison for life without their ears—the Sedition Act seemed almost gentle.

The problem was that, like all sedition laws, it was a political instrument and therefore could never be used with justice. Given the nature of the offense, guilt or innocence would always necessarily be seen through a political filter. Any doubt in that regard was resolved when the act was voted on by the Senate: Every member of the ruling Federalist party voted for it, and every member of the opposition Republican party voted against it. In a pair of presumably unintended desecrations of history, the act passed the Senate on July 4 (America's Independence Day) and was enacted into law on July 14 (France's Bastille Day).

Unfortunately for their own future, the federalists wielded their new weapon with a self-defeating instinct for overkill. Owners and editors of Republican newspapers were prosecuted with ferocious regularity, while court dockets could be searched in vain for news of any case against a Federalist publisher. This reflected the logic of the law: Those in power were the nation; those who opposed them were not; to criticize the nation was a crime; and to punish its critics was the duty of the people, as expressed through their appointed prosecutors. To the legitimate advantages conferred by public office, the Sedition Act added a profoundly illegitimate one: escape from full public examination of performance in office.

The event that finally killed the Sedition Act was the prosecution of James Callender in Richmond, Virginia, in 1800. He had printed an attack on the administration of John Adams called *The Prospect Before Us,* and was the last American citizen to be tried under the act. He was represented by four magnificent Virginia lawyers who saw a chance to attack the despised Sedition Act publicly: Edmund Randolph, George Haye, William Wirt, and young Phillip Nicholas—three lions of the bar and a ferocious cub. Randolph was the acknowledged "leading" lawyer in Virginia, and Wirt was a forensic poet, the most famous legal orator of his generation.

All of this did Callender no good at all—he might as well have been represented by the Three Stooges. Presiding Judge Samuel Chase was an ardent Federalist who understood perfectly why Adams had appointed him to try the case. He made no phony pretense to being unbiased. He had read *The Prospect Before Us* from cover to cover and did not need a trial to tell him it was libelous. As for the array of talent representing Callender, he announced before the trial began that he would "put the lot of them over my knee and teach them a lesson they will not soon forget."

He made good his boast, in an almost literal sense. Throughout the trial he shouted down the defense lawyers, making their efforts virtually useless. He had a rollicking good time rejecting their futile protestations: "In vain Haye protested against [the judge's rulings]. He was interrupted and contradicted, hurried, harried and baited, until the whole room roared with laughter, for there is nothing so infectious as the wit of the bench on which a bully sits enthroned."[3]

In his final argument, Wirt commenced a concerted attack upon the constitutionality of the Sedition Act. Chase halted him in midsentence, telling the jury that they were not to consider the argument. When Wirt attempted to resume it, Chase told him to be seated. Wirt courageously persisted, reading the portion of the Sedition Act that stated that the jury "should determine the law and the facts." The Constitution is the law, is it not, asked Wirt, and therefore to be determined by the jury. A "non sequitur, sir," thundered Chase, and Wirt was finally blown back into his seat.

Haye tried to pick up the argument, but Judge Chase checked him at every step. The lawyer fought the unequal battle as long as he could stand it and then returned to the counsel table and began to gather up his books and papers, preparatory to leaving the courtroom. As the defense lawyers moved toward the door, it occurred to Chase that he had perhaps gone too far. "Please to proceed, sir," he said, "and be assured you will not again be interrupted by me. Say what you will."

It was far too late. The lawyers left the courtroom and left Callender to his fate. The jury did the expected, sentencing the defenseless defendant to nine months' imprisonment. Five years later, Chase was impeached and tried by the Senate for, among other things, "indecent solicitude in the conviction of [Callender]." He was acquitted in a trial in which he received all of the due process rights he had denied to James Callender.

By the time of Chase's impeachment, the public revulsion created by the sedition prosecutions, and Callender's in particular, had rendered the Sedition Act a thoroughly dead letter. Shortly after taking office in 1801, the new president, Thomas Jefferson, pardoned all convicted defendants, to popular applause. In 1840 and again in 1850, two of the fines that had been exacted pursuant to the act's provisions were returned to the defendants' families. It would be generations before the crime of sedition would haunt the land again.

During the First World War the old ghost stirred and walked again. Fear and patriotism combined, as they nearly always do in wartime, to strangle political dissent. A fit heir to the Sedition Act, called the Espionage Act, was passed by Congress, and dozens of citizens were imprisoned once again for words.

One of these was Charles Shenck, a lowly Socialist party functionary who mailed—not composed, but *mailed*—circulars to potential army recruits urging them to express opposition to the draft. He was convicted under the Espionage Act, and the conviction was appealed to the U.S. Supreme Court, becoming the first significant First Amendment case since the amendment was adopted in 1791.

Many thought that the Sedition Act had taught the nation the irrevocable lesson that, in a democracy, words may not be made a crime simply because they conflict with governmental policy. No one really knew, because the First Amendment had been all but moribund for the 127 years of its existence, and no clear standard for the criminality of words had been established.

In what looks in retrospect like a failure of nerve, or of philosophy, Oliver Wendell Holmes wrote the decision of the Court, affirming Shenck's conviction. He presented a standard that seemed hopeful on its face. In light of the First Amendment, he wrote, speech is criminally punishable only if it creates a "clear and present danger" of illegal action. Fair enough, but the justice had another artful bromide in his rhetorical quiver. Freedom of speech is relative to time and place, he said; it does not, for example, permit one "to shout 'fire' in a theater." Shenck's exhortation to recruits might have been acceptable in peacetime, but in an environment of total war it constituted a "clear and present danger" to the welfare of the nation. Good metaphor, most critics say, bad decision.

The blood lust of the paranoid patriots gave Holmes ample chance to adjust his libertarian halo. A few months after *Shenck,* the closely similar case of *Abrams* v. *United States* came before the Court. Abrams was a Russian refugee who had thrown leaflets from the roof of a New York building in protest of American military intervention in Russia. A more pathetic threat to domestic tranquillity could hardly be imagined; but, presumably having no more formidable defendants on which to build a reputation, the U.S. attorney prosecuted and convicted Abrams and got him twenty years in the penitentiary.

The Supreme Court affirmed the conviction, but this time without Holmes's help. In a powerful, memorable dissent, Holmes became the first Supreme Court justice to tell his countrymen what the First Amendment could truly mean. Describing Abrams's crime as the "surreptitious publishing of a silly pamphlet by an unknown man," Holmes gave an unforgettable discourse on the protected status of unpopular opinion in a free society.

"Persecution for the expression of opinions seems to me perfectly logical," he began. "But when men have realized that time has upset many fighting faiths, they may come to believe, even more than they believe the very foundations of their conduct, that the ultimate good desired is better reached by free trade in ideas. . . . That at any rate," he continued, "is the theory of our Constitution. It is an experiment as all life is an experiment. . . . [But] while that experiment is part of our system, I think that we should be eternally vigilant against attempts to check expression of opinions that we loathe and believe to be fraught with death."

The government vigorously argued that, never having been declared invalid, the ancient law embodied in the Sedition Act still survived. That law permitted punishment of words that had a "bad tendency" vis-à-vis the official goals and aspirations of society. Holmes's main argument was based on essential philosophy but he paused briefly to deal with this historical point. "I wholly disagree," he wrote, "with the argument of the government that the First Amendment left the common law as to seditious libel in force. History seems to me against the notion. I had conceived that the United States through many years had shown its repentance for the Sedition Act of 1798 by repaying the fines that it imposed." This virtual afterthought would have reverberations in the future as loud as any words the great justice ever wrote.

Intellectuals tend to make the best legal arguments, not because they are smarter than their colleagues but because they are prone to think in metaphors and similes. The essence of all sound legal arguments is this: If A is like B, it should be legally treated like B. Such an argument is not about what *is*, which may win a jury verdict, but about what *ought to be*, which wins appeals.

Herbert Weschler was a professor at Columbia Law School. When the *New York Times* retained him to appeal the *Sullivan* judgment to the U.S. Supreme Court, he knew very little about libel law—but he knew a great deal about legal similes and the concept of what "ought to be."

A more pragmatic lawyer might have been overawed by the task. Eight times in its history, the Supreme Court had said what the Alabama Supreme Court had so emphatically repeated: The First Amendment does not apply to libel.

But, like James Otis and Thurgood Marshall, and—yes—John Lilburne before him, Weschler knew he could take the Court outside of its own history if he made it see a vision of better justice. That vision, he knew, must build upon what the Court had done in other circumstances. It must allow him to say, "Look, this is the real tendency you have followed, this is the true destiny of your prior work."

What was the simile? What was the five-hundred-thousand-dollar *Sullivan* judgment "like"? Surely, it was "like" all those fines under the Sedition Act that "history" had declared invalid, according to Holmes's dissent in *Abrams*.

As Weschler warmed to the simile, it became clear to him that a libel action by a public official was, in some ways, a greater danger to liberty than a sedition prosecution. Both are legal actions instigated by government representatives against citizens critical of government. But conviction in a sedition case requires proof according to the criminal standard of "guilt beyond a reasonable doubt," whereas a public official like Sullivan who sues for libel is required to prove his case only by the civil standard of a "preponderance of the evidence." Moreover, the monetary penalty under the old Sedition Act had been limited to two thousand dollars, whereas the amount of a civil libel judgment is limited only by the imagination and greed of the plaintiff and the fairness of the jury.

A was like B, and more, and should be treated accordingly. The logic of America's rejection of sedition prosecutions required it to reject public official libel suits as well.

The Supreme Court bought most of Mr. Weschler's simile. In a masterful opinion by Justice William Brennan, the Court declared that libel actions brought by public officials could prevail only if it were alleged and proved: (1) that the defendant had published false and damaging facts about the official, (2) *knowing* that the facts were false, or *in reckless disregard* of their truth. The proof in *New York Times* v. *Sullivan* obviously did not meet that lofty standard, and the judgment must fall. A monumental landmark in American legal history had been reached: Government punishment of governmental critics had essentially met its end.

In writing the epitaph for sedition in America, Brennan borrowed the solemn words of America's most poetic judge. " 'The First Amendment,' said Judge Learned Hand, 'presupposes that right conclusions are more likely to be gathered out of a multitude of tongues, than through any kind of authoritative selection. To many this is, and always will be folly; but we have staked upon it our all.' "

History has not recorded what happened to the proceeds from the sale of the ministers' cars. Presumably, the owners were reimbursed and were able to purchase comparable transportation that allowed them to continue to pursue the serious business of desegregation.

The so-called Public Official Rule had unanticipated consequences. The decisions that applied it in later years gave the press virtual carte blanche in reporting on government. They made it clear that officeholders and aspirants for officeholding could be covered and commented upon almost with impunity. As the press's fear of legal reprisal fell away, so did much of its respect, and it began to communicate a so-what attitude toward America's government and leaders to the general population.

Most political figures had never thought of suing for libel anyway, but nonetheless the knowledge that they were now *impotent* to do so had a profound effect. It made them seem somehow weaker in the press's eyes, more vulnerable, fairer game. If you could print things about them you could not print about anybody else, what did that say about their equality with—let alone, their superiority over—other citizens? If their lives could be made subjects of unverified published gossip, how much dignity were they really due? If the law had no regard for their reputations, why should the world?

The phenomenon was clearest at government's highest levels. Love them or hate them, the presidents who served in the thirty-year period preceding *Sullivan*—Roosevelt, Truman, Eisenhower, and Kennedy—were, in the nation's eyes, outsized and more than human.[4] Their successors—Lyndon (Check My Surgical Scar) Johnson; Richard (Tricky Dick) Nixon; Jerry (Stumble down the Stairs) Ford; Jimmy (Lust in His Heart) Carter; Ronald (The Amiable Dunce) Reagan; George (Read My Lips) Bush; and Bill (Slick Willie) Clinton—were nothing if not human.

Vilification had always been part of the bargain in American politics. When a politician entered the war for power, he knew that his opponents, aided and abetted by the press, would shoot at him with every verbal bullet they could get away with firing. But after 1964, the nature of that warfare began to subtly change. Vilification was increasingly accompanied by trivialization—the most dire fate a politician can endure. Worse, verified factual accuracy was no longer necessarily crucial to the decision to publish. Having a constitutional *right* to print nonreckless falsehoods about public officials, many newspapers acted as though they had a *duty* to do so.

Did Jack Anderson's report of vice presidential candidate Thomas Eagleton's arrest for drunk driving turn out to be a blatant, unsubstantiated lie? Too bad, but those things happen when First Amendment rights are being exercised. Was Eagleton entitled to a retraction and apology? Of course not—the lie was a mere mistake, and therefore constitutionally sanctioned. Did the *Washington Post* report as fact an irresponsible rumor accusing President Carter of wiretapping Blair House, the guest residence for visiting dignitaries? Well, we never believed he was capable of it anyway, the paper's editorialist explained—as though lack of belief *compensated* for publishing a false report.

A low-grade fever of factual degradation spread through the news media and into the body of our politics, gradually sapping its strength. This pathology could be traced to many cultural causes, but a primary one—make no mistake—was the loftily intended, mostly beneficial libertarianism granted by *New York Times* v. *Sullivan*.

The corresponding benefits were great, of course. The same press that callously trashed Eagleton tenaciously wrestled Nixon over Watergate. The weakness of the *Sullivan* principle was that it tended to diminish government; its strength was that it helped cut it down to size. It was, in both respects, much like the principle of democracy itself.

The reciprocal public and private engines of American society had done their work again. Racism had produced desegregation, desegregation efforts had produced governmental oppression, oppression had produced a constitutional press privilege, and the privilege had produced a new way of looking at, and reporting about, government and governmental leaders. In the American legal system, great wrongs have large effects not only because of the harm they cause, but because of the remedies that they require.

21

TRIAL BY JURY

*Our civilization has decided . . . that determining the guilt or innocence
of men is too important to be trusted to trained men. If it wishes for
light on that awful matter, it asks men who know no more about the
law than I know, but can feel the things I felt in the jury box.*

G. K. Chesterton

Fame used to be more closely related to achievement than it is today. In the old days, an obscure person could become famous, but
he generally had to *do* something. The fame of a Peter the Hermit
or a Joan of Arc might be distasteful depending on one's religious or
nationalistic persuasions, but there could be no doubt that it was
earned—and in that sense, real.

Modern communications technology has changed all that, of
course. In the age of TV Ascendant, we have learned that observation not only alters what is observed, it can, to all intents and purposes, create it. Why did Gary Hart's sex life destroy his career,
while John Kennedy's remarkably similar one had no effect at all on
his? Observation. Being unobserved, Kennedy's activities, on an important level of reality, did not exist at all. And Hart's had the great
significance they were "observed" to have.

Modern technology's power to raise the obscure to promi-
nence, and the trivial to importance, has had a deep effect on every
aspect of our lives—not least upon our hallowed legal system.

* * *

One April evening in 1991, a heartbreakingly ordinary series of events took place in Los Angeles, California. A drunken motorist named Rodney King refused to stop for police and led them on what newspapers always call a "high-speed chase." He was eventually stopped, pulled from his car, and brutally beaten in the course of being taken into custody. Around the country there were countless other citizens who could have told similar tales of similar arrests on other nights across the years. The difference in King's case, the thing that made him into one of the best-known and, indeed, important Americans of his generation, was nothing that he did or was. It was: observation.

By extraordinary happenstance, King's commonplace ordeal was captured on videotape by a resident of the neighborhood. That tape became celebrated as the most widely viewed and evaluated piece of evidence in the history of criminal justice, but it was more than that. It entered the consciousness of Americans as a grotesque, mobile work of art, a ballet of brutality and pain, that was played for them again and again until they could see it in their dreams. Where had they witnessed that terrible dance before, the lurching and desperate crawling away, the blind, stumbling seeking of surcease from agony? In a TV special depicting an animal kill on the African veldt? In the tricked-up finale to a professional wrestling match? Perhaps, but this was both human *and* real, and as old as law enforcement itself.

Never before had the public so totally made a criminal case its own. The people felt certain that the cops were guilty because they had seen the crime itself and had seen not only what the cops had done, but with what verve and concentration they had done it. They wanted those cops punished, not so much for King's sake as for the sake of all the future Kings, including just possibly themselves.

When the jury returned verdicts of "not guilty" on almost all the charges, the people were stunned. Seldom in memory had a jury verdict cut so painfully against public sentiment. The destructive riots in south Los Angeles were only its most visible and destructive by-product. All across the country, orthodox, peace-loving, authority-accepting people thought of that videotape and were baffled and enraged.

The violent local reaction to the verdict and the general non-acceptance of it were ominous portents for American justice. The jury had for centuries been the saving grace of the American and English legal systems. In the worst of times, it had been the one truly good thing about those systems. In the midst of the dark and bloody fifteenth century, John Fortesque had touted the jury as the emblem of the moral superiority of English justice, and in succeeding centuries it had impelled the government toward more rational and humane methods of determining guilt and innocence. Old brutalities were discarded and new rights were adopted because juries refused to convict.

More than that, juries had provided everyday sanctity for the administration of justice. They were the counterparts of representative government in the legislatures. They made the people the owners of the courts in the same sense that the ballot made them owners of Parliament and Congress. The owners might question the work product of their surrogates from time to time, but the system was theirs, and what it produced was therefore sanctified and legitimatized. A jury verdict was the great healer. It defined justice, it *was* justice, and it ended all debate.

Jury trial was in this sense the heir to the ancient trial by ordeal, in which guilt and innocence had been determined by whether a burn inflicted by a priest festered or healed within three days. The result—whatever it was—was accepted because it was the word of God. The jury verdict had become similarly sanctified as the voice of the people. It was not accepted because it was right, it was right because it was accepted.

Not so in *Rodney King*'s case. Suddenly, in *this* case, the country needed no jury to tell it where justice lay. Through the miracle of modern communications technology, the public had decided the case months before the jury was empaneled, and the verdict was unacceptable because it was *wrong*. As the voices of public outrage echoed across the land, a vital institution constructed by a thousand years of effort seemed to crack at its foundations.

It had been a long and curious journey. The jury system was not planned, or even intended, and what it ended up as was nothing like what it started out as. Its history was the product of conflicting motives, unanticipated events, lonely courage, and sheer accident. Jury trial was not so much an idea as an unself-conscious cultural creation. As Trevelyan said of its sister institution, Parliament, "No man made it, for it grew."

It was brought to life, ironically, by the French. In 829,

Charlemagne's son, Emperor Louis the Pious, decided that royal rights were not being adequately protected by the old trial method of using witnesses produced by the parties and devised a more favorable procedure called "The Inquest." He proclaimed that disputes involving royal rights would henceforth be settled by the "sworn statement of the best and most credible people of the district," who would give a judgment based upon their interpretation of national custom. The members of this inquest would, of course, be chosen by the emperor himself.

This was obviously no blow for popular freedom. The rights of the Crown were to be determined by the sworn conclusions of "responsible" gentry instead of by lesser folk chosen by litigants, who would be far more likely to hold antiroyal views. Nevertheless, Louis had created a citizen fact-finding body that in its future manifestations would become independent of government and a guardian of the rights and liberties of the people. No contemporary of Louis who learned of his proclamation could conceivably have guessed that a seed had been planted that would eventually grow into the most brilliant flower in England's constitutional garden. Certainly, Louis's intent was in exactly the opposite direction.

When William of Normandy conquered England in 1066, he brought the Frankish Inquest with him. As an alien ruler in an alien land, he required information above all other commodities. Adapting the inquest to that purpose, he compiled an inventory of his subjects' property holdings that, for comprehensiveness and specificity, had probably never been equaled by any similar survey in the history of the world. He cataloged everything but fingernail parings in great volumes known as the *Domesday Book,* acquiring the information by summoning the most credible men from every district and asking them such questions as:

> What is the name of the manor, who held it in the time of King Edward, who now, how many hides, how many plows, how many men, how many villains, how much was it then worth, and how much now; and all this at three times, the time of King Edward, the time when King William gave it, and now.

A government capable of such encyclopedic inquiries would obviously have no difficulty discovering from village leaders which of its serfs were reputed to have committed robbery or rape in the last twelve months, or which of two claimants was entitled by inheritance to a tract of land. When the king began to order such inquiries, as he later did, the jury system was truly launched.

Exactly one century after the Norman conquest, a momentous change occurred in English law. The astonishingly energetic King Henry II was busy standardizing England's system of justice and decided to make the inquest the means of initiating criminal charges against citizens. His Assize (ordinance) of Clarendon in 1166 was so clear in its wording and so rational in its purpose that it is hard for us of the twentieth century—with our ignorant sense of superiority—to associate it with the remote and supposedly unenlightened age from which it came. It said simply:

Inquiry shall be made in every county and in every hundred [subdivisions of counties, which averaged about 300 square miles in size] by the twelve most lawful men of the hundred and the four most lawful men of every [village] upon oath that they shall speak the truth, whether in their hundred or [village] there be any man who is accused or believed to be a robber, murderer, thief, or receiver of robbers, murderers or thieves, since the King's accession.

With these words, Henry in effect created the grand jury, which later produced the criminal trial jury as an offshoot. Not a bad day's work for a busy monarch who had no legislative research staff to assist him.

In 1215, a vital cog was stripped from the machinery of justice. The church decreed that its priests would no longer be allowed to conduct ordeals to determine the guilt or innocence of accused criminals, and the government was left with no reliable trial method. The grand jury could accuse a man of murder, but without a priest to throw him bound into water or to burn his flesh with hot iron, how could he be tried?

In 1219, a poor stopgap method was adopted. The king sent his justices a writ which acknowledged that, with the end of the ordeals, guilt had become largely a matter of suspicion. Weak proof, he declared, required weak punishments. Defendants convicted of great crimes would thereafter be jailed (for safekeeping); those suspected of medium crimes would be permitted to leave the country;

those suspected of lesser crimes would be set free after giving pledges to keep the peace.

The government was admitting its own helplessness and, worse, it was giving its citizens no reason to believe that its judgments were just. Whatever might have been said against a trial process which relied upon the burning of flesh, the ordeals had at least been definitive, and had more or less been accepted by the people. An acceptable replacement for them would have to be found.

In 1228, one Hamo De La Mare lost his horse and brought a criminal suit, called an appeal, against a local thug by the name of Elias, whom he accused of stealing it. Since it was a privately brought criminal case, it would normally have been settled by battle between Hamo and Elias, but Hamo was a man of peace, and he paid for the privilege of having a judge and jury consider the case in lieu of battle. This was an increasingly common practice in cases of private appeals, which had not had the benefit of grand jury inquiry.

The procedure that followed bore almost no resemblance to a modern criminal jury trial. Four juries of eight men each were selected from the vills of Chesnut, Waltham, Wormley, and Enfield. These thirty-two jurors were summoned before the court after Hamo and Elias had told the judge their versions of the facts. The jurors were told what the case was about and were given a day to investigate it, after which they were to return to the court and report.

The Waltham jurors reported that they "believed" that the horse originally belonged to Hamo because "all the countryside says so." The Enfield jury made a similar report. The Wormley jury could not discover whether the horse belonged to Hamo or not, and the Chesnut jury said that it did not know but "rather thinks that she did not." The four reports were factually complicated and based almost entirely upon hearsay information. The jurors were not so much judges of the facts as they were witnesses and investigators. Rather than rendering a single coherent verdict, they conducted four separate inquiries, which the judge was at liberty to accept or reject.

Judge Pateshull considered the jury reports and the statements made by Hamo and Elias, and then rendered a verdict and judgment:

> It is awarded that Elias lose his foot, and be it known that the King's council is dealing with him leniently, for by law he deserved a greater punishment.

England had not yet finally made up its mind whether it wanted judges or juries to decide its criminal cases, but it would do so shortly.

Juries eventually "won out" in the fact-finding contest, largely because judges did not want the job. Deciding criminal guilt was an ultrahazardous occupation in thirteenth-century England. When a Winchester grand jury declined to indict a notorious den of thieves in 1249, the jurors were swiftly sentenced to death for perjury on the ground that they had sworn "falsely" that the suspects were innocent. A second grand jury was convened, saw the light, and returned indictments that resulted in the hanging of approximately 112 men—the thieves and the recalcitrant members of the first grand jury. As a civic duty, jury service was, understandably, somewhere between "pikeman in the King's army" and "burier of plague victims" in popularity with the public.

The jury was also generally unpopular with defendants. Medieval jurors were often corrupt, being subject to bribery and intimidation by the rich and powerful. Moreover, many defendants sincerely believed that God should decide guilt—as in the old ordeals—instead of fallible men. (This view was fortified by the fact that a much higher percentage of convictions was occurring under the jury system than had occurred under the ordeals, in which the odds had been approximately even.) Surprisingly, defendants were given a choice, being subjected to jury trial only if they stated in open court that they were willing to "put themselves on the country." If they did not say these magic words, they could not be tried at all.

In 1275, the statute of Winchester provided a crude solution to this problem, directing that "those who refused inquests of felony [jury trial in felony cases] will be remanded to a hard and strong prison" in the hope that they would be coerced to change their minds. In later years, this procedure was "refined" into an elaborate series of tortures designed to coerce agreement to jury trial, culminating in the piling of stones upon the chest of the accused until he either expired or "put himself on the country." Centuries later, someone conceived the brilliant idea of proceeding with the trial over the defendant's objection by entering a not guilty plea on his behalf, instead of incarcerating, starving, and crushing him to death while waiting for him to change his mind.

Although it was the pride of the English criminal law, the medieval jury was to some extent a cat's-paw of the prosecution. In prosecutions of common folk at the assize trials, juries could usually convict or acquit at will, and often acquitted even guilty defendants to spare them the outlandishly severe punishments that were imposed for petty crimes. In the upper regions of the system, however, where the king's interests were directly engaged, juries were expected to convict and could be punished when they failed to do so.

A notorious instance of such punishment occurred in 1544, when a flashy and popular protestant named Nicholas Throckmorton was prosecuted for treason. The trial was so stacked against him that he would have been given little chance of acquittal if he had been clearly innocent—and Throckmorton was clearly guilty. Nevertheless, his popularity and brilliance in court combined to win him one of the more astonishing jury acquittals in English history. The jurors were not so fortunate. They were punished in place of the defendant they had "falsely" acquitted, the Star Chamber imprisoning and imposing a crushing fine of five hundred pounds on eight of them. The four others confessed that they had "offended in not considering the truth of the matter," and—except for their pride—emerged unscathed.

The jury was still far from being the independent sovereign of the legal system it would ultimately become. It would take some powerful people and events to make it so.

William Penn was born in one of those cracks in time when life truly changes. Three years before his birth, that great, slandered symbol of ancient tyranny, the Star Chamber, had been laid to rest. He lived his childhood in the midst of a pandemonium of religious and political struggles that were the birth pangs of a more rational, less zealous age to come.

When he was still a toddler, the English people did something they had never done before: They declared their king a traitor, and tried and executed him in accordance with formal legal process. (Not until the Nuremburg trials of 1946 would the exercise of raw political power be so self-consciously clothed in the trappings of the law.) Meanwhile, John Lilburne was demonstrating that the English trial system, with the jury at its center, was as capable of declaring the innocence of common folk as the guilt of a king. There was a growing sense that power was becoming more divisible, and in some small way the property of all. How much of that feeling young William Penn consciously shared in is unknown, but it was in the air he breathed.

By the age of twenty-six, he had immersed himself in religious and political turmoil of a most perilous kind. He had done so, paradoxically, by becoming a member of the Quaker church, a new religious sect whose creed was tolerance and peace. Since nothing could be more threatening to those whose authority depended upon the legitimacy of persecution and war, the government of King Charles II responded to the Quakers punitively. They treated these apostles of peace as enemies of the state—as they were in spirit—and prosecuted their appeals for religious toleration as crimes.

One evening in the summer of 1670, Penn was delivering a sermon to a small group of the faithful on Grace Church Street in London when he was arrested for sedition. Time stood still on that night, crouched in preparation for a long leap forward.

With notable exceptions—the Norman victory at Hastings, Alexander Graham Bell's telephonic summoning of Mr. Watson, the bombing of Hiroshima—it is always hard to tell precisely when a page of history has been turned. In a quiet vein, the trial of William Penn for "tumultuous assembly" in September 1670 was such an exception. It produced nothing less than the final emancipation of the criminal trial jury and the possibility of truly administering justice on behalf of the people.

The technical charge against Penn was that he had violated the Conventicle Act, which provided that only the Church of England could conduct meetings for worship. The indictment stated that he had disturbed the peace "by preaching to an unlawful assembly and causing a great concourse and tumult," but the very fact that he had conducted a worship service at all was a crime. He was tried before ten judges, including the lord mayor of London, and a jury. According to his own account of the trial, he conducted himself like a latter-day John Lilburne.

He began by refusing to plead to the charge, questioning whether the government had the authority under the common law to bring it. After a rancorous, and somewhat inane, debate with the recorder, he was confined to the bale dock, a sort of cage recessed below the level of the court. He was thereafter forced to conduct his defense out of sight—but certainly not out of voice range—of the court and jury.

After five days of trial and several hours of deliberation, the jury returned to the courtroom and, according to Penn's account, the following colloquy occurred:

RECORDER: How say you? Is William Penn guilty of the matter whereof he stands indicted in manner and form, or not guilty?

JURY FOREMAN: Guilty of speaking in Grace Church Street.

RECORDER: You had as good say nothing.

There followed a heated dispute between court and jury, in which the judges insisted that the jury find Penn guilty of "unlawful assembly." The jury refused to do so, merely repeating the useless finding that Penn had spoken on Grace Church Street. Finally, the recorder applied the age-old method of dealing with recalcitrant jurors:

RECORDER: Gentleman, you shall not be dismissed till you bring in a verdict which the court will accept. You shall be locked up, without meat, drink, fire or tobacco. You shall not think thus to abuse the court. We will have a verdict by the help of God or you shall starve for it.

According to Penn, the following stirring colloquy occurred as the jurors were being dragged off to jail:

PENN: My jury, who are my judges, ought not to be thus menaced. Their verdict should be free, not forced.

RECORDER: Stop that fellow's mouth or put him out of court.

PENN: Ye are Englishmen, mind your privilege, give not away your right.

The jury was imprisoned for two days and nights and fined forty marks. Then under the leadership of their most obstreperous member, Edward Bushell, they filed a writ of habeas corpus in the Court of Common Pleas and won a famous legal victory. In an opinion that would be quoted for generations to come, Chief Justice Vaughn finally gave the English jury full independence, making it as sovereign in its domain as the Parliament and king were in theirs. The verdict in a case is the exclusive province of the jury, he ruled. It is what the jury says it is, nothing more, nothing less, and nothing different, and jurors may not be coerced into agreeing with the court's view, nor punished for concluding otherwise. That crucial principle would never be effectively questioned again.

In the early years of American history, it was the independent jury, not great Bill of Rights principles, that most embodied the ideal of justice. The Salem witch prosecutions ceased when, and only when, the juries stopped convicting. Andrew Hamilton argued the defense of truth in *Zenger*'s case, but it was the jury that conferred that defense and gave it enduring reality in our law. Throughout the nineteenth century, New England juries brought in not guilty verdicts when the crime seemed silly or oppressive, on the accepted theory that they were "the judges of the law and the facts." On the frontier, the law was literally what the jury believed "a man ought or ought not do," irrespective of the instructions of the court. And in all the controversial cases through the years, when defendants were vilified, lawyers excoriated, and judges derided, seldom was a jury verdict criticized. Juries were the voice of the people, and when they spoke, it was *over*. Justice had been done—like it or not.

Although the jury was the voice of the people, it was not the people themselves. It was representative, not popular justice. It belonged neither to the public nor the government—being an impermanent, anonymous, agreed-upon *means* of deciding cases—and its verdicts were considered sacrosanct by both.

Until the Rodney King affair, that is.

When jurors enter the courtroom, they leave the world behind. They undertake a duty unlike any they have known in their lives, and to perform it, they are asked to engage in new and artificial ways of thinking. They are, in fact, asked to do superhuman things—things we know they cannot, and do not, do. They are asked to wipe from their minds testimony they were not supposed to have heard; resolve conflicts in evidence no mortal could resolve with any confidence; identify thoughts that flickered through the consciousness of people at precise moments months and years in the past; absorb and apply pages of complex instructions concerning legal principles they have never heard of. And, in reaching a verdict, they are asked to perform a feat of probably impossible schizophrenia: If they *believe* the defendant is guilty, they must nonetheless find that he is *not if* they have a reasonable doubt that he *is*. Each of them must find a way to agree with eleven random strangers on this elusive, difficult proposition, or their labors are in vain.

A jury does, on the other hand, have spectacular strengths that help it shoulder these quixotic burdens. Sincerity, for one thing. Those who see a jury in operation for the first time are struck by its dedication to the task. Jurors may be biased, ignorant, or stupid, but they are seldom cynical. Most of them want to do right, according to their view of right. They are, for the most part, that rarest of commodities: truly, totally dedicated public servants.

They are not left to wander aimlessly through fact and inference in reaching a decision. The judge gives focus to their deliberations by his instructions. He reminds them of the points at issue, summarizes the conflicting contentions, reminds them that emotion has no place in their deliberations, gives them formulas for weighing the evidence, and provides them with principles for deciding the case. All of this clarifies the process of decision-making and unifies the jurors' approach to it. It reminds them one last time that they are not a random group of individuals out to vindicate personal points of view but officers of the court with a defined duty to perform.

Then there is the power of group decision-making. Studies have shown that twelve jurors are a far more "accurate" decisional instrument than six, and that when the number falls below five, there is no contest at all. A twelve-headed decision-maker has an astonishing memory, a vast fund of common experience, hugely versatile analytic skills, and the counterpressures of opposed extremes of opinion, which drive its judgments toward the middle ground of rational moderation.

Finally, being both anonymous and impermanent, juries have no personal stake in the outcomes of the cases they decide, to divert them from the path of justice. Each juror is a stranger to the other jurors and to the trial participants, and once they pass out of the courtroom doors, they are unlikely ever to see any of them again. Outside of their families and close acquaintances, they will never be identified with their verdict. It will cost them no money, lose them no elections, and—except in the rarest of cases—subject them to neither abuse nor praise. Even when, as in the *King* case, the public rails against their verdict, almost no one knows their names. A jury has, in short, little motive other than to focus on its job with all of its twelve-headed virtuosity.

And of course, unlike the rest of us, a jury has a constant front-row seat. It sees all the faces, hears all the voices, absorbs all the psychic emanations. It inhales the atmosphere and experiences the environment of the trial in a way no outside "observer" can. Guilt and innocence can be asserted, argued, and reasoned through, but most of all it must be *perceived*.

Whether the critics of the *King* verdict were right or wrong, therefore, one thing is as certain as tomorrow: Their rightness or wrongness was a matter of uninformed accident. They were sincere and righteous, but—not to put too fine a point on it—they didn't have a clue. The cops may well have used force that was unjustified under the applicable police regulations; they may well have had the requisite criminal intent under the court's instructions; and all of this may well have been proven beyond a reasonable doubt—but none of the above could be determined by watching ninety seconds of a truncated videotape. If it could, there would have been no reason to conduct a full-scale trial. A few minutes with a VHS would have sufficed.

Yes, there was reason to doubt the verdict. But with the anger of all those ninety-second experts reverberating in their ears, the *King* case jurors were like playwrights or directors panned by critics who had seen only a portion of the play. "Perhaps our performance wasn't all that great," they may have thought, "but who are *they* to say?"

There was a remedy at hand for the *King* jury's perceived mistake. The cops could be retried in federal court, this time for violating King's civil rights instead of for plain, old-fashioned assault and battery. But wasn't that double jeopardy? Not technically. Even though they would be retried for the same actions, it would be under a different legal theory and by a different legal authority—federal instead of state. So it wasn't technically double jeopardy at all.

Everything went as hoped for. The federal prosecutors were very good. Unlike the state boys, they had the good sense to present King—who after all was the reason they were there—as a witness, and he did an effective, soft-toned job of it. Eschewing the tyranny of the tape, the federal prosecutors supplemented it with eyewitness and expert testimony that made the cops' actions into a flesh-and-blood, inexcusable crime. They struck unexpected pay dirt when a female police officer called as a defense witness broke into tears on cross-examination as she recalled the fearful head cracking King had sustained and the cops' locker-room banter about it afterward.

The greatest difference was in the jury. It was much "better balanced," having been harvested from multiethnic, multicultural Los Angeles, instead of the WASP police retirement community that had provided that "misguided" other jury. More importantly, the jurors presumably knew from the posttrial "events" of the first prosecution what was good for the peace of the city and the psyche of the country. The odds were strong that they would do what their fellow citizens wanted them to do.

And they did. After six days of intense deliberation, they returned what was widely described as a Solomonic verdict: convictions for the most vicious banger and the officer in charge and acquittals for the other two. Justice, but discriminating justice. Insurance against rioting without caving in to pressure. Sternness without vindictiveness. And, in the grand tradition of jury verdicts, a definitive end to the dispute. The first jury had screwed up for sure, the people thought, but this one had made things right again.

Funny, though, the chief prosecutor had an "attitude" when he appeared at the press conference. He stood there quiet and tough, a carpenter who had done a workmanlike job, and told the people of the press that the whys and wherefores of what had happened were, essentially, the jury's business and not theirs or his. He refused to be coopted into partnership with the clamoring journalists, despite every tactic they could devise. Was it the tape that did it? I wasn't in the jury room. Did you give the other two cops a free ride in order to get Koon and Powell? We presented what we had; the jurors made the distinctions. Were they pressured, do you think, by fear of provoking riots? I assume they decided it the way they saw it.

No, he seemed to be saying. No. After a thousand years of sweat and blood, we won't relinquish the peace to the tyranny of the mob. The public has been given back as much control of justice as justice can stand, and it must stop here and now. The jury is still the jury: the voice of the people, not its polling booth or recording device, however you may wish to make it so. Not yet, it's not.

In the name of all that has gone before us, and for the sake of all who will come after us, let us devoutly hope the man was right.

EPILOGUE

The "Trial of the Century"

Public opinion is less tolerant than any system of law.
GEORGE ORWELL

As this book was being completed, the O. J. Simpson double murder trial was grinding to a halt as well.[1] Pundits called it the Trial of the Century, making it the latest of perhaps a dozen criminal prosecutions to be given that title over the last ninety-five years. What features, if any, did it have that justified such a label? Was it a uniquely creative or instructive or representative event in our legal history, or merely a vast diversion for a bored nation? Did it measure up in any of the above respects to the "great" trials of the past? Let us see:

The Issues. Most "great" trials have dealt with important political issues. The last fifty years have produced several that qualify as "great" in that sense: the Alger Hiss perjury trials, which triggered a shameful era of communist witch-hunting; the Jack Ruby and Sirhan Sirhan prosecutions, which probed calamitous political assassinations; and the Watergate prosecutions, which reaffirmed America's commitment to constitutional government.

The Simpson prosecution was no trial of the century in that sense. Its subject matter was, sadly, quite ordinary for a 1990s' American trial—a brutal murder, allegedly committed by an enraged ex-husband. As a trial of the century, it was more akin to the Leopold-Loeb murder case in the 1920s, or the prosecution of Bruno Hauptmann for kidnapping the Lindbergh baby in the 1930s. Its importance was in the eyes of the beholders, and the beholders were drawn to it—at least at first—by motives no more profound than those that motivate readers of supermarket tabloids.

Length. When King Charles I of England was prosecuted and condemned to death for treason in 1648, the trial was completed in five days. Not counting the interminable jury selection process, the

259

O. J. Simpson trial spanned eight months, one week, and four days. Its pace was amazingly ponderous. Things that should have taken minutes took hours, and things that should have taken hours took days. It took Judge Lance Ito almost as long to decide how many hairs should be cut from Simpson's head for laboratory analysis as it had taken Thomas More's court to decide to cut off his entire head. Babies were conceived and almost brought to term, businesses were formed and placed in bankruptcy, and baseball teams trained for, began, and almost played out their seasons between the opening statements and the verdict in the Simpson trial.

But, while it sometimes seemed as though the Simpson prosecution would *last* a century, it by no means qualified as the Trial of the Century on the basis of its length. The longest criminal trial in recent times was a day-care sexual abuse prosecution in California that lasted almost three years. The previous record holder was the 1983 Hillside Strangler prosecution, which took two years to try after a preliminary hearing that lasted for six months! The Simpson trial was slow and ponderous in part because it was uniquely prominent—not the other way around.

Brilliance of Defense Counsel. Some trials have been made "great" by the performances of counsel. John Peter Zenger without Andrew Hamilton or *Paxton*'s case without James Otis would have made no marks on history. Daniel Webster and Clarence Darrow converted several ordinary trials into memorable events by the virtuosity of their performances. Despite much media nonsense about Simpson's Dream Team, however, none of his lawyers bore the remotest resemblance to Darrow. They were pragmatists, not poets, and they performed the uninspiring job of doing what they had to do, as exasperating as it often was to viewers.

That job consisted of—in the words of Rumpole of the Bailey—"pouring sand into the gearbox of justice." As Simpson sat placidly in their midst, looking like a delegate at a bar association convention, his squadron of lawyers took turns asserting every real and imagined right they could conjure up on his behalf: making every conceivable objection, offering testimony to impeach and counter the prosecution's impeaching and countering testimony, taking two days to put on fifteen minutes' worth of proof, cross-examining endlessly and repetitively until the witness's direct testimony was a vague, muddled, and distant memory in the jury's mind, and bickering, bickering, bickering with prosecution counsel.

The effect of all of this was to slow the trial down, cut its logic into small pieces, and create the illusion that doubt existed—*must* exist—somewhere in that slow-moving pile of evidentiary rubble.

These tactics were far from novel or creative. They are as old as the adversarial trial system and are as frequently used as the financial resources of defendants will permit. They are based on a simple and long-understood syllogism: The job of defense counsel is to create doubt; delay, complexity, and confusion create doubt; therefore, it is the job of defense counsel to create delay, complexity, and confusion. The Simpson team's performance was denounced as abrasive and time-wasting, which—since they were criminal defense lawyers—must have given them a glow of inner satisfaction. It was not a performance for the ages, but what it lacked in brilliance it made up for in effectiveness—they won.

Constitutional Innovations. Many of the cases in this book gave momentum to the development of a constitutional principle. Not the *Simpson* case, although there were some fascinating applications of existing principles.

The right to confront accusers, for example. The California rules of court extend this right to the pretrial stages of a case, making it into a right to *prepare* for confrontation. In the Simpson case, each side was required to give notice of the witnesses they intended to produce far in advance, so that no in-court surprises would occur. It was not sufficient to be able to confront; the confrontation must be painstakingly prepared for. This process often made the lawyers look timid and ridiculous—"No fair, you didn't tell us you were going to use him, so now you *can't*"—and made the trial even slower and more wooden. But it probably enhanced the truth-producing capacity of the process and was likely worth the aggravation it caused.

For all the solicitude shown it, the right of confrontation was curiously—and, one must say, erroneously—withheld from the defendant at a crucial stage. Simpson's lawyers asked to recall Detective Mark Fuhrman to the stand and cross-examine him as to whether he had committed perjury on certain subjects during his previous testimony. When questioned out of the jury's presence, he invoked his Fifth Amendment privilege. Denied their right to confront him before the jury on the vital issue of his truthfulness, defense counsel requested that the jury be instructed that Fuhrman had declined to testify and the jurors be allowed to make whatever inferences they chose. The request was presented to the California Supreme Court, which—somewhat amazingly—ruled that *Simpson's* jury could not be told about *Fuhrman's* invocation of the Fifth. Why not, the nation's lawyers wondered. Fuhrman's not on trial. If the jury inferred he committed perjury, it would do him no legal harm.

The legal harm to Simpson, on the other hand, was obvious. The key government witness had refused to defend the truthfulness of his own testimony, and Simpson's lawyers were never permitted to confront him before the jury to establish that salient fact. Shades of Sir Walter Raleigh!

The constitutional principle most visibly on display was Simpson's Fifth Amendment privilege against self-incrimination. As the day appointed for his testimony approached, the national game of "Will he or won't he?" became intense. The ABC and NBC legal experts solemnly disagreed as to whether he would or wouldn't. We learned that Simpson had been cross-examined by his own lawyers in a mock weekend session and had done badly. Finally the moment arrived. Simpson told Judge Ito in the jury's absence that he was innocent of the crimes but nonetheless wished to invoke his privilege not to testify.

Meanwhile, he had already virtually testified in several different ways. At the time of his arrest he had made a heartfelt public statement of innocence, which, if the jurors didn't hear, they must have heard *about*. As part of the defense's opening statement, Simpson stood before the jury and displayed injuries that his lawyers contended prevented him from assaulting and killing two able-bodied adults. Later in the trial, when the prosecution stupidly asked him to try on the incriminating bloody glove, he struggled histrionically to do so and mouthed to the jury, "It's too *small*." Then, of course, there was the statement of innocence to Judge Ito obviously intended to be conveyed to the jurors during spousal visits. Surely all of this testifying without testifying, using the sword of communication while retaining the shield of silence, was a brilliant Dream Team innovation.

These were good tactics, but hardly innovative. Nonverbal demonstrations by nontestifying defendants are nothing new in modern criminal trials. There have even been cases of defendants relying on their privilege not to testify, then making final jury arguments asserting their innocence. We may remember that the technique of communicating to the jury, while invoking a privilege not to testify, was perfected by the inventor of the privilege—Freeborn John Lilburne himself. He told his judges and the jury all about the case, much more than most of them cared to hear, but refused to swear to any of it or submit to cross-examination. Simpson's pantomimes will no doubt be imitated in future trials, but, effective though they were, they were nothing new.

The Verdict. When the verdict came in, many considered it the Injustice of the Century. How was an acquittal possible—and after only four hours of deliberation! How could the system survive if juries cavalierly ignored overwhelming scientific evidence of guilt? One of the prosecutors told the jury in his final argument: "You *know* he's guilty. *Everybody* knows he's guilty." And, seemingly, almost everybody did.

The hostility of the popular reaction was heightened by the false assumption that the jurors had found Simpson innocent (if he didn't do it, who did, for God's sake?). Of course, they had found no such thing. In the humane tradition of the common law, their verdict merely said they had a reasonable doubt as to his guilt. Verdicts that are actually based on reasonable doubt, as Simpson's may have been, inevitably seem irrational and wrong (despite her acquittal, who doubts that Lizzie Borden killed her parents?).

Many people seemed stunned that the verdict might have been influenced by race. Nothing new there either, of course. A Ph.D. candidate researching a thesis on "the influence of race in American trials" would encounter an embarrassment of riches. If Race sullied Lady Justice in the *Simpson* case, he assaulted no virgin. The attacker and victim knew each other well.

The critics of the verdict seem most incensed by the thought that it was intentionally dishonest. The jurors hadn't tried to decide guilt or innocence; their intent had been to "send a message" to the Los Angeles police force and others like it all around the country. They had acquitted Simpson regardless of his guilt, the theory went, because the hands of the police were soiled with the filth of corrupt investigations, perjury, and racism, in this case and in many others through the years.

The police did have a sorry history, and Detective Fuhrman was disgusting, the critics conceded, but two wrongs don't make a right. The lack of discipline displayed by the jury was a threat to the integrity of the legal system. If a jury could apply its own law, what was the use of having law at all?

But every experienced trial lawyer knows that juries send messages all the time. Verdicts are regularly returned bearing jury messages of support for the police, disapproval of various "lifestyles," outrage at shoddy business practices, dislike of murder victims, and many other points of view that have nothing to do with guilt or innocence. The Simpson team's tactic of using police misconduct as a "defense" probably occurs every day in some courtroom in this country.

Jury messages have, in fact, played an honored role in our legal history. Constitutional heros John Lilburne, William Penn, and John Peter Zenger had two things in common: They were guilty under the law, and they were acquitted by juries that were sending messages. The Lilburne acquittal was a rejection of the use of treason laws to suppress political opinions; the Penn acquittal was a vindication of religious freedom; and the Zenger verdict was an early declaration of American independence from English rule. O. J. Simpson is certainly no William Penn, but—who knows—his jurors may one day be considered the Edward Bushells of their time. Their message was just, even though their verdict, perhaps, was not.

Public Observation and Involvement. If the Rodney King trials had penetrated the American psyche, the Simpson trial thoroughly saturated it. It was impossible to escape the case, on television or in conversation. The thumb of a channel surfer could never be fast enough, the rebuke of an uninterested dinner companion never sharp enough, to deflect the quenchless flow of information and comment about the "O. J. trial." It was in the air we breathed, and in the end many of us all but choked on it.

Physics says that the observation of a thing changes its nature, and that principle surely applied to the Simpson trial. Lawyers, witnesses, and the judge played to the cameras—just as the Scopes trial participants had played to the assembled press seventy years before—and their self-consciousness altered the essence of the trial. More significantly, the millions of Americans who observed the trial minute by minute on television became vicarious participants in it, to an even greater degree than in the *Rodney King* case. It was, finally, technology that set the *Simpson* case apart from its predecessors. It was the Lizzie Bordon trial, with cameras in the courtroom.

Hundreds of years ago when justice was mostly by hue and cry, guilt was decided, and punishment administered, with the knowledge of very few people. Grave wrongs must have been inflicted regularly, with hardly anyone the wiser. When the state took over the administration of justice, England's proudest boasts were its jury system and the openness of its trials. With the invention of printing, actual transcripts of great trials like More's and Raleigh's could be circulated at large, and public reaction helped force liberalization of the system. In the latter nineteenth century, the press began to publicize the details of major trials almost instantaneously, and the good and bad effects of public scrutiny were accelerated. Now, with the *Simpson* case, most of the nation had vicariously participated in all phases of a prominent trial, critiquing and arguing over its every nuance. This incredible scrutiny reached its zenith when the forewoman of the jury submitted herself to questioning at a televised post-trial news conference, in an attempt to justify the verdict.

Suppose this is a harbinger of things to come. What if, every five years or so, we have a similar participatory extravaganza, in which the techniques employed and results produced are universally dissected, analyzed, and trashed.

There would surely be pressures, over time, for a more "commonsense" approach to justice. The requirement of a unanimous jury verdict is already under attack in some quarters because of the prospect that the Simpson jury would be hung. Simpson's rapid acquittal, if repeated in future televised cases, may bring pressure to bear on the reasonable doubt standard. "Technical" rules of evidence designed to shield the jury from unreliable and prejudicial information may fall into disfavor. The exclusion of unconstitutionally seized evidence may become even more unpopular than it is today.

In ancient Athens, criminal prosecutions were tried before juries ranging in size from five hundred to twelve hundred men, depending upon the importance of the case. The size and anonymity of these bodies made them a true "voice of the people," and in many ways they were a hedge against tyranny. But they had the shortcomings of large popular assemblies as well. They made trials into oratorical contests in which emotional presentations counted for more than factual truth. In the most famous trial in Greek history, an Athenian jury condemned Socrates to death because his views were unpopular, thereby shaming Athens' proud reputation as the home of free expression.

If 100-million-member vicarious juries become common in this country, will we have similarly shameful results? What will happen to the great principles of American justice if the *Simpson* case turns out to be the prototypical Trial of the *Twenty-First* Century? We may all have a chance to find out.

NOTES

1   Nationalizing English Justice

1. The West Saxons were one of the several Saxon kingdoms that constituted England from the sixth to the tenth centuries A.D.

2. It is said that on a trip to Rome at the age of six, Alfred recited his own lineage as follows: "I am Alfred son of Ethelwulf, son of Egbert, son of Ealhmund, son of Eafa, son of Eoppa, son of Ingild, son of Cenred, son of Ceolwold, son of Cutha, son of Cuthwine, son of Ceawlin, son of Cynric, son of Creoda, son of Cerdic, son of Elesa, son of Esla, son of Gewis, son of Wig, son of Freawine, son of Freothogar, son of Brand, son of Baeldag, son of Woden, son of Fralaf, son of Finn, son of Godwulf, son of Eat, son of Taetwa, son of Beaw, son of Sceldwa, son of Heremod, son of Itermon, son of Hathra, son of Hawla, son of Bedwig, son of Sceaf, who was the son of Noah and born in the Ark. My father is the King of the West-Saxons, in the German parts of Britain." The line seems too short to reach to Noah, but the Saxons were less worried about such things than we are.

3. "The rapid extension of the King's peace until it becomes . . . the normal and general safeguard of public order, seems peculiarly English." Sir Frederick Pollack and Frederic William Maitland, *The History of English Law Before the Time of Edward I*, Cambridge University Press, London (Reissued Second Edition, 1968), vol. I, p. 45.

4. F. W. Maitland, coauthor of the nineteenth-century classic *The History of English Law*.

5. In its final stages of development, of course, the King's peace was extended to nonviolent crime. "[T]o all appearance, [larceny] was the last of the great crimes to which that elastic phrase was applied. This was natural, for to say of the thief that he has broken the King's Peace is to say what is hardly true until those words have acquired a non-natural meaning." Pollack and Maitland, *History of English Law*, vol. II, p. 495.

2   The Rule of Law

1. See chapter 1, *Nationalizing English Justice*.

2. Roger of Wendover, *Chronica sive Flores Histriarum*, ed. H. O. Cox (Eng. Hist. Society, 1841); see also Elizabeth Longford, *The Oxford Book of Royal Anecdotes*, Oxford University Press, Oxford (1989), p. 9.

3. Roger of Wendover, pp. 64, 263.

4. William McKechnie, *Magna Charta*, Burt Franklin, New York (1914), pp. 45, 46.

5. *The Institutes of the Laws of England* was painful required reading for American law students well into the nineteenth century.

6. G. M. Trevelyan, *History of England*, Longman Group Limited, London (1988), p. 205.

7. The provisions of Magna Charta were generally restricted to "freemen," a classification that—as the tongue-in-cheek author of the opinion of course knew—had nothing to do with penal incarceration (see p. 22).

8. The Petition of Right was a statement of the basic rights of Englishmen that Parliament enacted into law as a statute. It was formulated under the leadership of Edward Coke in opposition to the autocratic rule of King James I, and in particular to his practice of arbitrarily imprisoning his adversaries.

9. But see chapter 4, Binding Precedent.

10. Much of the impetus for discovering these rights was provided by the religious struggles that racked England in the sixteenth century, featuring defendants who appealed to the "higher law" of conscience in their prosecutions. See chapter 5.

11. The appellation "Great" initially referred to its length, rather than to its importance, as we now interpret it.

12. The mythic power of the charter began to be felt very early. On the day it was sealed, an order was addressed to every sheriff requiring that it "should be publicly read" in every shire of England. Thus, "[m]uch of the awe and romance which through the ages has come to surround the Great Charter was already in the ears and eyes of those who first heard its terms proclaimed and saw in the hands of the King's officer the actual document sealed with the King's great seal." Doris Stenton, "After Runnymede," *Magna Carta Essays,* University Press of Virginia, Charlottesville, Va. (1965), p. 10.

3   The Bar Is Born

1. "[T]he phenomenon of attempt to administer justice without lawyers, a feature of all utopias, a feature of all revolutions from Jack Cade's rebellion to the French Revolution, to the Russian Revolution, is ... universal...." Roscoe Pound, *The Lawyer from Antiquity to Modern Times,* West Publishing Company, St. Paul, Minn. (1953), p. 136.

2. Winston S. Churchill, *History of the English-Speaking Peoples,* Dodd, Mead Company, New York (1958), vol. I, pp. 286, 288.

3. Churchill, *History of the English*, p. 291.

4. As noted, English criminal trials usually employed the physical test of the ordeal to establish guilt or innocence. (See chapter 2.)

4   Binding Precedent

1. Ruth Marcus, "Court Declines to Overrule Roe, But Limits Permitted on Abortion," *Washington Post* (June 30, 1992), p. 1A.

2. Ibid.

3. Jon Carroll, "Justice Prevails Against All Odds," *San Francisco Chronicle* (July 1, 1992), p. E12.

4. Bruce Fein, "Court Sets Precedent over Truth," *USA Today* (July 6, 1992), p. 10A.

5. John Leo, "The Quagmire of Abortion Rights," *US News & World Report* (July 13, 1992), p. 16.

6. The pipe rolls were long sheets of parchment rolled up on a rod, like a window shade.

7. Jerome Frank, *Courts on Trial,* Princeton University Press, Princeton, N.J. (1949), p. 263.

8. Frank, *Courts on Trial,* p. 267.

9. The most dramatic example of all was furnished by the decision in *Ashford* v. *Thornton* (1817), in which an English court granted a defendant's request to have his guilt determined in a battle to the death with his accuser. When the stunned accuser protested that trial by battle had not been seen in England for centuries, the presiding judge placidly responded, "The general law of the land is in favor of the wager of battle, and it is our duty to pronounce the law as it is, and not as we may wish it to be. Whatever prejudices therefore may exist against the mode of trial, still it is the law of the land, and the court must pronounce judgment for it."

10. John Austin, *The Province of Jurisprudence* (1832), in Frank, *Courts on Trial,* p. 264.

11. Benjamin Cardozo, *Cardozo on the Law,* Legal Classics Library, Birmingham, Ala. (1982), p. 149.

12. Frank, *Courts on Trial,* p. 289.

13. Frank, *Courts on Trial,* p. 263.

14. "[T]he political question point in Mr. Justice Frankfurter's opinion was no more than an alternative ground."

15. "The political question principle as applied in *Colgrove* has found wide application commensurate with its function as 'one of the rules basic to the federal system and this Court's appropriate place within that structure.' "

5   Man Against the State

1. Richard Marius, *Thomas More,* Alfred A. Knopf, New York (1984), p. 406.

2. Latter-day Protestant writers tended to attribute their own religious tolerance to More. In his seminal *Lives of the Lord Chancellors,* Lord Campbell wrote that More's character came "as near to perfection as our nature will permit," and that "with all my Protestant zeal, I must feel a higher reverence for Sir Thomas More than for Thomas Cromwell or for Cranmer" [minions of Henry VIII who helped do More in]. He then made the astonishing misstatement that "before the Reformation, [More] was as warm a friend as Locke to the principle of religious toleration" (Lord Campbell, *Lives of The Lord Chancellors of England*, Cockcroft & Company, New York [1878], pp. 76, 77, 81). More's most notable twentieth-century biographer, R. W. Chambers, treated More's religious faith as simply another admirable quality in a flawless character. He essentially avoided discussing More's theology and never suggested that it led him to brutal words and deeds. He explicitly compared More to Socrates.

3. Leonard W. Levy, *Origins of the Fifth Amendment,* Oxford University Press, New York (1968), p. 80.

4. For example, Darrow made his most memorable speech immediately at the end of a long argument in support of a motion to quash the indictment. He insisted on making it even though the judge had just announced adjournment of the court for the day. The argument's timing, its defiance of the judge's order of adjournment, and its prepared-in-advance quality suggest that it was intended more

for the morning headlines than for the fundamentalist judge, who wasn't about to grant the motion.

6   The Right to Confront Accusers

1. Leonard W. Levy, *Origins of the Fifth Amendment,* Oxford University Press, New York (1968), pp. 25, 26.

2. Sir James Fitz James Stephen, *A History of the Criminal Law of England,* Macmillan and Co., London (1883), vol. I, p. 402.

3. Even as pro-prosecution and pro-judge a commentator as James Stephen found the judges' interpretation of the law "extremely curious." Stephen, *History of Criminal Law,* vol. I, p. 335.

4. "The brutality which [Coke] showed in the prosecution of Sir Walter Raleigh has never been forgotten. But after he became Chief Justice an astonishing metamorphosis took place, for he now showed the same devotion and courage in advancing the claims of the common law that he had previously shown in support of the crown." Arthur L. Goodhart, "Law of the Land," *Magna Carta Essays,* University Press of Virginia, Charlottesville (1966), p. 43.

5. Pyrnne was a printer whose vitriolic criticisms of high society offended the Crown and led to repeated punishments for libel (see chapter 8). Lilburne was a famed radical who was tried for sedition and later for treason (see chapters 8 and 9). Scroggs and Jeffreys were the presiding judges in the Popish Plot and Bloody Assizes trials, respectively, which are generally considered the most brutal episodes of sustained injustice in English history. All of the above occurred in the mid- to late seventeenth century.

6. The right of confrontation is also a principle of constitutional law. The Sixth Amendment guarantees that criminal defendants "shall have the opportunity to confront witnesses against them." Because the hearsay rule resolves most witness confrontation issues and is more familiar to lawyers than the confrontation clause, the Sixth Amendment right of confrontation is seldom invoked in court.

7   Judicial Review

1. Sir James Fitz James Stephen, *A History of the Criminal Law of England,* Macmillan and Co., London (1883), vol. II, p. 207.

2. A mandamus is an order issued by a court to the judge of a lower court, or other government official, requiring him to perform a stated official action.

8   The Death of a Scapegoat

1. The chamber's image remains constant. In the 1980s, the producers of a third-rate movie about vigilante justice calculated that the masses would get the point if they called it *The Star Chamber.*

2. E.g., "[T]he Star Chamber sent innocent men to the gallows ignorant of both their accusers and the charges against them." William Manchester, *A World Lit Only by Fire,* Little, Brown and Company, Boston (1992), p. 34.

3. William Bollan, *The Freedom of Speech and Writing upon Public Affairs Considered,* S. Baker, London (1766), p. 51, quoting a "treatise written by [an unidentified] person well acquainted with the proceedings of this court."

4. After extensively researching the issue, Professor Max Radin con-

cluded that "there was apparently nothing secret about the actions of [Star Chamber]," "The Right to a Public Trial," 8 *Temple Law Quarterly* (1932), p. 381. Most knowledgeable authorities, including the U.S. Supreme Court, have agreed.

5. "The most striking characteristic of the [Star Chamber] was its moderation. It was surely the mildest-mannered tribunal that ever sentenced a criminal, considerate in its procedure, gentle in its punishments, and failing altogether to live up to the reputation of ruthlessness that the Star Chamber has enjoyed since the Seventeenth Century." C. G. Bayne, quoted in Theodore Plucknett, *A Concise History of the Common Law*, Little, Brown and Company, Boston (Fifth Edition 1956), p. 182.

6. Calculated in wages, five hundred pounds in the seventeenth century was roughly equivalent to thirty-five thousand pounds, or approximately fifty thousand dollars, today.

9   The Privilege Against Self-incrimination

1. "Any system ... which permits the prosecution to trust habitually to compulsory self-disclosure as a source of proof must itself suffer morally thereby." John Wigmore, *Evidence in Trials at Common Law,* Little Brown and Company, Boston (Third Edition, 1940), vol. VIII, p. 309.

2. Sir James Fitz James Stephen, *A History of the Criminal Law of England,* Macmillan and Co., London (1883), vol. I, p. 535.

3. Stephen, *History of the Criminal Law*, vol. I, p. 542.

10   Freedom of the Press

1. He dismissed the case in mid-trial in exchange for a tentatively worded acknowledgment of error by CBS.

2. Hamilton's invitation to the jury to overrule the judge, and apply a defense of truth to the alleged libel, is startling to modern lawyers, who are used to treating legal issues as "questions for the court." Hamilton was well within his rights, however, since the then-prevailing view was that the jurors were the "judges of the law, as well as the facts." See chapter 21, Trial by Jury.

3. Leonard W. Levy, *Emergence of a Free Press,* Oxford University Press, New York (1985), p. 16. Many of the cases involving Colonial suppression of free expression described in this chapter and elsewhere in this book are taken from Professor Levy's remarkable study.

4. In *Peck* v. *Tribune Company* (1909), the Supreme Court held that the plaintiff, who was a nurse and a teetotaler, had a viable libel claim against the publisher of an ad that pictured her endorsing a brand of whiskey. To the defendant's argument that drinking whiskey is not generally considered disgraceful, and is therefore not actionable, Justice Holmes replied that "libel is not a matter of majority vote." In a sense, *criminal* libel is.

5. The Union borrowed this baroque definition from Jack London, who invented it.

6. It must be said that the vicious prosecutions of pacifists under the Espionage Act in the 1920s, and of communists and "fellow travelers" under the Smith Act in the 1950s, do not offer much comfort in that regard.

11   Unreasonable Searches and Seizures

1. Sir Frederick Pollock and Frederic William Maitland, *The History of English Law Before the Time of Edward I,* Cambridge University Press, London (Reissued Second Edition, 1968), vol. II, p. 579.

2. After the argument, the magnanimous Gridley was quoted as saying, "I raised up two eagles and they plucked out both my eyes."

3. See chapter 15, Unreasonable Searches and Seizures, Continued. (The Exclusionary Rule).

12   The Bill of Rights

1. In the mid-twentieth century, the U.S. Supreme Court finally settled on Madison's view, that postpublication sanctions, as well as prepublication restraints, are subject to First Amendment limitation. It is likely, though unprovable, that most of the Framers agreed with Jefferson's contrary view.

2. See chapter 4, Binding Precedent.

3. See chapter 19, Equality as Law, Continued (The Eclipse of Judicial Restraint).

13   Constructive Treason

1. The other is "giving aid and comfort" to an enemy of the United States.

2. Albert J. Beveridge, *The Life of John Marshall,* Houghton Mifflin Company, Boston (1919). Unless otherwise indicated, the quotations relating to the Burr trial throughout the chapter were taken from Beveridge's biography.

3. Or if the defendant confessed to such an act "in open court."

4. Blennerhassett's diary of the trial contains frequent references to Martin's drinking and its lack of impact upon his performances: "Martin was both yesterday and today more in his cups than usual, and though he spared neither his prudence nor his feelings, he was happy in all his hits. . . . Luther Martin has made his final immersion into the daily bath of his faculties."

5. Lisle was an elderly lady who was beheaded in the latter seventeenth century for compassionately nursing wounded men who turned out to be in rebellion against the king.

14   Equality as Law

1. It will be noted that, in addition to its obvious moral defects, this statement represents the doctrine of original intent at its worst.

15   Unreasonable Searches and Seizures, Continued

1. Bradley's opinion, however, does quote extensively the splendid eloquence of Lord Camden. Having rejected the banjo music, Bradley needed some Beethoven.

2. Beginning in 1967, the Court decided a series of cases that successively shrank the scope of the Fourth Amendment, holding, for example, that seizures could include "mere evidence" as well as "instrumentalities" and "fruits" of crimes; that unlawfully seized evidence could be used for certain purposes on cross-examinations; that searches made pursuant to certain unconstitutional arrests were

valid; and that the right to attack unconstitutional seizures in federal habeas corpus procedures was limited in certain instances.

16 The Right of Privacy

1. Newspaper editor Emile Gauvreau, quoted in *Editor and Publisher,* September 10, 1932.

2. "Pen-um-bra. A partial shadow between regions of complete shadow and complete illumination." *American Heritage Dictionary,* Houghton Mifflin Co., Boston (1992).

17 Nationalizing American Justice

1. Judge Parker's career is memorialized in a book by J. Glaston Emery appropriately titled *Court of the Damned* (1959).

2. Reprinted in Nashville's morning newspaper, *The Tennessean,* on March 7, 1982, in a special section devoted to the *Frank* case.

3. Jerome Frank, *Courts on Trial,* Princeton University Press, Princeton, N.J. (1949), p. 32.

4. Frank, *Courts on Trial,* pp. 23, 24.

5. Taken from an account of the hanging in the *St. Louis Globe-Democrat,* August 18, 1915, reprinted in John D. Lawson, *American State Trials,* F. H. Thomas Law Book Co., Saint Louis (1918), vol. 10, pp. 413, 414.

18 The Right to Counsel

1. Those committed to looking on the bright side of things will be pleased to learn that the defendants were spared capital punishment on their retrials, their sentences being "confined" to seventy-five years' imprisonment.

19 Equality as Law, Continued

1. For example, Frankfurter's seeming reluctance to join the majority may have assisted his later efforts to persuade the Court to order desegregation "with all deliberate speed," instead of commanding "prompt" or "immediate" obedience to its decision, when it entered the order implementing the decision in 1955.

2. Quoted in Bernard Schwartz, *Super Chief,* New York University Press, New York (1983) p. 86.

3. At least one of Frankfurter's biographers asserts such a thesis. See H. N. Hirsch, *The Enigma of Frankfurter,* Basic Books, Inc., New York (1980), p. 195.

20 Freedom of the Press, Continued

1. Sir James Fitz James Stephen, *A History of the English Criminal Law of England,* Macmillan and Co., London (1883), vol. II, p. 348.

2. Mary Patterson Clarke, *Parliamentary Privilege in the American Colonies,* Yale University Press, New Haven, Conn. (1943), p. 117.

3. Frederick Trevor Hill, *Decisive Battles of the Law,* Harper & Brothers, New York (1907), p. 20.

4. Subsequent revisionism has, of course, reduced Roosevelt and Kennedy to sometimes distressingly human dimensions.

Epilogue   The Trial of the Century

1. For the benefit of any future reader who may not know the facts of the case, Simpson was a former football star who was prosecuted for murdering his former wife, Nicole, and her friend Ronald Goldman in June 1994.

INDEX

OCT 278 1999 INDEX